D0913114

A Fistful of Rubles

A Fistful of Rubles

THE RISE AND FALL OF THE RUSSIAN BANKING SYSTEM

JULIET JOHNSON

CORNELL UNIVERSITY PRESS   ITHACA AND LONDON

First published 2000 by Cornell University Press

Printed in the United States of America

Library of Congress Cataloging-in-Publication Data

Johnson, Juliet Ellen, b. 1968
    A fistful of rubles : the rise and fall of the Russian banking system /
Juliet Johnson.
        p. cm.
    Includes index.
    ISBN 0-8014-3744-X (cloth : alk. paper)
    1. Banks and banking—Russia (Federation) 2. Finance—Russia
(Federation) I. Title.
    HG3130.2.A6 J64 2000
    332.1'0947—dc21

                                                        00-009763

Cornell University Press strives to utilize environmentally responsible
suppliers and materials to the fullest extent possible in the publishing
of its books. Such materials include vegetable-based, low-VOC inks
and acid-free papers that are recycled, totally chlorine-free, or partly
composed of nonwood fibers. Books that bear the logo of the FSC
(Forest Stewardship Council) use paper taken from forests that have
been inspected and certified as meeting the highest standards for
environmental and social responsibility. For further information, visit
our website at www.cornellpress.cornell.edu.

Cloth printing
10 9 8 7 6 5 4 3 2 1

FSC FSC Trademark © 1996 Forest Stewardship Council A.C.
     SW-COC-098

Contents

Contents

Figures and Tables

Preface: The Power of Trust

The ruble lived, the ruble lives, the ruble will continue to live.
—Russian Finance Minister Boris Fedorov, 1992

What do democratic politics and banking have in common? While the cynics among us may guess venality, or the pursuit of power, the underlying answer is that both rely on trust to survive. A democratic political system is undermined if its citizens do not trust it to represent their political and economic interests. Likewise, if a bank loses the trust of its clients, they will withdraw their money and the bank will collapse. Money itself is an ephemeral, trust-based phenomenon, existing as a means of payment and a store of value only as long as people widely believe it to be capable of doing so.

In the 1990s, Russia faced the challenge of building public trust in its young democracy and in its newly liberalized banking system—tasks made doubly difficult by Soviet-era legacies of political prevarication and command economics. By 1998, Russia had failed at both of these tasks. An article in the newspaper *Komsolmol'skaia pravda* neatly summed up the state of the emerging Russian banking system. It told the story of an elderly pensioner who lost her entire life savings of one million rubles because she had stored the money in her basement, where it was eaten by rats. The paper observed that "the lady, having studied a variety of Russian state and commercial banks, concluded that her cash was safest in the cellar."[1]

---

1. "Rats Devour Villager's Savings," *Associated Press*, November 2, 1994. At November 1994 exchange rates, she had about $300.

Instead of developing a stable, law-based political and economic system, post-Soviet Russia became known as the "Wild East," a country where order had been replaced by a society "without limits" (*bezpredel'*). Murder, financial scams, casinos, and cronyism characterized Russian life, especially in the capital city of Moscow. Russia's bankers, now grown wealthy and influential, occupied the center of this seedily compelling world. Indeed, the influence of the Russian banking system on the emergence of market democracy during this period of transformation was overwhelmingly negative. Its politically autonomous yet technically underdeveloped central bank carried out monetary policy in a secretive, uncoordinated, destabilizing manner. Worse, its commercial bankers played an increasingly important role in the political system, with the most powerful banks acquiring state property cheaply and forming a so-called financial-industrial oligarchy. The bankers and the state both came to depend upon each other for survival, while most Russian enterprises withdrew further and further from the cash-based economy. In 1998, after undergoing ten years of economic "reforms," the Russian financial system collapsed.

This book explores these pathological developments by tracing the causes, processes, and ultimate effects of institutional change in Russia's banking system from the initial decision to break up the Soviet central bank in 1987 through the aftermath of the August 1998 banking crash. It argues that in Russia, a disastrous combination of perverse, Soviet-era institutional legacies and misguided, Western-inspired policy choices led to the creation of a banking system so parasitic that it ultimately undermined Russia's economic transformation. In particular, the liberalization of the Soviet financial system while the rest of the command economic structure remained intact led to an "irony of autonomy." Even though this liberalization granted banks more freedom from central government control, autonomy did not contribute to the development of competitive, market-oriented, or efficient institutions. On the contrary, it spawned banks that served to enrich the few while failing to help build a market economy in Russia. Even after they became independent, Russia's commercial banks continued to turn to the state for sustenance. At the same time, the Russian government became dependent on the political and financial support of the most prominent bankers in order to maintain its control over the country.

In researching this book, I spent eight months in three fascinating Russian cities between 1994 and 1997. These included Moscow, Russia's capital and largest city; Riazan', a depressed, mid-sized industrial town about 200 kilometers southeast of Moscow; and Volgograd (formerly Stalingrad), a large industrial and agricultural city on the Volga River in southern Russia. Since the early Soviet era, Moscow has been the country's unquestioned political and financial center. As of January 1998, over one-third of all Russian banks were headquartered in Moscow, including

19 of the 20 largest. Riazan' and Volgograd, on the other hand, represent relatively average regions demographically, economically, and politically. Neither city was a major exporter of a single commodity (like Tiumen', an oil-producing region of Siberia), nor a semi-autonomous economic region that operated as a tax haven (like Dagestan or Bashkortostan). Nor did these regions enjoy a special political status (like Tatarstan). Volgograd had a slightly larger-than-average financial market, while Riazan's was slightly smaller.

My research in these cities involved interviewing numerous Russian bankers, policymakers, entrepreneurs, and academics; reading archival issues of local newspapers and journals; participating in banking conferences in Moscow and St. Petersburg; and analyzing primary source materials on Russian and Soviet banking from the Association of Russian Banks, the Financial Services Volunteer Corps, Dialog Bank, Inkombank, the Interbank Financial House, the Central and East European Legal Initiative, the Barents Group, the Riazan' Pedagogical University, the Central Bank of Russia, Volgograd State University, the Russian State Duma, and the Russian Federation Council, among others.

In this book, I have used the most reliable statistics available from both Western and Russian sources. However, the quality of financial statistics in the 1980s and 1990s leaves much to be desired. The Central Bank of Russia has changed its methodology over time. Little consistency exists between one information source and another. Russian accounting standards, on which many of these statistics are based, inflate bank assets in comparison with international accounting standards. Moreover, banks have had every incentive to cook their books throughout the transformation period. As a result, exact figures should be treated with caution. Even a statistic as seemingly straightforward as the number of banks in a region may be slightly off, depending on whether or not defunct banks have been included. In many instances the relative relationship among statistics, rather than the discrete figures themselves, reveals the more important and valid findings.

In crafting this book I have inevitably amassed financial, professional, and personal debts as large and unrepayable as those of the Russian banking system. For supporting my research and writing, I thank the Social Science Research Council, the American Council of Teachers of Russian, the Center of International Studies at Princeton University, the Council on Regional Studies at Princeton, the Brookings Institution, and Loyola University Chicago. I also appreciate receiving permission to reprint material from two earlier essays: "Misguided Autonomy: Central Bank Independence and the Russian Transition," which appeared in Andreas Schedler, Larry Diamond, and Marc Plattner, eds., *The Self-Restraining State: Power and Accountability in New Democracies* (Lynne Rienner, 1999); and "Russia's

Emerging Financial-Industrial Groups," *Post-Soviet Affairs*, vol. 13, no. 4, pp. 333–365 (©V.H. Winston & Son, Inc., 360 South Ocean Boulevard, Palm Beach, Fla. 33480. All rights reserved). Chapter three is a substantially revised and updated version of the former, while revised sections from the latter appear in chapters five and six.

I owe endless gratitude to those Russians in Moscow, Riazan', and Volgograd who revealed the secrets of their marvelous, maddening country to me. In Riazan', I particularly thank the Central Bank's indefatigable regional director Tamara Pigilova, Sergei Kostikov of the Riazan' Pedagogical University, and Oleg Churbanov and the entire staff of PRIO-Vneshtorgbank. In Volgograd, Evgenii Komarnitskii of RIT Bank and Daniil Zakharov of Russkaia Nedvizhimost' went out of their way to explain the intricacies of Russian regional banking to me. In particular, though, I thank Nadezhda Filipovna, who gave me unique insights into Russia's past and present and taught me to make authentic blini. In Moscow, thanks go out especially to Peter Derby at Dialog Bank, Aleksandr Zagriadskii at the Association of Russian Banks, Liuba Ternova at the Federation Council, Garegin Tosunian at Tekhnobank, the Interbank Financial House, and Duma member Pavel Medvedev. In addition, while in Russia I benefited enormously from discussions with Michael McFaul and Michael Davey, and from the friendship of Karen Bradbury, Laura Kennedy, and Chris Boffey.

When asked about how best to design the Russian financial system, the central bank's once and future director Viktor Gerashchenko observed that "We hardly need to take the United States as a model. It is a country with its own painfully specific features. We must not forget that it is 200 years old and has been settled mainly by rebels, adventurists, and misfits, by what one may call dissidents who did not get on in their native civilizations and were drawn to the undeveloped continent, where they could do, think up, and try whatever they liked."[2] Stephen Cohen and Nancy Bermeo happily allowed me to do, think up, and try whatever I liked (within reason), and supported me throughout my work. Kathleen Thelen's theoretical insights on institutionalism inspired my own. Larry Diamond sparked my interest in democratization, encouraged me to pursue graduate study in political science, and persuaded me through his example that an academic life could actually be exciting. Andrew Barnes and I went through graduate school, fieldwork, and writing together; I cannot imagine having a better colleague or friend. Joel Hellman graciously answered my early, naive questions about Russian banking when

2. Quoted in Vitalii Kovalenko, "Viktor Gerashchenko: Reform Is Not a Horse, It Will Not Save Us Itself," *Rossiiskaia gazeta*, April 24, 1993, 5, trans. FBIS-SOV, April 28, 1993, 35–36.

he did not need to do so. My colleagues at Princeton, Brookings, and Loyola were interested and supportive throughout this process. Roger Haydon of Cornell University Press first snapped up the manuscript and then tore it apart, both of which I thoroughly appreciated. Clancy Broxton worked over the multi-fonted endnotes and bibliography, while Daniel Karnes expertly designed the maps in chapter five. My family, especially my mother Margaret and my brother Erik, provided the foundation upon which I have built my work and my life. This book is dedicated to the memory of my father, Roger Johnson, who loved the Wild West.

Most importantly, though, I want to thank my husband Ben Forest. He made finishing this book much more pleasant than I could ever have imagined, and I believe he hopes I never write another one.

JULIET JOHNSON

Budapest, Hungary

Note on Transliteration

I have transliterated Russian words using the Library of Congress system throughout the text and notes, except where doing so might cause confusion. For example, I refer to Yeltsin, not El'tsin, and when "ia" or "iu" would appear at the beginning of a word, I transliterate "i" with a "y" (e.g., Yaroslavl', not Iaroslavl'). Unless otherwise specified, all translations from Russian are my own.

Abbreviations

ADR	American depository receipt
AEA	American Economics Association
ARB	Association of Russian Banks
ARKO	Agency for the Reconstruction of Credit Organizations
BIS	Bank for International Settlements
BOF	Bank of Finland
CBR	Central Bank of Russia
CIS	Commonwealth of Independent States
CPSU	Communist Party of the Soviet Union
EBRD	European Bank for Reconstruction and Development
ECU	European Currency Unit
FIG	Financial-industrial group
FIMACO	Financial Management Company, Limited
FSU	Former Soviet Union
FSVC	Financial Services Volunteer Corps
GDP	Gross domestic product
GKO	Short-term treasury bills (Gosudarstvennye kratkosrochnye obligatsii)

HIID	Harvard Institute for International Development
IBEC	International Bank for Economic Cooperation
IMF	International Monetary Fund
LDPR	Liberal-Democratic Party of Russia
MFK	International Financial Company (MFK Bank)
NGO	Nongovernmental organization
OECD	Organization for Economic Cooperation and Development
OFZ	Federal bonds (Obligatsii federal'nogo zaima)
OMRI	Open Media Research Institute
ONEKSIM	United Export-Import (Bank)
RFE / RL	Radio Free Europe / Radio Liberty
RKTs	Payments / clearing center (Raschetno-kassovyi tsentr)
RSFSR	Russian Soviet Federated Socialist Republic
SBS	Stolichnii Bank Sberezhnii
SOE	State-owned enterprise
TsNTTM	Center for Scientific-Technical Creativity of Youth
USAID	United States Agency for International Development
USSR	Union of Soviet Socialist Republics

A Fistful of Rubles

CHAPTER ONE

The Politics of Money

Large banks are rich. Money, in every country, is an influential
force. And when the political system is not stable, everybody strives
to use money as a political tool.

—**Moscow banker, 1995**

In April 1996, in the throes of Russia's divisive presidential
campaign pitting incumbent Boris Yeltsin against Communist Party leader Gennady Zyuganov, a letter signed by thirteen prominent bankers and businessmen appeared simultaneously in almost every major Russian newspaper. Dubbed the "Appeal of the
Thirteen," the letter implored the candidates to come to a political compromise before the June elections. A clear threat embedded within the
letter warned that "those who encroach on Russian statehood . . . must
understand that domestic entrepreneurs have the necessary resources
and will to influence excessively unprincipled and uncompromising
politicians."[1] Within days, even the communist Zyuganov had met pri-

---

1. "Get Out of the Impasse!" *Kommersant-Daily*, April 27, 1996. With the exception of AvtoVAZ director Nikolaev and Vympelcom president Mikhailov, the signatories are either
bankers or directors of enterprises then controlled by bank-led financial-industrial groups.
They included B. A. Berezovskii (president of LogoVAZ), V. A. Gorodilov (chairman of the
board of Sibneft oil), V. A. Gusinskii (chairman of the board of the Most Group), A. N. Dun-
dukov (president of Yakovlev Bank), N. B. Mikhailov (president of Vympelcom), S. V. Mu-
ravlenko (president of Yukos oil), L. B. Nevzlin (president of Rosprom), A. V. Nikolaev
(president and general director of AvtoVAZ), D. L. Orlov (chairman of the board of
Vozrozhdenie Bank), V. O. Potanin (president of ONEKSIMbank), A. P. Smolenskii (president of Stolichnii Bank Sberezhnii), M. M. Fridman (chairman of the board of Al'fa Group),
and M. B. Khodorkovskii (chairman of the board of Menatep bank).

vately with the signatories in an effort to allay their concerns. In post-Soviet Russia, no politician could afford to ignore the influence of Russia's most powerful bankers. Indeed, Yeltsin's ultimate victory in the July runoff election, despite his single-digit approval ratings earlier in the year, resulted in great part from the monetary and media support of these financiers. Yeltsin reciprocated after the election by giving two of them, ONEKSIMbank president Vladimir Potanin and LogoVAZ director Boris Berezovskii, key positions in his administration.

The relationship between bankers and politics significantly affects the character of the economic system that emerges in post-communist states, for good or for ill. After the fall of the USSR, both West and East briefly embraced the teleological assumption that the end of history had arrived and that post-communist states had embarked on a one-way journey to democracy and the market. Unfortunately for Russia, its financial system developed in a dramatically distorted manner that reinforced and politicized ties between banks and the state. This eventful evolutionary process culminated in the implosion of Russia's financial markets in August 1998, undercutting the reputation of the Central Bank of Russia (CBR) and threatening the very survival of the biggest commercial banks.

This book explains why and how this transformation occurred. I argue that the interaction of perverse, Soviet-era institutional legacies and misguided, Western-inspired economic policy choices led to the creation of a parasitic banking system in Russia. Policies under both Gorbachev and Yeltsin decentralized and liberalized the banking system, while simultaneously allowing the rapid privatization of state-owned property. Policymakers assumed that increasing the formal separation of the economy from the state would yield a competitive environment in which market-oriented financial institutions would flourish. However, the shotgun approach to transformation neglected the lengthy and more difficult process of economic and political institution building. The depressed industrial and agricultural sectors suffered from entrenched, Soviet-era inefficiencies that would take years to overcome, while the state-owned savings bank enjoyed a near-monopoly on household deposits. As a result, even though the state had freed Russia's banks to attract depositors and invest in profitable enterprises, just as capitalist banks do, because of Soviet-era legacies the banks could not reliably make money by engaging in these activities. They could, however, succeed by searching out political patrons, operating in the poorly regulated gray areas of the hybrid economy, and participating in the high-stakes game of property redistribution. For bankers, the road to wealth in Russia lay in politics.

The Russian government, despite its overall policy commitment to decentralizing the economy, found itself equally tempted to enter into cozy relationships with Russia's leading banks. The introduction of national, regional, and local elections, with the concomitant rise of political party activity, gave Russia's bankers an unprecedented opportunity to enter the political system as campaign financiers, lobbyists, and even candidates. Institutional deficiencies, such as the lack of a treasury system, encouraged state agencies to place their funds in commercial banks in a process that inevitably became heavily politicized. The dismantling of the command economy meant that the state lost its main means of generating revenue well before it could introduce a functioning tax system, leading the state to turn regularly to the banking system for financial succor. In particular, the government became heavily dependent on Russian banks' regular purchases of state treasury bills (GKOs), offered at extremely high interest rates. Finally, the Russian government could justify these actions by arguing that its support for (and reliance on) the commercial banks actually contributed to building capitalism in Russia.

Russia's half-hearted democratization process, which undercut the state's capabilities without notably strengthening the rule of law or representative institutions, further encouraged these pathological developments. The personalization of party politics, Yeltsin's reliance on executive decrees to implement major economic policies, the confrontations between the president and the parliament, and the continual yet unpredictable replacement of Yeltsin's governments lent a constant air of uncertainty to Russian politics. This political uncertainty, when combined with the vagaries of economic liberalization and the free-for-all of privatization, encouraged extremely short-term thinking among Russia's bankers. They did not want to make money next year, next month, or even next week, but right now. So, although Russia's bankers prospered by reforging and exploiting their ties with the democratizing state, the atmosphere of uncertainty gave them additional incentives not to sink equally deep roots into the Russian economy. Rather, the banks eschewed long-term investment and institutional development in Russia in favor of capital flight and speculative, short-term domestic transactions. The banks and the state supported each other, while leaving the bulk of the Russian economy out in the cold.

In developing this analysis, I explore the history of the entangling connections between domestic bankers and democratic politics in Russia, beginning with the 1987 decision to dismantle the Soviet state bank and concluding with the fallout from the 1998 Russian financial crisis. Based on the work of David Stark and László Bruszt, I have divided my analysis into two distinct periods: *extrication* and *transformation*. Extrication describes the process that occurs between the first attempts to confront the socialist state's legitimacy and the final downfall of the regime (whether through capitulation, compromise, or electoral competition). Transformation describes the subsequent process of "transform[ing] the fundamental institutions and property relations of these societies."[2] For Russia, extrication began in 1987 with Gorbachev's first calls for democratization within the Communist Party and ended in late 1991 with the disintegration of the Soviet Union. Transformation began immediately afterwards, and continues, haltingly, to this day.

During the extrication period, the Soviet banking system became significantly liberated from direct state ownership and control. This decentralization occurred both because of politically motivated actions from above (primarily during the sovereignty battle between the Soviet central government and the Russian Republic) and because of opportunistic activity from below. The Soviet state bank (Gosbank) split up, the resulting "specialized" banks became commercialized, and new cooperative and private banks appeared, all well before the collapse of the Soviet Union. This financial liberalization took place before the Soviet state eased control over other sectors of the economy, timing that became critical to subsequent institutional developments.

Banking reform in the USSR officially began on January 1, 1988, when the state dismantled Gosbank to create a two-tiered banking system. This disaggregation resulted in little practical change, though, until the strains in the fabric of the Soviet system began to show. In 1990, the Russian government transformed the Moscow branch of Gosbank into the CBR so that it could serve as a counterweight to Gosbank in Russia's struggle for sovereignty. Both the Soviet and Russian governments took numerous steps to increase the political independence of their respective central banks during this period, giving the banks more power in the battle for control over Russia's financial resources. The central bankers, in turn, took every opportunity to expand their spheres of influence within Russia. This political battle for sovereignty provided no incentives for the central bankers to increase their technical capabilities or to stop funneling cheap credits to state enterprises, and the state took few active measures to promote such reforms. Indeed, these policies created a Russian central bank with political autonomy vis-à-vis both the Russian government and the commercial banks, but with little technical capacity to carry out market-oriented central banking tasks. When the Soviet Union collapsed and the CBR swallowed Gosbank, Russia entered the post-Soviet era with a relatively autonomous central bank whose institutional framework and actors had changed relatively little.

Meanwhile, unanticipated consequences of the May 1988 Law on Cooperation permitted commercial banks to appear and flourish during the extrication period. Gorbachev intended this law to give individuals and

2. David Stark and László Bruszt, *Postsocialist Pathways* (Cambridge: Cambridge University Press, 1998), 52.

state enterprises the freedom to open their own cooperative ventures, thereby encouraging the development of an alternative, semi-free market in the USSR. Yet as a result, small, undercapitalized cooperative banks began to proliferate wildly. The barriers to entry in this loosely regulated market were political, not financial. As Most Bank founder Vladimir Gusinskii observed, "In those days, everyone needed a government patron to 'raise' him. The act of entrepreneurship consisted of establishing a good patron—just as in any bureaucratic system."[3] Commercial banks in Russia, whatever their formal, legal origins and status, were born with an inextricable tie to the state.

To complicate matters, beginning in September 1990, the state allowed the specialized banks that had emerged from Gosbank to "commercialize" themselves in a rapid process that splintered the centralized system and gave shares in the resulting banks to their enterprise customers. Since this took place during the power struggle between the Russian Republic and the central Soviet government, commercializing the banks was not part of any planned economic transition program. Neither the Soviet nor the Russian government established the institutional groundwork for completing the process or for managing and regulating the new banks that emerged. As a result, hundreds of small, poor banks and a few massive, centralized banking networks emerged. During this period, all of these banks grabbed as much autonomy as possible while continuing their traditional economic mission of channeling state credits to industrial enterprises and agriculture. Like the new banks, the former state banks entered the post-Soviet period firmly entrenched in the economic system but burdened with a dangerous reliance on the state, a reliance inherited from the past and reinforced during the process of commercialization.

After the collapse of the USSR, the Yeltsin government briefly attempted to carry out a Western-inspired radical reform program known as shock therapy. The clash of shock therapy policies (especially price liberalization and rapid privatization) with these hybrid financial institutions had detrimental consequences for the Russian banking system and for the polity as a whole. The CBR's political freedom led to a battle of wills among the CBR, the Yeltsin government, and the parliament over shock therapy policies, while unaddressed institutional legacies in the financial system made it all but impossible for the CBR to control the money supply. This combination of central bank autonomy and persistent Soviet-era roadblocks contributed to the failure of shock therapy, the poorly executed breakup of the ruble zone, and unpredictable monetary policy.

3. Quoted in David Remnick, "The Tycoon and the Kremlin," *New Yorker*, February 20 and 27, 1995, 118–29.

Table 1.1. Year-end banking sector indicators

	1991	1992	1993	1994	1995	1996	1997	1998	1999
Number of licensed commercial banks[a]	1360	1713	2019	2517	2295	2030	1697	1476	1349
Number of bank branches[b]	na	3135	4539	5440	5581	5123	4425	4453	3923
Number of foreign-owned banks[c]	1	2	15	na	19	23	26	30	32
Banks with authorized capital above 20 billion redenominated rubles (%)	na	na	na	1.2	3.6	9.3	17.0	28.0	40.1
Banks headquartered in Moscow city (%)	na	22	27	37	39	41	42	45	45
Loss-making banks as percent of all banks	na	4.8	9.9	23.7	22.9	19.9	15.8	23.6	17.5
Licenses revoked by CBR (cumulative)	2	7	25	65	303	562	852	1004	1028
CBR refinancing rate (%)	20	80	210	180	160	48	28	60	60
Commercial bank credit to the non-financial sector (as % GDP)	na	33.6	20.4	19.6	12.0	10.4	9.6	14.1	11.3
Average bank equity/asset ratio	na	na	11.2	10.9	8.9	13.8	12.8	na	na
Interest rates (period average) deposit rate	na	na	na	na	102	55	16.4	25.7	8.5
lending rate	na	na	na	na	320	147	46.2	41.7	32.1
Membership in the Association of Russian Banks (ARB)	415	570	733	954	1067	1006	868	707	660

Sources: CBR, *Bulletin of Banking Statistics;* OECD, *Economic Survey: Russian Federation, 1997* (Paris: OECD, 1998); Bank of Finland, "Russian Economy: The Month in Review" <http://www.bof.fi/env/eng/it/mreview/mreview.stm>; ARB, personal communication.
[a] Credit institutions licensed to perform banking operations
[b] Except Sberbank outlets and Vneshekonombank branches
[c] Fifty percent or higher foreign ownership

Table I.2. Year-end economic indicators

	1991	1992	1993	1994	1995	1996	1997	1998	1999
GDP (billion rubles)[a]	1.4	19.0	171.5	610.7	1540.5	2145.7	2478.6	2696.4	4476.1
Percent change in real GDP (year average)	-5.0	-14.5	-8.7	-12.7	-4.1	-3.5	0.8	-4.6	3.2
CPI inflation	161.0	2506.1	840.0	204.4	128.6	21.8	10.9	84.4	36.5
Producer price inflation	345.0	3279.1	895.0	233.0	175.0	25.6	7.4	23.2	57.0
Industrial production (% change)	na	-18.2	-14.2	-20.9	-3.0	-4.0	1.9	-5.2	8.1
Broad money supply (% change)	125.9	642.6	416.1	166.4	125.8	30.6	28.4	21.0	57.2
Government balance (as % GDP)	na	-4.1	-6.5	-11.4	-5.4	-7.9	-6.7	-4.9	-1.7
Domestic public debt (as % GDP)	na	35.7	26.3	18.9	14.4	19.9	28.4	39.6	19.7
GKO annual return rate	na	na	103.2	136.8	100.8	38.7	36.6	na	na
Ruble / dollar exchange rate	169	415	1247	3550	4640	5570	5974	20.65[a]	27.00[a]
Foreign exchange reserves (billion $)[b]	na	na	5.8	4.0	14.3	11.3	12.9	7.8	8.5
Foreign direct investment (billion $)	na	na	na	0.6	2.0	2.5	6.6	2.8	2.9
Loans disbursed by IMF annually (billion $)	0	1.1	1.6	1.6	5.3	3.7	2.0	6.5	0.6
External public debt (billion $)	96.8	107.7	112.7	119.9	120.4	125.0	124.6	149.3	158.8
Estimated capital flight (billion $)	na	11.0	13.1	19.7	18.5	16.3	17.9	>23.7	>15.9

Sources: CBR, *Bulletin of Banking Statistics*; Russian Economic Trends, "Monthly Update" <http://www.hhs.se/site/ret/update>; OECD, *Economic Survey: Russian Federation, 1997 and 1999/2000* (Paris: OECD, 1998 and 2000); Bank of Finland, "Russian Economy: The Month in Review" <http://www.bof.fi/env/eng/it/mreview/mreview.stm>; EBRD, *Transition Report 1998* and *Transition Report 1999* (London: EBRD, 1998 and 1999); calculated from IMF, "Summary of Disbursements and Repayments: Russian Federation" <http://www.imf.org/external/country/RUS/index.htm>; and Vladimir Tikhomirov, *The Political Economy of Post-Soviet Russia* (London: Macmillan, 1999) and "Regulation of Capital Flows and Capital Flight from Russia," ms, April 2000.

[a] Redenominated rubles
[b] Excluding gold

Commercial banks, meanwhile, sought to further cement close ties with the state because such political connections proved to be the most stable, lucrative source of profit. Although shock therapy promised to break the power of Soviet-era managers, it actually reinforced these networks and inadvertently gave the largest Moscow commercial banks (along with the raw material export industries) the leading role in the Russian economy. The unstable political, economic, and institutional situation surrounding the young banks allowed them to consolidate their positions and make "money for nothing." These banks could be profitable without being productive by relying on central bank credits at negative real interest rates, conducting foreign exchange operations, facilitating export–import operations and capital flight, handling government monies, developing the interbank credit market, and granting expensive short-term loans. All of these activities exploited their ties to government ministries, the CBR, and state-run enterprises. The banks used this growing economic power to reinforce their political positions. They served as important sources of campaign finance in the 1993 and 1995 parliamentary elections and developed strong lobbying organizations.

As inflation slowed and the CBR began to crack down on fly-by-night banks in 1994 and 1995, the commercial banking community split into the strong and the weak. The subsequent emergence of financial-industrial groups (FIGs) reconnected banks, industries, and the state in a way eerily reminiscent of the Soviet period. Two kinds of FIGs appeared: industry-led and bank-led. The industry-led FIGs typically combined poor regional banks with suffering industrial or agricultural enterprises in an unsuccessful attempt to use their collective power to lobby the government for more money and to attract outside investment. In contrast, Russia's leading banks established FIGs as a way to protect their already powerful positions in the economy. By astutely exploiting their status as the only domestic interest group with ready access to financial resources, several well-connected Moscow banks persuaded the Russian government to give them large shares in major Russian export companies for rock-bottom prices—the infamous 1995 cash privatization scheme known as loans-for-shares. By late 1995, a small number of politically powerful banks, founded with the appropriated resources of the Soviet state, had assumed control over many potentially profitable Russian companies. The banking system had become firmly concentrated in Moscow, with favored banks in the capital stretching their branch networks to challenge troubled regional banks. The critical financial support the banks provided to Yeltsin's 1996 presidential election campaign helped to ensure the continuation of this process of mutual entanglement and enrichment. The state, the big banks, and the largest enterprises remained irretrievably intertwined.

Despite their considerable economic and political muscle, though, the banks at the center of these FIGs remained unable and unwilling to perform many market-oriented tasks. They had still not developed the ability or desire to evaluate borrowers, grant long-term loans, or restructure the enterprises they had acquired, and so remained reliant on short-term sources of speculative profit. On August 17, 1998, the Russian government's GKO default, ruble devaluation, and declared moratorium on foreign debt payments laid bare this glaring structural weakness in the banking system. For the Moscow bankers, already hurting from the government's tighter monetary policy and restrictions on authorized banks, these events were catastrophic. One after another, Russia's largest banks defaulted on their loans and contracts, destroying their credit ratings and, in the process, becoming technically bankrupt. The Russian government, not surprisingly, chose to bail out many of these banks, but the crash dealt an expensive body-blow to most of Russia's would-be financial "oligarchs"—and, by extension, to the entire concept of market reform. More generally, in the aftermath of the crisis the state reestablished many formal connections with Russia's banks at all levels of power, epitomizing the frustrations of this decade-long attempt to build democracy and capitalism in the heart of the former Soviet Union.

Bankers and Democracy

In order to understand how policymakers could fail so dismally in crafting the post-communist Russian banking system, we first need to step back and examine the political context in which this development occurred. The simultaneous attempt to introduce democracy and the market economy in Russia (and indeed, in the majority of post-communist states) demanded a dramatic reconfiguration of business-state relationships. Not only did these states need to make new kinds of connections between the political and economic spheres, they had to deal with the pervasiveness of previous, mostly undesirable ones. Therefore, democratization presented new problems and new opportunities to these emerging banking sectors.

Market economies can exist and even thrive without political democracy, but no democracy has ever survived long without a market economy. Ever since John Locke, most Western scholars have argued that democracy and economic progress naturally, over the long term, go hand in hand. Political democracy supports the civil liberties that can enhance economic development. Ideally, these liberties ensure that a free media will root out growth-sapping corruption; elections will make politicians accountable for sub-par economic performance; the rule of law will protect markets and contracts, making economic transactions safe and predictable; technology will flow unimpeded; resources will be allocated efficiently (that is, without state interference); individuals will have the freedom to innovate; and the amount and quality of available economic information will be superior. Economic development, in turn, creates and maintains the middle class that helps underpin democracies.[4] Indeed, as democracies become wealthier, they also grow more stable over time.[5] This complementarity has apparently already manifested itself in the post-communist world, inasmuch as the most democratic post-communist countries have enjoyed the most economic success as well.[6]

Yet democracy and the market also exist in tension with one another. Whereas democracy reifies and institutionalizes the notion of political equality, capitalism operates on the ideal of competition and legitimates inequality. Inequality in economic resources, in turn, leads to an inequality in political influence because wealthier banks, corporations, and individuals have greater means with which to press their interests. Moreover, elected officials know that their fates are intimately tied to the fortunes of the economy, and so have strong incentives to support and protect business interests. As a result, business organizations generally play a more prominent and privileged role in democratic polities than do other kinds of interest groups or individuals.

Business interests, however, do not inevitably support democratic politics (or free markets, for that matter). When business is secure in the knowledge that representative political institutions work to its advantage, business will support them.[7] If business interests find democracy a potential threat to their livelihood, as was the case in Russia in 1996, they may take active measures to subvert or manipulate it. Less directly, if business interests become so powerful that they can use their political influence to concentrate society's wealth in their own hands, it can damage the legitimacy of the democratic system. Business interests, in short, may support and protect political democracy while simultaneously possessing the capa-

4. For example, see Barrington Moore, *Social Origins of Dictatorship and Democracy: Lord and Peasant in the Making of the Modern World* (Boston: Beacon, 1966); Seymour Martin Lipset, *Political Man: The Social Bases of Politics* (New York: Doubleday, 1960); and Dietrich Rueschemeyer, Evelyne Huber Stephens, and John D. Stephens, *Capitalist Development and Democracy* (Chicago: University of Chicago Press, 1992).

5. Adam Przeworski and Fernando Limongi, "Modernization: Theories and Facts," *World Politics* 49 (1997): 155–83.

6. M. Steven Fish, "The Determinants of Economic Reform in the Post-Communist World," *East European Politics and Societies* 12 (1998): 31–78.

7. As Charles Lindblom famously observed, "The mere possibility that business and property dominate polyarchy opens up the paradoxical possibility that polyarchy is tied to the market system not because it is democratic, but because it is not." Charles Lindblom, *Politics and Markets* (New York: Basic Books, 1977), 168–69.

bility to undermine it. As a result, both central banks and commercial banks face special challenges and take on special roles in a democratic context.

Central Banks and Democratic Politics

Central banks, as government agencies, guardians of the money supply, and overseers of commercial banking systems, are inherently political institutions. The actions of central banks can affect the rate of inflation, whether an economy grows or stagnates, and who wins or loses financially. In many countries with underdeveloped financial and taxation systems, the central bank also provides an important source of government revenue. A central bank can bail out favored commercial banks, play a key role in foreign policy by manipulating exchange rates, and sometimes even wield immense direct control over foreign economies whose monetary systems use or are pegged to its currency. Central banks, therefore, can strongly influence democratic politics by providing monetary stability and by adopting policies that privilege certain societal groups over others. For example, a central bank hoping to fight inflation might raise domestic interest rates, but at the risk of increasing unemployment and sending the economy into recession.

For central banks in post-communist democracies, the main policy debate revolves around the extent and desirability of central bank independence from government control. Supporters of independence argue that central banks should be insulated from democratic accountability in order to prevent politicians from misusing their power.[8] Political incumbents might, for example, be tempted to increase the money supply before an election, knowing that the temporary boost in economic activity could help their chances while the potential inflation would not strike until after they had safely achieved victory. Advocates of independence also point out that effective monetary policy and banking supervision are inherently technical, difficult tasks requiring a high level of consistency and planning, and as such may best be left to "apolitical" professionals. Many economists support this through studies showing that countries with independent central banks are, over time, more likely to enjoy low rates of inflation. Since democracy often fails in states with annual inflation rates

8. For example, see William Nordhaus, "The Political Business Cycle," *Review of Economic Studies* 42 (1975): 169–90; John Williams, "The Political Manipulation of Macroeconomic Policy," *American Political Science Review* 84 (1980): 767–95; Edward Tufte, *The Political Control of the Economy* (Princeton, N.J.: Princeton University Press, 1978); and John Goodman, *Monetary Sovereignty: The Politics of Central Banking in Western Europe* (Ithaca, N.Y.: Cornell University Press, 1992).

of over 30 percent, an independent central bank, though undemocratic itself, thus might help maintain a democratic political system.[9] In addition, in post-communist countries, independent central banks give a strong signal to international financial markets that the government will maintain economic stability even at the risk of domestic strife.

On its face, the argument seems compelling. Radical economic transformation requires a strong state that can implement sometimes-unpopular reforms. Democratization demands just the opposite, that the state become more responsive to and representative of the diverse interest groups in society. If an independent central bank can provide economic stability and serve as a scapegoat for painful yet vital economic reforms, the chances for a successful transition should intuitively be greater.

However, the case for central bank independence rests on contested empirical and normative grounds.[10] Although studies have demonstrated a connection between low inflation and independent central banks, there seems to be no relationship between independent central banks and economic growth in general. In addition, even the correlation between inflation and independence may be spurious, resulting not from central bank independence per se but either from a societal consensus supporting low inflation or from the influence of domestic financial interests preferring low inflation.[11] Independent central banks may, on occasion, actually harm domestic economies by pursuing too-cautious monetary policies contributing to recessions. For such reasons, critics like former World Bank chief economist Joseph Stiglitz have argued that central banks should be accountable to democratic processes.[12] If the economic case for independence, then, does prove ephemeral, on what basis can democratizing post-communist states justify creating undemocratic institutions? Moreover, given the influence of Soviet-era legacies, politically independent central banks in post-communist countries may not behave in ways that Western central bankers expect or desire.

9. Adam Przeworski, Michael Alvarez, Jose Antonio Cheibub, and Fernando Limongi, "What Makes Democracies Endure?" in *Consolidating the Third Wave Democracies: Themes and Perspectives*, ed. Larry Diamond (Baltimore: Johns Hopkins University Press, 1997).

10. See Sheri Berman and Kathleen McNamara, "Bank on Democracy: Why Central Banks Need Public Oversight," *Foreign Affairs* 78, no. 2 (1999): 2–8, for an excellent, nontechnical summary of this point of view. In addition, see Paul Bowles and Gordon White, "Central Bank Independence: A Political Economy Approach," *Journal of Development Studies* 31, no. 2 (1994): 235–65; and David Levy, "Does an Independent Central Bank Violate Democracy?" *Journal of Post-Keynesian Economics* 18, no. 2 (1995–96): 189–211.

11. See Adam Posen, "Why Central Bank Independence Does Not Cause Low Inflation: There Is No Institutional Fix For Politics," *AMEX Bank Review: Finance and the International Economy* 7 (1994): 41–54.

12. Joseph Stiglitz, "Central Banking in a Democratic Society," Tinbergen Lecture, Amsterdam, the Netherlands, October 10, 1997.

Intriguingly, in spite of this debate, relatively independent, Western-style central banks did emerge rather quickly in most post-communist democracies, with many explicitly adopting the German Bundesbank as their model.[13] The active, intensive efforts of Western central bankers bear much of the responsibility for this development.[14] During the late 1980s and early 1990s, these central bankers increasingly emphasized the importance of creating politically autonomous central banks capable of promoting macroeconomic stability (stability in exchange rates, interest rates, and inflation rates) during post-communist transformations.[15] International Monetary Fund (IMF) deputy managing director Richard Erb summarized this viewpoint in a 1994 address to Eurasian central bankers: "Since the 1980s, there has been a convergence in the thinking with respect to two ideas about central banking: first, that a central bank's main mission should be to pursue and maintain price stability as the best strategy for sustainable economic growth; and second, that to achieve its main objective, a central bank should be independent from political influences."[16] Western central bankers had strong incentives to facilitate the creation of independent central banks in Eurasia and East Europe; after all, the international financial system itself cannot remain stable over the long term without the cooperation of individual central

13. Although the absolute level of independence gained by central banks in post-communist democracies has varied, the relative increase in independence has been extremely striking in every case. See, for example, Sylvia Maxfield, *Gatekeepers of Growth: The International Political Economy of Central Banking in Developing Countries* (Princeton, N.J.: Princeton University Press, 1997); and Pierre Siklos, "Central Bank Independence in the Transitional Economies: A Preliminary Investigation of Hungary, Poland, the Czech and Slovak Republics," in *The Development and Reform of Financial Systems in Central and Eastern Europe*, ed. John Bonin et al. (Brookfield, Vt.: Edward Elgar, 1994).

14. Western central bankers have thus created an epistemic community (defined as a group with a unified "set of principles and causal beliefs" and a "shared policy enterprise"). Peter Haas, "Knowledge, Power, and International Policy Coordination—Introduction," *International Organization* 46, no. 1 (Winter 1992): 1–35.

15. For example, twenty-three central banks from around the world cooperated with the Bank for International Settlements (BIS) and the International Monetary Fund to provide technical assistance to all fifteen central banks in the former Soviet Union. The BIS, IMF, and European Commission coordinated similar programs for Eastern Europe. See Joan Nelson, "The Politics of Economic Transformation: Is Third World Experience Relevant in Eastern Europe?" *World Politics* 45 (1993): 433–63; Jeffrey Sachs and David Lipton, "Remaining Steps to a Market-Based Monetary System in Russia," in *Changing the Economic System in Russia*, ed. Anders Åslund (London: Pinter Publishers, 1992), 127–61; Christine Kessides et al., *Financial Reform in Socialist Economies* (Washington, D.C.: World Bank, 1989); Federal Reserve Bank of Kansas City, *Central Banking Issues in Emerging Market-Oriented Economies* (Kansas City, Mo.: Federal Reserve Bank of Kansas City, 1990); and Thomas Willett et al., eds., *Establishing Monetary Stability in Emerging Market Economies* (Boulder, Colo.: Westview, 1995).

16. International Monetary Fund, *Central Banking Technical Assistance to Countries in Transition* (Washington, D.C.: IMF, 1994), 131.

banks in major states.[17] Ironically, then, the Western "advice package" for post-communist states included both political democracy and nondemocratic central banks. Influenced by this international consensus, for post-communist democracies, independent central banks came to symbolize their reassertion of sovereignty and desire to join the international financial community.

Commercial Banks and Democratic Politics

Less studied, but no less important, are the ways in which commercial banks affect democratic politics. While we often worry about state interference in banking activities, commercial banks themselves also wield power over the state. In past decades, bankers clearly influenced major political and economic decisions in the United States and Western Europe. As Ron Chernow has observed, the House of Morgan, "much like the old Rothschilds and Barings, seemed insinuated into the power structure of many countries. . . . the old Morgan partners were financial ambassadors whose daily business was often closely intertwined with affairs of state."[18] Although public outcry and state regulation eventually reined in the political power of bankers like J. P. Morgan, banks still retain significant political influence in Western democracies.

Commercial banks play four separate roles in democratic political systems: as interest groups, agents, patrons or clients, and (de)stabilizers. Two characteristics differentiate these roles: whether they represent formal or informal relationships between bankers and the state, and whether they give bankers direct or indirect influence over state actors. Each of these roles, depending on the precise nature of bank-state interactions, can have a positive or negative impact on the state's representative political institutions and overall economic development.

As an *interest group*, commercial bankers formally and directly influence democratic politics. Practically every democratic state has a powerful banking lobby to protect the interests of its members; the Association of Russian Banks (ARB) was founded even before the collapse of the USSR. Banking associations lobby to influence a variety of political decisions, such as the content of financial laws or key economic appointments. Individual banks and bankers may also lobby the government directly, and top government officials may have regular meetings with leading bankers to

17. See Peter Evans, "The Eclipse of the State? Reflections on Stateness in an Era of Globalization," *World Politics* 50, no. 1 (October 1997): 62–87; and John Goodman, "Monetary Politics in France, Italy, and Germany: 1973–85," in *The Political Economy of European Integration,* ed. Paulo Guerrieri and Pier Carlo Padoan (Savage, Md.: Barnes and Noble, 1989).

18. Ron Chernow, *The House of Morgan: An American Banking Dynasty and the Rise of Modern Finance* (New York: Atlantic Monthly Press, 1990), xii.

Table 1.3 The political influence of commercial bankers in the democratic state

	Direct Influence	*Indirect Influence*
Formal relationship	Interest group • Organized lobbying • Campaign finance • Positions within state	Agent • State ownership • Authorized banks • Tax collector
Informal relationship	Patron-Client • Preferential loans • Media control • Payoffs/corruption	(De)Stabilizer • Hold household deposits • Make investment loans • Facilitate capital flight

canvass their views on economic issues. Similarly, banks and bankers' associations may provide campaign funds for politicians they perceive to be supportive of business and financial interests. In some cases bankers may even run for office themselves, or be selected to serve in appointed government positions. This role can enhance democratic politics inasmuch as it provides an important interest group with a formal means of participating in the political system, increasing the group's support for democratic institutions. If the influence of banking interests becomes too strong relative to other interest groups, though, bankers can use their power to extract excessive resources from the state, to the detriment of the rest of the economy.

As *agents*, banks have a formal relationship with the government but do not directly influence the political system. In this role, banks carry out state programs and affect the state's revenue flows. State-owned banks may be encouraged or forced to grant loans for political reasons (such as implementing an industrial support policy) rather than for more narrow, profit-oriented ones. They may also serve as a source of state finance, either by loaning money directly to the government or by purchasing government treasury bills and other state debt instruments. This role has been particularly important in many post-communist states, which have needed to replace lost revenues as they have decentralized their economies faster than they have developed efficient taxation systems.[19] For example, many post-communist states have resisted privatizing their state savings banks, because control over household deposits represents a lucrative source of financing.

Like state-owned banks, commercial banks support the state budget by trading in treasury bills. Without a lively domestic market for state debt,

19. Kaja Sehrt, "Banks vs. Budgets: Credit Allocation in the PRC, 1984–1997" (Ph.D. diss., University of Michigan, 1999).

the central bank cannot conduct open-market operations and the government loses out on an important source of revenue. Commercial banks can also serve as conduits for state budget funds to needy economic sectors or regions, profiting by charging fees, collecting interest, or investing the money temporarily before passing it on. They can act as "authorized banks," holding the accounts of government agencies and thus acquiring significant deposit resources. In some cases, including in Russia, banks served as tax collectors by confiscating the bank account resources of tax debtors for the state.

As agents, banks can support the state by implementing state programs and protecting state monies, ensuring the smooth flow of resources from the state to the economy and back again. The role presents two potential dangers, though. If the state has too much control over its agent banks, it may be tempted to rely on and abuse bank resources. This can lead to a state that overspends, to a redistribution of banking system resources from the private economy to the state, and to an accumulation of bad debt in the banking system. On the other hand, if the agent banks have enough power to manipulate the state, they can use earmarked government resources for their own purposes. Russian banks, for example, were accused of regularly diverting government funds intended for medium- and long-term agricultural loans to the more lucrative Russian treasury bill market.

As *patrons* and *clients*, commercial bankers can affect the political system directly through informal means. This role covers a whole range of reciprocal favors and relationships between bankers and politicians. Banks can give preferential loans to politicians or members of politicians' families. Banks can attempt to buy votes on important issues. Banks can affect a politician's image by manipulating coverage in media sources controlled by the bank. Banks might hire a politician, former politician, or a politician's relative in order to curry favor in the halls of power. Banks may even contribute to a politician's favorite charity or pet project. As the Russians say, it is no coincidence that leading Moscow banks contributed large sums of money to Mayor Yurii Luzhkov's expensive reconstruction of the imposing Church of Christ the Savior.

In return, politicians can ensure that their preferred banks get lucrative government contracts or control over state funds, arrange for the forgiveness of tax debts, speak for the banks in the legislature, and in general protect the bankers from political, economic, and regulatory intervention. While this role can, in some cases, help to bind bankers to the democratic political system, in most respects patron-client relationships between bankers and politicians undermine democracy. Informal relationships, in this instance, are usually corrupt relationships, weakening the rule of law, privileging certain banks over others, and hiding the connections between money and power from public view.

Finally, commercial banks can act to *stabilize* or *destabilize* the democratic polity in indirect and informal ways through their everyday business activities. They carry out this role by holding household deposits, making investments and small-business loans, and trading in currency. When the public trusts the banking system, they will deposit their savings in banks or invest it in other ways, thereby activating funds for economic development. Banks, if they reliably collect these deposits and seek to make loans to a variety of promising businesses, seed the growth of the small business sector. If the banking system performs these tasks well, it can engender and sustain the development of the middle class, which is important to the maintenance of democracy.

Banks can undermine economic growth, though, by facilitating capital flight, granting too many risky loans (for example, by loaning to connected parties), and treating depositors poorly. Between 1992 and 1997, over two times more money left Russia than Russia borrowed from international banks and financial institutions. Russia's citizens, burned repeatedly by inflation, fly-by-night banks, and confiscatory currency reforms, strongly preferred to keep their savings in dollars or goods than in rubles. Banks can also contribute to the de-legitimization of the economic sphere by engaging in criminal activities and illicitly harming their competitors. This role becomes particularly important in post-communist states. Not only do these countries need to develop a middle class from scratch, but because of the simultaneous political and economic transformation, citizens of these states psychologically equate democracy and the market. If one proves to be criminalized or unstable, then the other's reputation suffers as well.

At the extreme, major financial crises culminating in bank runs and closures can and do bring down governments, both authoritarian and democratic. Russian prime minister Sergei Kirienko's dismissal after the financial collapse of August 1998 represents neither the first nor the most dramatic such episode. The majority of post-communist states experienced severe banking crises in the 1990s, crises which directly contributed to political upheaval in less stable states such as Romania, Bulgaria, and Albania. In post-communist states, the interaction of banks and bankers with their democratizing political systems has significantly affected the character of the economic transformation process, despite the literal absence of a recognizable banking sector in these countries prior to the 1980s. In the Russian banking system's evolution, democratization provided the political context for the clash of policy choices with Soviet-era legacies, to which we now turn.

Institutional Transformation

Every post-communist state began its banking reforms in the same way, by splitting up the state monobank into a central bank and specialized banks. Afterwards, each faced a similar set of problems. How could the central bank transform itself from an allocator of credit to a guardian of the currency? How could individuals receive the financial training necessary to run a banking system? How could these states handle the legacies of unprofitable lending practices, overspecialization, and bad debt riddling their banks? How (and how fast) should they privatize state banks and allow the creation of new banks? How would the banking system's evolution interact with other rapid changes taking place in their political and economic systems?

Despite the daunting size of the task, Western social scientists eagerly and optimistically supported the efforts of these states to redesign their Soviet-style banking systems. It was felt that such institutional design would not only be possible, but progressive. Certainly there would be major technical obstacles to overcome, but with intelligence, will, and planning, policymakers could guide their states towards the free market.[20]

Yet attempts to create healthy, market-oriented financial systems often backfired. In Russia, institutional designs intended to decentralize the financial system and wean it from state connections had precisely the opposite effect, reinforcing both formal and informal ties between the financial system and the state. Despite similar problems, no other country experienced bank proliferation comparable to Russia's. The penetration of foreign banks and the asset share of state-owned banks varied widely among countries, and did not correlate particularly well with overall economic or political success. Moreover, while bankers and politicians remained intertwined throughout the region, no other state developed a banking sector nearly as politically active (or destructive) as Russia's. Given the initial optimism, what happened?

Poor policy choices engendered by two fundamental Western and Russian misperceptions about the nature of institutional change in revolutionary situations contributed to this perverse outcome. The first misperception lay in characterizing institutional change as a rapid, discontin-

---

20. The titles of many scholarly and popular books on Russian economic reform expressed this optimism. For example, see Anders Åslund, *How Russia Became a Market Economy* (Washington, D.C.: Brookings Institution, 1995); Bridget Granville, *The Success of Russian Economic Reforms* (London: Royal Institute of International Affairs, 1995); Richard Layard and John Parker, *The Coming Russian Boom* (New York: Free Press, 1996); A. E. Sizov, *The Russian Economy: From Rags to Riches* (Commack, N.Y.: Nova, 1995); The World Bank, *Russian Economic Reform: Crossing the Threshold of Structural Change* (Washington, D.C.: World Bank, 1992); and Alexander Elder, *Rubles to Dollars: Making Money on Russia's Exploding Financial Frontier* (New York: New York Institute of Finance, 1998).

Table 1.4. Banking development in Eastern Europe and the former Soviet Union

	Number of banks (of which foreign-owned)		Asset share of state-owned banks	
	1994	1997	1994	1997
Russia	2,517 (na)	1,697 (26)	na	29.0%
Albania	6 (3)	9 (3)	97.8%	89.9
Bulgaria	40 (1)	28 (7)	na	66.0
Croatia	50 (na)	61 (7)	55.5	32.6
Czech Republic	47 (13)	41 (15)	19.2	17.9[a]
Hungary	43 (17)	41 (30)	62.8	12.0
Poland	82 (11)	83 (29)	72.3	47.5
Romania	20 (3)	33 (11)	80.4	80.2
Slovak Republic	19 (4)	25 (9)	66.9	48.7
Slovenia	44 (6)	34 (4)	39.8	40.1
Armenia	41 (1)	30 (1)	1.9	3.4
Azerbaijan	210 (1)	99 (3)	77.6	80.9
Belarus	48 (na)	38 (2)	69.2	55.2
Estonia	22 (1)	12 (3)	28.1	0.0
Georgia	226 (1)	53 (8)	67.9	0.0
Kazakhstan	184 (6)	82 (22)	na	45.4
Kyrgyzstan	18 (3)	20 (3)	77.3	9.8
Latvia	56 (na)	32 (15)	7.2	6.8
Lithuania	22 (0)	11 (4)	48.0	48.8
Moldova	21 (1)	22 (4)	0.0	0.0
Tajikistan	na	24 (0)	na	na
Turkmenistan	na	15 (3)	na	68.3
Ukraine	228 (1)	227 (12)	na	na
Uzbekistan	31 (1)	30 (3)	46.7	70.6

Source: EBRD, *Transition Report 1998* (London, EBRD, 1998).
[a] However, even in 1997 the state still controlled the four banks that dominated the Czech banking sector, retaining significant shares (from 45% to 65.7%) in each.

uous process in post-communist states, while the second held that democratic, market-oriented institutions would emerge of their own accord once the state withdrew from the economic arena. As a result, both Western advisors and the Russian executive branch advocated a "trickle-down" institutional design program inappropriate for the political, economic, and institutional conditions in the country.

These misperceptions led observers to predict a rapid economic transition once the government liberalized prices, achieved macroeconomic stability, and privatized state property. Many spoke as if the fall of the Communist Party and the discrediting of the command economic system had created a virtual *tabula rasa* on which policymakers could inscribe a new, market-oriented institutional framework. By this logic, once the government had lifted restrictions on economic activity, individuals would shed the habits of the past and begin to engage in market-oriented economic activities as *Homo Sovieticus* gave way to *Homo economicus*. These misperceptions ensured that Russia's efforts at economic reform would focus primarily on liberalization instead of on actively building new mediating political and economic institutions. This exacerbated the poorly controlled decentralization process begun under Gorbachev, and at the same time hindered the development of the state's legal and regulatory structures.

The Window of Opportunity

The first misperception was that an expansive "window of opportunity" for institutional design, comparable to periods of punctuated equilibrium in evolutionary history, had opened in the post-communist world. Evolutionary biologists use the term punctuated equilibrium to describe sharp breaks in the evolutionary process. These breaks occur when an ecosystem receives a shock so severe that the evolutionary paths of species within it do not just bend but disappear, shattering the pattern of path dependency that regularly characterizes evolution. As adopted by political science, punctuated equilibrium implies that during system-wide crises, institutions can be rapidly changed in fundamental ways.[21] Revolutionary situations radically weaken or destroy old, inertia-bound, autonomous institutional forms and allow policymakers to either restructure these institutions or create entirely new ones.

But while post-communist states have certainly undergone a period of revolutionary institutional change, they have not experienced discontinuous change.[22] Instead of a *tabula rasa*, the Soviet system bequeathed Russia a dazzling array of institutional forms that refused to vanish on command. Even in revolutionary situations, policymakers ignore the existing institutional landscape at their peril. Institutional legacies are important be-

---

21. Stephen Krasner, "Approaches to the State," *Comparative Politics* 16 (1984): 223–46.

22. The nature of the changes (a fundamental, rapid, and simultaneous restructuring of political, economic, and ideological systems) meets any definition of revolution that does not require the changes to be violent. A few of the many works characterizing this transformation as revolutionary include: Timur Kuran, "Now Out of Never: The Element of Surprise in the East European Revolution of 1989," *World Politics* 44 (1991): 7–48; Michael McFaul, "State Power, Institutional Change, and the Politics of Privatization in Russia," *World Politics* 47 (1995): 210–43; Minxin Pei, *From Reform to Revolution: The Demise of Communism in China and the Soviet Union* (Cambridge, Mass.: Harvard University Press, 1994); and Nicolai Petro, *The Rebirth of Russian Democracy: An Interpretation of Political Culture* (Cambridge, Mass.: Harvard University Press, 1995).

cause they structure the initial power relations among the actors. Some actors, by virtue of their particular institutional advantages, are in a better position than others to grasp the opportunities presented by a period of political and economic upheaval. These well-positioned actors can use the old institutional mechanisms to advance themselves in a new, uncertain environment. For example, even though Gosbank played a fairly insignificant role in the economic life of the USSR, its control over household savings, the currency printing presses, and the flow of foreign currency gave this institution enormous power. This revealed power, in turn, provided new political and economic opportunities for individual bankers that had nothing to do with policy elites' design plans for the central bank.

The initial institutional context does not, however, simply establish unequal power relationships. It defines the nature and difficulty of the transformatory task at hand. The more inhospitable the institutional context is to the changes the state envisions, the more difficult it will be to carry these changes out. Moreover, the lack of certain institutions (such as a market-oriented legal framework) is as important to the eventual outcome as the presence of sclerotic and resistant ones. In other words, the original structure makes some kinds of institutional adaptations easier— and therefore more likely—than others. A window of opportunity may open during transitions, but it is a window crisscrossed by the spider webs of history. Whoever jumps through cannot help but be covered in the webs—and as anyone who has ever run through a spider's web knows, it takes a long time to peel off the invisible, sticky residue.

Trickle-Down Design

This brings us to the second fundamental misperception: that the state can encourage the development of market-oriented institutions primarily by withdrawing from and liberalizing the economy in a trickle-down approach to institutional design.[23] In trickle-down design, policymakers do not attempt to affect institutional frameworks directly. Instead, they either replace institutional actors or introduce broad, decentralizing changes designed to alter the preferences and behavior of already existing actors. This may include passing laws that merely rescind powers the government had previously reserved for itself (for example, removing prohibitions on currency trading). These kinds of measures, in theory, cause the actors to adapt existing institutions to better serve the state's

---

23. I have argued elsewhere that state-led institutional design can be characterized as either passive ("trickle-down") or active ("state as architect"). See Juliet Johnson, "Path Contingency in Post-Communist Transformations," *Comparative Politics*, forthcoming.

new goals. In this trickle-down approach, market-oriented institutions emerge spontaneously from the bottom up once elites present individuals with the correct incentives to build them.

The simplest version of trickle-down institutional design involves changing the leadership of institutions directly. By putting a monetarist in charge of a post-communist central bank, for example, political leaders would expect the new director to implement tight monetary policies, requiring that director to adapt the central bank's framework to forward this goal. Disaggregation and privatization of already existing institutional structures also represent straightforward trickle-down measures. For example, simple privatization of industrial and agricultural enterprises changes only their ownership, not their form. Such privatization aims to provide owners with incentives to restructure these enterprises and make them profitable. That is, altering the status of institutional actors either by introducing new owners or transforming old managers into owners would encourage them to fire unneeded employees, alter production strategies, and find new markets for their products if necessary.[24] Finally, trickle-down institutional design encompasses broad, decentralizing macroeconomic policy measures such as price liberalization, currency convertibility, and trade liberalization. While these measures often have purposes and importance beyond institutional design, as design policies they rest on the assumption that such macroeconomic changes can predictably produce certain microeconomic ones. As Anders Åslund, an economist and advisor to the Russian government, argued, "the introduction of an adequate economic system should lead to structural changes, raising economic efficiency."[25]

In attempting to guide their transitions, Russian policymakers relied heavily on trickle-down institutional design. Western theories and policy prescriptions advocating trickle-down techniques characterized them as efficient, faster, more controllable measures, and argued that the broadest measures (like price liberalization) could serve to change a large number of institutions all at once. These policies often contained a broader ideological justification, inasmuch as proponents firmly believed in limiting the state's role in the economy. Although this viewpoint proved contentious in the West itself, Russia received consistent advice supporting trickle-down design. As Joseph Stiglitz has provocatively written:

---

24. For example, see Maxim Boyko, Andrei Shleifer, and Robert Vishny, *Privatizing Russia* (Cambridge, Mass.: MIT Press, 1995); and Vladimir Andreev, "The Privatization of State Enterprises in Russia," *Review of Central and East European Law* 18, no. 3 (1992): 265–75.

25. Åslund, *How Russia Became a Market Economy*, 7.

Following the fall of the Berlin Wall, two schools of thought had emerged concerning Russia's transition to a market economy. One of these, to which I belonged, consisted of a melange of experts on the region, Nobel Prize winners like Kenneth Arrow, and others. This group emphasized the importance of the institutional infrastructure of a market economy—from legal structures that enforce contracts to regulatory structures that make a financial system work. . . . We emphasized the importance of fostering competition—rather than just privatizing state-owned industries—and favored a more gradual transition to a market economy. . . . The second group consisted largely of macroeconomists, whose faith in the market was unmatched by an appreciation of the subtleties of its underpinnings—that is, of the conditions required for it to work effectively. These economists typically had little knowledge of the history or details of the Russian economy and didn't believe they needed any. . . . The great strength, and the ultimate weakness, of the economic doctrines upon which they relied is that the doctrines are— or are supposed to be—universal. . . . Unfortunately for Russia, the latter school won the debate in the Treasury Department and in the IMF.[26]

The reform approach characterized as shock therapy represents a package of such universally applicable trickle-down policies. The chief advocates of shock therapy, a group of Western scholars led by Jeffrey Sachs, argued that rapid, pro-market institutional change could be achieved in post-communist countries by quickly implementing measures such as price, trade, and financial liberalization; macroeconomic stabilization; and privatization.[27] The shock therapists explicitly advised post-communist states to use such methods to destroy their old command-oriented institutions in a "big bang," evoking a metaphorical destruction and rebirth of the economic universe.

Despite high expectations, actual institutional outcomes usually proved disappointing. Advocates of trickle-down design often lay the responsibility for suboptimal results on the shoulders of policy elites, blaming fail-

26. Joseph Stiglitz, "What I Learned at the World Economic Crisis," *New Republic*, April 17, 2000.

27. See Josef Brada, "The Transformation from Communism to Capitalism: How Far? How Fast?" *Post-Soviet Affairs* 9, no. 2 (1993): 87–109; Jeffrey Sachs, "Poland and Eastern Europe: What Is to Be Done?" *Economist*, January 13, 1990 (one of the first of many statements in favor of shock therapy in post-communist states); Kevin Murphy, Andrei Shleifer, and Robert Vishny, "The Transition to a Market Economy: Pitfalls of Partial Reform," *Quarterly Journal of Economics* 107 (1992): 889–906; Richard Ericson, "The Classical Soviet-Type Economy: Nature of the System and Implications for Reform," *Journal of Economic Perspectives* 5, no. 4 (1991): 11–27; Joan Bennett and Maxim Boyko, "Savings and Stabilization Policy in a Pre-Post-Socialist Economy," *Journal of Money, Credit, and Banking* 27, no. 3 (1995): 907–19; and Andrew Berg, "Does Macroeconomic Reform Cause Structural Adjustment? Lessons from Poland," *Journal of Comparative Economics* 18 (1994): 376–409.

ures not on the trickle-down policies themselves but on a lack of "political will" among top policymakers to carry these policies through to their necessary conclusions.[28] Likewise, the perception that "new blood" could shake up old institutions explains the excitement in the Western press whenever Yeltsin replaced key members of his government. For example, Yeltsin's March 1998 decision to fire Prime Minister Viktor Chernomyrdin (1992–98) and bring in the unknown young technocrat Sergei Kirienko sent one kind of message; his May 1999 replacement of Prime Minister Yevgenii Primakov with Interior Ministry head Sergei Stepashin sent another. The technocrats' perceived need to have more freedom and power to design institutions implicitly justified authoritarian measures, because slower, more democratic policy-making processes might allow short-sighted interest groups to block reformist programs. When Yeltsin violently disbanded the elected Russian parliament in October 1993, he claimed that he did so because reactionary representatives had impeded his market reform efforts. Similarly, Anatolii Chubais, as Presidential Chief of Staff, "called for the establishment of a 'dictatorship inside the government' to facilitate democracy in society."[29]

But, as Stiglitz points out, proponents of trickle-down institutional design underestimated the role of institutional legacies in affecting the character of change, particularly in the post-Soviet states. Without simultaneous broad-based institution building, trickle-down policies aimed at changing individual incentive structures can backfire. Sachs, for example, supported early financial liberalization across the board in post-communist states, arguing that postponing it until after enterprise privatization would hinder the restructuring process:

> Special and urgent attention should be directed to commercialization and privatization of the large state banks. It might be thought, erroneously, that the banks could be among the last enterprises to be privatized, but the experience of Eastern Europe teaches otherwise. Commercial banks have a vital role to play in the governance of industrial enterprises . . . When the commercial banks are themselves bureaucratic organs of the state, the incentive to carry out these functions is naturally dulled. . . .[30]

28. See, for example, Jeffrey Sachs, "Poland and Eastern Europe: What Is to Be Done?" in *Foreign Economic Liberalization: Transformations in Socialist and Market Economies*, ed. Koves and Marer (Boulder, Colo.: Westview, 1990); and Andrew Berg, "Does Macroeconomic Reform Cause Structural Adjustment?" As Sachs states, "It is up to politicians with vision and daring to create the conditions for Eastern Europe's economic transformation" (p. 246).

29. Quote in Robert Orttung, "Chubais Calls for Discipline," *OMRI Daily Digest,* October 29, 1996.

30. Jeffrey Sachs, "Privatization in Russia: Some Lessons from Eastern Europe," *AEA Papers and Proceedings,* May 1992, 47.

However, as Ronald McKinnon and Jacek Rostowski have argued, in order for commercial banks to function as banks at all there must be a suitable economic framework in which they can operate.[31] Giving financial institutions autonomy from the state leads to unanticipated, non-market-oriented outcomes in a country that has an existing institutional environment at odds with the market, and lacks both a supporting external infrastructure (such as enterprises with hard budget constraints, enforceable and well-defined property rights, and effective bank regulatory bodies) and a supporting internal institutional framework (computer technology, the ability to evaluate borrowers, and a functioning payments system). Without viable private enterprises, to whom could banks make loans? Without a legal infrastructure to ensure property rights, how could potential borrowers legitimately provide collateral? Under such circumstances, the banks could not act like banks. Similarly, the first stage of Russia's privatization program caused widespread bewilderment and served only to return control of most large enterprises to their Soviet-era managers.[32] These managers, in turn, did not find that private ownership encouraged them to fire unnecessary workers or seek profits; instead, Russian industry spiraled further downwards in a cycle of barter, inter-enterprise debt, and wage arrears. Unfortunately, as the following chapters demonstrate, modern market behavior does not emerge spontaneously from the wreckage of a liberalized command economy; it requires the support of a complex, wholly unnatural institutional infrastructure that Russia did not possess. Disembodied, the "invisible hand" putrefied and became corrupt.

31. Jacek Rostowski, "Problems of Creating Stable Monetary Systems in Post-Communist Economies," *Europe-Asia Studies* 45, no. 3 (1993): 445–61; and Ronald McKinnon, "Financial Control in the Transition from Classical Socialism to a Market Economy," *Journal of Economic Perspectives* 5, no. 4 (1991): 107–22. This follows Nelson and Winter's critique of neoclassical economics, in which "the problem of providing the basic institutional underpinnings of a system of voluntary exchange is assumed away" (p. 363). Richard Nelson and Sidney Winter, *An Evolutionary Theory of Economic Change* (Cambridge, Mass.: Harvard University Press, 1982).

32. See Lynn Nelson and Irina Kuzes, *Radical Reform in Yeltsin's Russia: Political, Economic, and Social Dimensions* (Armonk, N.Y.: M. E. Sharpe, 1995).

CHAPTER TWO

The Political Origins
of Russia's Banks

Everybody in this country knew that the banking system was very
profitable. So, after the introduction of the market economy, enterprises found that they had some money. How to use that? Let's start
a bank! Okay guys, let's start a bank.

—Moscow banker, 1995

The paradoxical old saying "the more things change, the
more they stay the same" captures the spirit of the tumul-
tuous final period in Soviet history. The great Soviet socialist experiment begun by Lenin and the Bolshevik Party came to an end as
the Soviet Union disintegrated; democracy and capitalism replaced communism as the declared ideological aspirations of many of the USSR's
leaders; and the country that had once shunned the decadent West began
importing Western economic advisors, goods, and popular culture.

Nevertheless, much of the institutional framework of the Russian political and economic system in 1992 remained startlingly familiar to those
who had studied the Soviet Union in years past. Political patronage and
Soviet-era economic connections formed the backbone of Russian power
politics. Old institutions had new missions, but often the same managers
and resource bases. Meanwhile, many of those who attained influential
positions in the newly created institutions of the "democratic" Russia of
1992 had used privileged positions in the Soviet system to facilitate their
climb.[1] In short, Russia's banking system was not created from scratch in

---

1. It should be noted that Boris Yeltsin himself had been a candidate member of the Soviet Politburo.

1992, but was inherited from the Soviet system following an era of reform and retrenchment under Gorbachev.

The substantial liberalization of the Soviet financial sector represented a key component of this politically driven decentralization of power in the Soviet Union. It resulted in the creation of a banking sector that, by 1991, enjoyed far more economic autonomy than the enterprises it was meant to serve. This liberalization (and the subsequent proliferation of commercial banks) took place in two waves. The first wave, beginning in 1987–88, encompassed a reform from above and a revolution from below. From above, Gorbachev's team divided Gosbank into state-owned specialized banks and a central bank. From below, cooperative and commercial banks, encouraged by Gosbank and by the government, arose to take advantage of the more relaxed economic environment. Political and institutional infighting then kicked off a second wave of bank proliferation in 1990, as the networks of specialized banks broke up and were "commercialized" during the battle for monetary sovereignty between Gosbank and the Central Bank of Russia. In 1987, the Soviet Union had one bank—Gosbank. By January 1992, the rapid, politicized liberalization process had bequeathed 1,360 banks to Russia alone.

The Soviet Banking System

The Soviet economic system, based from the beginning on the eventual abolition of private ownership of the means of production, became strictly centralized after 1928 under Stalin. Gosplan (the State Planning Commission) made decisions on the production and allocation of goods (codified in five-year plans) and Goskomtsen (the State Committee on Prices) set prices for many goods in the economy. About sixty central ministries, headed by the Council of Ministers, coordinated this massive state economic bureaucracy. The Communist Party of the Soviet Union (CPSU) controlled all socially important positions through the *nomenklatura* system, in which the Party approved each individual's advancement to the higher ranks of the political, economic, or cultural apparatus.

The USSR's monobank system, typical of a command economy, was developed for nonmarket redistributive and accounting purposes. Over half of the assets of the banking system at any given time were credits to the government.[2] The Council of Ministers directly controlled Gosbank and the Ministry of Finance. Gosbank's director sat on the Council of Ministers, and the Council nominated the members of Gosbank's board. All

2. Kimio Uno, "Privatization and the Creation of a Commercial Banking System," in *What Is to Be Done? Proposals for the Soviet Transition to the Market*, ed. M. J. Peck and T. J. Richardson (New Haven: Yale University Press, 1991), 169.

monetary transactions went through Gosbank, as specified by the USSR Constitution. Besides its main branches in each of the fifteen union republics and sub-branches in autonomous republics, territories, and regions, Gosbank controlled three subordinate banks: Stroibank (the All-Union Bank for the Financing of the Investments of the USSR), Sberbank (the Savings Bank), and Vneshtorgbank (the Foreign Trade Bank). In addition, Gosbank and Vneshtorgbank had foreign subsidiary banks in London, Paris, Frankfurt, Luxembourg, and Vienna. The oldest and most prominent were Moscow Narodny Bank, founded in London in 1919, and Eurobank, founded in Paris in 1925.

The mammoth Stroibank managed and financed government investment with short- and long-term credits. Sberbank, the monopoly household savings bank which was incorporated into Gosbank in 1963, offered demand deposits, time deposits, current accounts, conditional accounts, and lottery accounts (accounts with a lottery drawing for interest payment). The Soviet state provided few quality goods for consumers to purchase, and consumers often spent months or years on waiting lists for items such as cars. As a result, Soviet citizens kept their surplus cash (known in economic terms as the "monetary overhang" or "repressed inflation") in Sberbank. Sberbank supplied funds for state investments by floating loans to the government with these deposits, serving as a reliable and lucrative source of state finance. Vneshtorgbank and its affiliated banks abroad financed trade among the Eastern Bloc countries and between the socialist and capitalist spheres. These were the only Soviet banks that handled hard currency.

The separation of cash money (*nalichnye*) and noncash money (*beznalichnye*) into a dual monetary circuit represented an important but often overlooked component of the Soviet banking system. For instance, an enterprise that was allocated *beznalichnye* in the planning process could use the credits in its *beznalichnye* account to purchase inputs from other state enterprises, but could not take this money out of the bank as cash (*nalichnye*) in order to pay wages or make purchases from private firms. This dual monetary circuit allowed Gosbank to give soft credit to enterprises with few adverse macroeconomic consequences under the command economy. Until 1990, when this system began to break down, there was little correlation between the growth of the broad money supply and the rate of open inflation. In short, the banking system served as an administrative means of channeling money to state enterprises and financing the government. Banking in the Soviet period was a low-status, low-paid profession dominated by women.

After Leonid Brezhnev's death in 1982, Soviet leaders began to view their economic system with a more critical eye. While the Soviet Union had suffered no economic crisis in the strict sense of the word, certainly the command economy had failed to maintain high levels of growth and to produce quality consumer goods. Moreover, the technological revolution elsewhere in the world proved difficult to replicate in the less flexible environment of a centrally planned economy. A common joke boasted that the mighty Soviet Union produced the world's largest microchips. As Gorbachev later admitted, "we came to realize that the country was living beyond its means. That holes in the budget were being covered through the Savings Bank, through credits. That we were heading for the abyss."[3] Gorbachev believed in the ultimate viability of socialism as an economic system for the USSR, and felt at first that its shortcomings could be addressed by reforming the economic bureaucracy and restoring discipline to the workplace.

This reform process began in the institutional context of a longstanding command economy: few laws governed market relations, private property barely existed, there was no market-based taxation system, the ruble was nonconvertible, and enterprises received copious soft credits from the financial system and fulfilled their part of the "plan" any way that they could. Economic reform attempts from 1985 through mid-1986, which focused on acceleration (*uskorenie*), quality control monitoring (*gospriemka*), and discipline (primarily campaigns against alcohol consumption and corruption), immediately ran up against these institutional barriers and stalled.

Rather than pulling back in the face of failure, however, Gorbachev and his advisors pressed ahead and initiated a wider debate, this time over both economic and political reform. Gorbachev believed that the forum for debate over economic policy needed to be broadened beyond the cautious, conservative Soviet Communist Party leadership. Political openness (*glasnost'*), therefore, represented a means to an end—the revitalization of Soviet socialism. This decision and its manifestations in the parallel policies of restructuring (*perestroika*) and democratization (*demokratizatsiia*) catalyzed the first significant changes in the economic institutions of the Soviet Union. Gorbachev's bold action rolled though the Soviet system like a tidal wave, leaving both liberation and devastation in its wake.

Reform from Above: The Breakup of Gosbank

The Law on the State Enterprise, drafted by Gorbachev's economic reform team and introduced at the June 1987 Central Committee plenum, represented a significant attempt to impose financial accountability and autonomy on state enterprises. In theory, enterprises would

---

3. Mikhail Gorbachev, "Strengthen the Key Element of the Economy," *Pravda* and *Izvestiia*, December 10, 1990, 1–2, trans. *Current Digest of the Soviet Press* 42, no. 49 (1990): 9.

have to support themselves with their own profits and would face bankruptcy if unsuccessful over a long period of time. Soviet reformers felt that the imposition of a harder budget constraint on enterprises would require transforming the passive state banking system into one that took an active role in allocating economic resources. This simple assumption—and the decisions that followed from it—led the state banking system to change much more rapidly than did the enterprises it served.

A major part of the government program broke up Gosbank, creating a standard two-tiered banking system.[4] The official split occurred in January 1988, only six months after the initial legislation had been passed. Gosbank itself became a true central bank, freed from serving clients and responsible for managing monetary policy. It retained only its major offices in the republics, large cities, and oblasts (equivalent to a small province or large county). Although the government would continue to direct credit policy, Gosbank received the power to set the interest rates on this credit in coordination with the Ministry of Finance and Gosplan. The state foreign trade bank (formerly Vneshtorgbank, now renamed Vneshekonombank) and the state savings bank (Sberbank) remained under Gosbank's control.

The rest of Gosbank split into three specialized banks, or spetsbanks. Agroprombank (the agro-industrial bank) and Zhilsotsbank (the bank of housing and social development) emerged from Gosbank proper, while Stroibank became Promstroibank (the industrial-construction bank). Not only did the spetsbanks gain more control over personnel, but Gosbank transferred cash reserves and the interbank clearing system to them.[5] The spetsbanks, though, did not receive permission to set their own interest rates or make their own credit policies. As a result, this reform created a whole new layer of squabbling banking bureaucracies that still had few incentives to operate in a market-oriented way.[6] No one delineated clear

4. The Council of Ministers resolution that created the spetsbanks, "O sovershenstvovanii na povyshenie effektivnosti ekonomiki," was introduced on July 17, 1987, as a part of a package of ten decrees (collectively entitled "O korennoi perestroike") that supplemented the 1987 Law on State Enterprises. See Garegin Tosunian, *Bankovskoe delo i bankovskoe zakonodatel'stvo v Rossii: Opyt, problemy, perspektivy* (Moscow: Akademiia narodnogo khoziaistva, 1995), 105 and 118; and Gertrude Schroeder, "Anatomy of Gorbachev's Economic Reform," *Soviet Economy* 3, no. 3 (1987): 219–41.

5. V. S. Zakharov, "Stanovlenie sistemy kommercheskikh bankov Rossii," *Den'gi i kredit* 8 (1998): 24–27.

6. Indeed, leading Soviet economist Nikolai Petrakov had implicitly warned of this possibility in late 1987, stating that "The radical perestroika of the country's economic mechanism outlined by the 27th Party Congress and discussed in detail at the June 1987 Central Committee Plenum can be fully realized only through fundamental changes in the planning of prices and finances and the enhancement of the role of the banking system in economic management." He stressed, among other measures, that automatic credits to enterprises

lines of authority between Gosbank and the spetsbanks, or determined how the spetsbanks were to draft credit plans, organize payments, or restructure their accounting systems. According to the law, the Council of Ministers controlled the spetsbanks. However, the legislation also created an All-Union Council of Banks consisting of the director of Gosbank, the directors of the main spetsbank offices, and representatives from other government economic ministries. This administrative reshuffling set the stage for major conflict between Gosbank and the Soviet economic ministries, whose access to credits was supposed to be reined in by these reforms.

It also led, predictably, to a proliferation of paperwork and growing acrimony between Gosbank and spetsbank staff. From the beginning, Gosbank opposed the spetsbank reforms as an affront to its control over the Soviet financial system. The head of the regional Gosbank office in Riazan' observed in 1989 that:

> In practice, perestroika of banks has not been carried out. It has just been a structural reorganization . . . in the worst traditions of the stagnation period . . . It is impossible not to mention that as a result of the reorganization of Gosbank . . . it has been allocated the role of simple coordinator of the spetsbanks' activities, without levers of influence over them. . . . The new system of banks not only doesn't contribute to economic reform, but in reality has become a brake on it.[7]

In response to the threat from the spetsbanks, Gosbank began to look for ways outside of legislative parameters to increase its own power to regulate the spetsbanks and to dilute their importance in the financial system as a whole. Using typical Soviet-style management techniques, Gosbank issued vast quantities of telegrams, orders, directives, and so forth in a vain attempt to micromanage the spetsbanks from above. In addition, Gosbank set credit limits for the spetsbanks that the latter felt were far too low, and refused to allow the spetsbanks the minor interest rate flexibility granted to them in the original legislation.

The spetsbanks, for their part, increased their staffs to build up a wall against Gosbank, while failing to monitor or to restrict credit to the enterprises that they served. Total bank credit grew by about 10 percent each year in 1988-89, compared with less than 5 percent growth in 1987.[8]

---

should be eliminated. Nikolai Petrakov, "Prospects for Change in the Systems of Price Formation, Finance, and Credit in the USSR," *Soviet Economy* 3, no. 2 (1987): 135–44.

7. Tamara Pigilova, "Kakoi bank nam nuzhen," *Priokskaia pravda*, October 14, 1989, 2.

8. Tomás J. T. Baliño, David S. Hoelscher, and Jakob Horder, "Evolution of Monetary Policy Instruments in Russia," *Working Paper of the International Monetary Fund*, December 1997, 8.

Within a year, the share of managerial personnel in the banking system rose from 17.2 percent to 19.7 percent, the number of bankers increased by about 18,000, and the operating budget of the banks increased by 18.5 percent.[9] The introduction of the spetsbanks created an administrative mess, while the spetsbanks received little real autonomy in setting interest rates or allocating credit, and enterprises continued to operate on soft budget constraints as before. As a Russian banking text dryly put it, "the reorganization of 1987 begat more negative than positive moments."[10]

In response to this unexpectedly unhelpful evolution of the banking system, in March 1989 the Council of Ministers passed another equally ineffective resolution making the spetsbanks responsible for financing their operations out of their own revenues (a policy called *khozraschet* in Russian). Policymakers thought that this would give the spetsbanks the profit motive they had sorely been lacking. However, as Gosbank retained control over the spetsbanks' credit resources, this merely increased the tension between Gosbank and the spetsbanks while failing to solve the problem of credit misallocation.

The spetsbank reform administratively decentralized the banks without simultaneously increasing their responsibilities or technical capacities and without reforming the external institutional environment. It did not address the question of ruble convertibility, caused bureaucratic proliferation and infighting, retained state control over sectoral investment decisions, and told banks to allocate credit on a for-profit basis without giving them the training, tools, incentives, or authority to do so. In short, it was doomed to failure from the beginning.

Why were these reform efforts so limited? First of all, few Soviet leaders supported more extensive banking reforms at that point in time. As Leonid Abalkin, a leading economic advisor to Gorbachev, stated, "We do not intend to evolve into [a Western, market-type model] and do not consider it to be ideal. Ours is more complex and not a market model."[11] Soviet leaders had only just accepted the idea of reintroducing cooperative enterprises, and full-scale enterprise privatization and democratic elections remained in the future. In fact, these initial financial reforms were actually less radical than those undertaken during the New Economic Policy (NEP) era of the 1920s, during which Soviet leaders introduced a parallel gold-backed currency, permitted currency trading, and

9. Nikolai Garetovskii, "Voprosy sovershenstvovaniia bankovskoi sistemy," *Den'gi i kredit* 11 (1989).

10. Yu. Korobov et al., *Bankovskii portfel' #1* (Moscow: Somintek, 1994), 199. Ironically, Promstroibank Russia was one of the primary sponsors of this textbook series.

11. Leonid Abalkin, "The New Model of Economic Management," *Soviet Economy* 3, no. 4 (1987): 299.

abolished the compulsory placing of state loans. The architects of *perestroika* wanted to retain control over monetary and credit mechanisms during this period of uncertainty and change. Further development required a firmer jolt, one in which the spetsbanks and Gosbank willingly participated.

Revolution from Below: The Rebirth of Commercial Banks

The Soviet government's first fundamental attempts at creating a revitalized socialist economy centered on the restructuring of economic bureaucracies, the introduction of *khozraschet*, and the revival of cooperative enterprises. Gorbachev himself, along with many leading Soviet economists, promoted cooperatives as a return to Leninist economic principles as practiced under the NEP.[12] The May 1988 "Law on Cooperation" officially opened these floodgates by legally permitting the creation of cooperatives, including cooperative banks.

Although the state intended cooperatives to form a new, productive economic sector to supplement the state-owned one, state enterprises themselves either created or "sponsored" a full 80 percent of these cooperatives.[13] While this should not be surprising considering the difficulty of acquiring the access and capital needed to found a cooperative from scratch, it undermines the popular notion that cooperatives represented a true alternative to the state-run economy. Rather than emerging as a complementary set of institutions that independently increased economic activity in the USSR, cooperatives grew out of state institutions and often served to transfer resources laterally, from the state sector to private hands. This created a need for banks to manage these funds, and because the spetsbanks did not serve the cooperative sector, such banks had to operate outside the state system.

Cooperative banks themselves represented only a small portion of the overall cooperative movement, and so their emergence seemed insignificant at the time.[14] According to the law, these credit institutions would aid in the development of cooperatives and had the right to get loans from

12. For one of the most famous statements advocating a return to NEP-era policies, see Nikolai Shmelev, "Avansii i dolgi," *Novyi mir* 6 (1987), trans. *Current Digest of the Soviet Press* 39, no. 8 (1987): 1–7. For the first authoritative Soviet-era article to discuss cooperatives in a positive way, see B. Mar'ianovskii, "Kooperativnye formy khoziaistvovaniia pri sotsializme," *Voprosy ekonomiki* 7 (July 1985): 47–57.

13. Anthony Jones and William Moskoff, *Ko-ops: The Rebirth of Entrepreneurship in the Soviet Union* (Bloomington: Indiana University Press, 1991), 22–23.

14. By January 1990 approximately 200,000 cooperative enterprises operated in the USSR, of which only a handful were banks. Indeed, a book on the cooperative movement devoted only three pages to cooperative banks (Anthony Jones and William Moskoff, *Ko-ops.*)

the state, in effect meaning that they could get loans at favorable interest rates as long as they had a good relationship with a spetsbank branch. The Soviet Union officially registered its first cooperative bank, the Chimkent Union Bank, on August 24, 1988. The first registration of a cooperative bank on Russian territory, Patent Bank in Leningrad, occurred just two days later. The Council of Ministers followed this up in September 1988 with another law allowing the creation of commercial banks. In the understatement of the year, a top Gosbank official happily observed that "Cooperative banks will help overcome the monopolization of banking services."[15] So they did. By the end of 1988, the USSR had registered 77 commercial and cooperative banks, and by August 1990 it had registered 358 new banks.[16] By condoning the creation of barely regulated cooperative and commercial banks, Gorbachev's government unwittingly liberalized the new Soviet financial system early on in the reform process. Yet formal legal liberalization alone does not explain why so many small, undercapitalized banks appeared so quickly.

Gosbank, the central spetsbank divisions, state-owned enterprises, and the new cooperative sector all had strong incentives to participate in the creation of these new banks—incentives born of the command-era economic structure and the first round of perestroika. Under director Nikolai Garetovskii, Gosbank (still smarting from the spetsbank reforms) wanted to foster an alternative banking stratum that could compete with the mammoth, troublesome spetsbanks. In fact, although it is generally believed that nonstate banks appeared only after the Law on Cooperation had passed, Gosbank had informally allowed a few of these banks to begin operations earlier. The Law on Cooperation *ex post facto* gave Gosbank a way in which to register those banks that already existed, and made it far easier for others to follow.

The battle between Gosbank and the spetsbanks heated up further in August 1989, when the USSR Supreme Soviet appointed Viktor Gerashchenko, a former Vneshekonombank executive, to head Gosbank. With the ascent of Gerashchenko, Gosbank began to take a more active role in policy-making. He had firm ideas about the path on which the banking system should embark and rejected the earlier spetsbank reforms as inadequate.

As a result, instead of creating a diversified yet controlled state-owned banking system, the spetsbank reforms unexpectedly encouraged Gosbank to participate actively in the formation of an alternative, parallel banking system. Gosbank's attitude helps to explain its light regulation of

15. V. Zakharov, Vice-Chairman of Gosbank, quoted in "Cooperatives' Bank Is Set Up," *Izvestiia*, August 26, 1988, 1, trans. *Current Digest of the Soviet Press* 40, no. 34 (1988): 21.

16. Yu. Korobov et al., *Bankovskii portfel'* #1, 200.

the emerging commercial banking sector. Indeed, Gosbank set few formal requirements for registration, and these first appeared only in January 1989 after 41 banks had already been registered.[17] Commercial banks required a minimum of five million rubles of start-up capital, while cooperative banks required only 500,000, amounts so low that many groups could muster the wherewithal to found a bank.

Similarly, the central spetsbank administrations realized that by founding affiliated banks they could transfer centrally allocated resources to these banks and make money outside of the command economic system. For example, they could divert cheap credit resources from the state to their new banks, which could in turn loan out the money at higher interest rates to enterprises in the credit-starved cooperative sector. Promstroibank, which managed the initial bank registration procedures before Gosbank reassumed control in 1989, became a shareholder in about 50 new banks.[18] Agroprombank helped to found at least 16 commercial banks, while Sberbank and Vneshekonombank participated actively in this process as well.

Both the newly created cooperatives and existing state organizations also saw the tangible benefits that founding a bank could provide. Not only did banks provide a convenient way to move state resources into private hands, but they could operate in the interstices of the devolving command economy. They could take advantage of controlled exchange rates, the dual monetary circuit, the differential between state and private interest rates, and so forth to earn significant profits. For example, a state enterprise could sell raw materials or goods to a cooperative at a low price, the cooperative could sell the resulting product on the private market for cash at a higher price, and the cooperative could then put the proceeds in its affiliated bank. As Gorbachev himself admitted, "a great many aspects of the development of the cooperative movement were not well thought out. . . . a channel was formed for converting noncash money into cash. Billions of rubles are involved here."[19]

The barriers to entry into this loosely regulated market were political, not financial. Just to get a banking license required the approval of Gosbank's regional office, its head office, the Ministry of Finance, and the local Soviet. It is not surprising, then, that 17 of the 20 largest new commercial banks as of April 1990 had been founded by state enterprises and political organizations. As Joel Hellman observes, "Together, these 17

17. Joel Hellman, "Breaking the Bank: The Political Economy of Banking Reform in the Soviet Union" (PhD diss., Columbia University, 1993), 139.
18. International Monetary Fund et al., *A Study of the Soviet Economy: Volume 2* (Paris: IMF, 1991), 117.
19. M. S. Gorbachev, "Communique on the Work of the 28th Congress of the CPSU," *Pravda,* July 3, 1990, 1, trans. *Current Digest of the Soviet Press* 42, no. 27 (1990): 5.

banks (or only 6% of the total number of commercial and cooperative banks at the time) held 54% of the aggregate starting capital of the new banking system."[20]

In fact, in his survey of 64 commercial banks in 1990, Hellman found that over half had been created either by USSR ministries, regional soviets, or Communist Party organizations. Likewise, a 1991 report issued by international financial institutions noted that about half of the new banks had been organized by enterprise sectors and regional organizations, while the other half were founded by "institutions owned by various associations and organizations and by governmental bodies."[21]

Moreover, the state in essence instituted a new system of privileges during this period by officially restricting many profitable activities to favored groups. These included forming joint ventures, earning the legal right to convert noncash money into cash (a privilege granted to the Komsomol's new Centers for Scientific-Technical Creativity of Youth, or TsNTTMs), receiving preferential state credits, carrying out export-import operations, and acquiring real estate. Both the new banks and the spetsbanks became intimately involved in such activities.

As a result, Soviet banks facilitated the phenomenon that became known as *nomenklatura* privatization. *Nomenklatura* privatization refers to the way in which those in positions of economic and political power in the Soviet system (*i.e.*, the *nomenklatura*) took advantage of economic decentralization by appropriating state resources for themselves.[22] Transferring assets through these new banks and cooperative enterprises allowed well-placed actors within certain Soviet organizations to ensure their own positions in the changing economy, which in turn accelerated the Russian Republic's political transformation process by providing this powerful group with a tangible stake in a more decentralized economic system. As central control over the economy began to break down, the transfer of assets also gave rise to the intertwined problems of increasing official corruption and the penetration of organized crime into the financial system.

This symbiotic process of financial liberalization and *nomenklatura* privatization begat two kinds of commercial banks in the first wave of bank creation—zero banks and industry banks—differentiated by their relative independence from or subordination to small groups of enterprises. A

20. Hellman, "Breaking the Bank," 149–50.

21. International Monetary Fund et al., *A Study of the Soviet Economy: Volume 2*, 114–15.

22. On the process of nomenklatura privatization, see Simon Kroll and Heidi Johnson, "Managerial Strategies for Spontaneous Privatization," *Soviet Economy* 7, no. 4 (1991); Yegor Gaidar, "Kak nomenklatura 'privatizirovala' svoiu vlast'," *Literaturnaia gazeta*, November 9, 1994, 10; and Ol'ga Kryshtanovskaia, "Transformatsiia staroi nomenklatury v novuiu rossiskuiu elitu," *Obshchestvennye nauki i sovremennost'* 1 (1995).

high percentage of the so-called zero banks, created primarily by party-affiliated bodies, spetsbanks, and other "nonproductive" organizations, arose in Moscow and enjoyed substantial financial autonomy from their founders. Industry banks, on the other hand, were created throughout the USSR by Soviet ministries and state enterprises. While the ministry banks gained some independence after the collapse of the Soviet Union (and thus of their affiliated ministries), most banks created by specific enterprises found their operations closely tied to and defined by their founders. Such banks came to be known as "pocket banks."

Zero Banks

Cooperatives and educational organizations founded several well-known zero banks, including Inkombank, Most Bank, and Stolichnii Bank, in order to facilitate and profit from perestroika. Vladimir Vinogradov, then working at Promstroibank, started Inkombank (the Moscow Innovation-Commercial Bank) in 1988. With the support of Leonid Abalkin, then deputy prime minister, and Vitalii Groshev, rector of the Plekhanov Institute for Economics, Vinogradov received his first 10,000 rubles from the Moscow City Soviet under the auspices of the Komsomol "Youth Housing Complex" initiative.[23] Inkombank's first shareholders—who raised another 4.5 million rubles for the bank—included the Plekhanov Institute, the popular newspaper *Literaturnaia gazeta*, the Main Department for Science and Technology of the Moscow City Executive Committee (Mosgorispolkom), and Gosbank's Credit-Financial Scientific Research Institute, among others.[24] With such patrons and with clear money-making opportunities, Inkombank then had little difficulty acquiring further start-up capital, raising the total to ten million. As Anatolii Mironov, chief of corporate advertising at Inkombank, put it, "In 1988, only 'middleman' firms worked on the market. When these firms started to get a large enough turnover of funds, that demanded new banking capacity. [These banks] were still small . . . but, like our bank, they were founded with a lot of enthusiasm. Our bank started in only two or three rooms!"[25] Vinogradov explained that "Perestroika came around, and the establishment of commercial banks was allowed. . . . I gathered like-minded people and, despite all difficulties, started a bank. . . . I cannot say

23. Victor Sergeyev, *The Wild East: Crime and Lawlessness in Post-Communist Russia* (Armonk, N.Y.: M. E. Sharpe, 1998), 126.
24. Vladimir Vinogradov, ed., *Kratkaia entsiklopediia* (Moscow: Entsiklopedicheskaia tvorcheskaia assotsiatsiia, 1993), 55, 64, and 70.
25. Anatolii Mironov, Chief of Corporate Advertising, Inkombank, interview with author, June 14, 1995, Moscow.

that we began to make good money right away. However, we worked 18 hours per day."[26] Although the bank began with statutory capital of only 10 million rubles, it had risen to 320 million by September 1991. According to Inkombank's figures, it enjoyed almost 3 million rubles in pure profit in 1989, rising to 13.6 million by 1991. In a common pattern for Soviet-era zero banks, Inkombank worked primarily with short-term loans, military conversion operations, and on the interbank credit market. In the increasingly inflationary environment of 1991, it also invested in land, real estate, and precious metals.[27]

Stolichnii Bank emerged from a successful construction cooperative called Moscow-3, which built dachas for Moscow party leaders and others. Director Aleksandr Smolenskii used profits from the construction company (whose original financing sources remain obscure) to start Stolichnii in 1989. According to Smolenskii, when he founded the bank he had only one goal: "To evade the state bank."[28] Vladimir Gusinskii, a former theater director and the founder of Most Bank, also started his meteoric rise with a construction cooperative. Although he downplayed his beginnings—"we built garages and such"—Gusinskii was no weekend carpenter.[29] In 1986, for example, the 34–year-old Gusinskii organized Goodwill Games events for the Moscow Komsomol (Communist Youth League). Soon he branched out, first starting a joint-venture consulting company and then Most Bank. Most Bank had a close relationship with the Ministry of Foreign Economic Relations and the Moscow city government, and located its headquarters in city hall. Through its connections, Most Bank managed to obtain control over several buildings in downtown Moscow and made quick profits in Moscow real-estate transactions.[30] Although many Russians believe that the bank's name signifies Bridge ("Most" in Russian), Gusinskii claimed that he named the bank after seeing a MOST decal on a Washington, D.C., automatic teller machine.[31]

Other powerful new zero banks arose as spetsbank proteges. For example, in 1989 Agroprombank and Sberbank participated in the founding of Tokobank, the bank which received the first general hard currency license in the USSR and—before its bankruptcy in the crash of 1998—

26. Quoted in Edgar Cheporov, "Vladimir Vinogradov: How Is Money to Be Made?" *Literaturnaia gazeta* 32 (August 11, 1993): 14.

27. Vinogradov, *Kratkaia entsiklopediia.*

28. Quoted in David Hoffman, "Russian Banker Reaches Pinnacle of Capitalism," *Washington Post*, October 17, 1997.

29. Vladimir Gusinskii, public lecture, Georgetown University, September 26, 1995.

30. Kryshtanovskaia, "Transformatsiia staroi nomenklatury v novuiu rossiskuiu elitu."

31. David Remnick, "The Tycoon and the Kremlin," *New Yorker*, February 20 and 27, 1995, 118–29.

rose as high as ninth on the list of largest Russian banks by assets (in 1993). In 1989, Vneshekonombank, Promstroibank, and Sberbank cooperated with four foreign banks to found what became one of the largest and most prominent banks in Russia, the joint-venture bank International Moscow Bank.[32] Nor did this occur only in Moscow; the head of the Leningrad office of Promstroibank represented the "main force behind the opening of the first three commercial banks in Leningrad."[33]

Soviet party organizations often used their resources to help start banks as well. Elites in these organizations could read the handwriting on the wall and wanted to protect their financial futures. The Komsomol, for example, established and invested in a number of commercial banks as a natural outgrowth of their TsNTTM organizations. Finist Bank was the Komsomol's leading bank in the Soviet era. Founded as the Commercial Youth Bank in 1988, the Komsomol's Central Committee started Finist's operations with 250 million rubles and added another 500 million by 1990, making it one of the largest commercial banks in the country.[34] Later, though, Menatep became the most prominent Komsomol bank. In 1986, Menatep founder Mikhail Khodorkovskii was the vice-secretary of the Komsomol committee for the Moscow Institute of Chemistry and Technology. As he describes it:

> We—I and several of my friends—decided to organize a youth cafe and discotheque. This was quickly transformed into a fund for youth initiatives, and then—after the Central Committee's resolution on centers for scientific-technical creativity of youth (TsNTTM)—into such a center. The resolution contained within it a good legal basis from which to start making money. We took up this task. When the center received its first 164,000 rubles, I asked my friends . . . to let me manage this money.[35]

He soon founded a cooperative (the Menatep Group) on the basis of the center, and engaged in computer resale (among other activities). But when he needed a bank loan to continue the cooperative's work, Zhilsotsbank turned him down, saying "If only [you] were a bank. . . ." Khodor-

32. Gosbank USSR director Viktor Gerashchenko held the reins at International Moscow Bank between his firing as CBR director in 1994 and his rehiring in 1998. See Viktor Gerashchenko, "Mezhdunarodnyi Moskovskii Bank: Pioner Rossiiskoi bankovskoi sistemy," *Den'gi i kredit* 8 (1998): 30–33.
33. Hellman, "Breaking the Bank," 151–52.
34. Stephen Solnick, *Stealing the State* (Cambridge, Mass.: Harvard University Press, 1998), chap. 4.
35. Mikhail Khodorkovskii, in *Biznesmeny Rossii: 40 istorii uspekha* (Moscow: OKO, 1994), 170–71.

kovskii then persuaded Zhilsotsbank to cooperate in founding the Commercial Innovation Bank for Scientific and Technological Progress (MENATEP) in December 1988. Khodorkovskii stated that "We put 2.5 million rubles into it from the center's profits and began to work. We met with practically no obstacles from the government—a rare combination of circumstances." Menatep thrived due to its good political connections and its savvy manipulation of the transitional economic situation.

Unlike the Komsomol, the CPSU itself remained reticent to disclose its appropriation of the country's wealth. Banks such as Rossiia, which the Leningrad oblast' Communist Party organization brazenly set up in Lenin's revolutionary headquarters, the Smolny Institute, were rare. As Hellman observes, "Frequently, party-affiliated institutions would create 'dummy organizations' to mask their involvement in the commercial bank."[36]

Nevertheless, it soon became clear that the CPSU regularly "privatized" its resources through the emerging banking system. This process took place all over the country, as local, regional, and central Communist Party bodies became involved in banking. For example, in 1989 the local Communist Party committee in Riazan' contributed significantly in founding the leading commercial bank in the city. The KGB, too, spread its money widely through the new banking system. Journalist Yevgeniia Albats' investigation, for example, revealed that the KGB had invested the equivalent of about 120 million dollars in six hundred new firms and banks.[37]

The process picked up speed after the February 1990 decision to rescind Article Six of the Soviet constitution, which had guaranteed the Communist Party's political monopoly in the USSR. After that, orders came directly from the Politburo to begin systematically transferring the Party's resources into both new and established banks.[38] Subsequent parliamentary hearings and investigations into the CPSU's financial activities confirmed what many had guessed:

> The Politburo of the CPSU Central Committee made several secret resolutions aimed toward direct concealment in commercial structures of the property and monetary resources actually accumulated at the expense of the nation. Based on this, at all levels of the party hierarchy, there was mass founding of party banks . . . in 1990–1991. Thus, 34.4 million rubles were deposited . . . at the Avtobank, 500 million rubles at the USSR Trade Union

36. Hellman, "Breaking the Bank," 174.
37. Stephen Handelman, *Comrade Criminal: Russia's New Mafiya* (New Haven: Yale University Press, 1995), 104.
38. For a detailed description of this phenomenon, see Handelman, *Comrade Criminal,* 100–113.

Bank, 150 million rubles at the Tokobank, 500 million rubles at the Unikombank, 90 million rubles at the Main Moscow Construction Bank . . . and so on.[39]

These investigators found over one billion rubles of Party money in Russian banks, and certainly this represented only a small percentage of the funds that the CPSU actually managed to transfer into friendly, "private" hands. The upshot is that even Russia's zero banks, despite their operational autonomy and formal, legal origins, were born inextricably tied to the state.

Industry Banks

Industry banks emerged early on as an unintended consequence of Gorbachev's "Law on Cooperation" and the accompanying legislation that allowed state-owned enterprises to open their own banks. Soviet economic ministries and their affiliated enterprises created the largest and most influential industry banks; in fact, few ministries passed up the opportunity to participate in founding a bank. Neftekhimbank, for example, was founded in 1988 with capital from the petrochemical and refining industries, including the USSR Ministry of the Petroleum Refining and Petrochemical Industry and over 37 affiliated enterprises. As S.M. Polotskii, a deputy minister involved in its creation, stated, "the bank will primarily promote a renewal of our vitally important industry and an increase in the output of consumer goods . . . Karl Marx, as you know, assigned banks to the sphere of production."[40] The USSR Ministry of Motor Vehicles, USSR Ministry of Finance, Vneshekonombank, Promstroibank, and enterprises in the automotive industry established Avtobank in 1988.[41] Its board chair previously worked in the USSR Ministry of Finance. Montazhspetsbank was created by the USSR Ministry of Assembly and Construction Work in June of 1989; Moscow trade union associations founded Profbank in 1990; the USSR Ministry of Construction for the Southern Regions founded Stroinovatsiia Bank; and the USSR State Supply Committee was a major founder of Tokobank.[42] Not only did these

39. Russian Supreme Soviet, parliamentary hearings, "About the Illegal Financial Activity of the CPSU," February 8, 1992, trans. *Demokratizatsiya* 4, no. 2 (Spring 1996): 275.

40. S. M. Polotskii, quoted in A. Nikitin, "Bank Issues Invitation," *Pravda*, January 9, 1989, 4, trans. *Current Digest of the Soviet Press* 41, no. 2 (1989): 28.

41. Ye. Aksakalian, "Passenger Cars for Shareholders in the Automotive Bank," *Izvestiia*, February 17, 1988, trans. *Current Digest of the Soviet Press* 41, no. 7 (1989): 21.

42. Association of Russian Banks, *Assotsiatsiia Rossiiskikh Bankov: Spravochnik* (Moscow: Intelbridge, 1994).

banks have extensive access to financial resources because of their ministry connections, but they gained a significant amount of operating freedom after the breakup of the USSR, when their founding Soviet ministries lost their missions. They began and remained closely tied to their founding sectors, but not to one or a few specific enterprises.

The rapidly proliferating pocket banks did not enjoy this benefit of the Soviet breakup. As the law in practice allowed almost anyone with connections to open a cooperative venture, many state enterprises took the opportunity to turn their financial departments into cooperative banks. Although Soviet banking legislation required that no single entity control over 35 percent of a bank's shares, enterprises easily evaded this statute. This increased their access to government credits, gave them more control over their own banking operations, and provided a mechanism through which to embezzle money from the state by transferring credits and resources from the state-owned enterprise to the cooperative. Most pocket cooperative banks worked closely with the numerous cooperative enterprises created by the state-owned enterprises. People began calling them pocket banks because the enterprise directors literally kept the banks "in their pockets," creating them in order to feed off of the loopholes in the old system.

This phenomenon became particularly prominent outside of Moscow and Leningrad, where far fewer zero banks and many more pocket banks emerged. For example, in 1992, Volgograd had eleven pocket banks, four large offspring of the specialized banks, and no zero banks. In Riazan' Kombainbank represented a typical small pocket bank. The finance department of the Combine Factory founded the bank in March 1991, and installed its deputy director as the bank's president. Kombainbank technically had nine founders, but the other eight were enterprises closely associated with the Combine Factory. The factory gave the bank much of its 5 million ruble charter capital as well as its office space. Its premises alone revealed the "unbanklike" nature of this bank—it was inconspicuously tucked into a few rooms of a factory-owned apartment complex at the edge of the city. Its activities naturally centered around the factory. As its director, Valentina Afanas'eva, observed, "We don't have any 'services,' so to speak, because we don't accept deposits."[43] Other typical pocket banks included Mosstroibank, created in April 1989 as a cooperative bank by a group of Moscow construction companies looking to get out from under Zhilsotsbank's thumb; Aeroflot bank, founded in December 1988 by several aerospace enterprises; Dal'rybbank, founded in June 1989 by Vladivostok enterprises involved in the fishing industry; and AvtoVAZbank. Av-

43. Valentina Dmitrievna Afanas'eva, director, Kombainbank, interview with author, March 15, 1995, Riazan'.

toVAZ, a large auto factory in Togliatti, founded the bank in October 1988 with Promstroibank, Vneshekonombank, and Sberbank: its main shareholders became automakers AvtoVAZ and KamAZ, along with the automobile distributor LogoVAZ (run by Boris Berezovskii).[44]

The emergence of banks under these freewheeling conditions, before enterprise privatization had occurred and before the government had any intention of creating a fully market-based environment for their operations, led to an almost uncontrollable proliferation of undercapitalized, poorly regulated, less-than-professional banks. The most typical, persistent problem for pocket banks was overlending to their own shareholders at favorable interest rates. These banks harbored fatal flaws from birth because they had been specifically founded to serve the needs of one enterprise or group of enterprises; indeed, enterprises often legally codified this purpose in their bank's charter. Yet this represented only the first wave of pocket bank creation. The commercialization (*aktsionirovaniia*) of the spetsbanks in the second wave drowned the USSR in hundreds of additional *de facto* pocket banks, with all of their attendant problems.

The War of the Banks

Economic policy represented a major source of conflict between Soviet leader Mikhail Gorbachev and Russian leader Boris Yeltsin. Yeltsin pushed for ever-more radical reforms and devolution of decision-making power to the republics, while Gorbachev stressed unity and more deliberate action. Yeltsin and Gorbachev used these contrasting policy stances as political tools with which to justify vesting political and economic sovereignty in either the Russian or Soviet government, respectively. Western economic advisors supported Yeltsin's plans without expressing great concern for their political nature and ramifications. The Western consensus that all liberalization is good liberalization gave a veneer of theoretical respectability to this political dogfight, and put Yeltsin on the side of the angels.

After the election of the Congress of People's Deputies for the Russian Republic in March 1990 and Yeltsin's ascension as its head, Russia distanced itself further from the Soviet government and finally declared its sovereignty on June 12, 1990. In this political context, Gosbank's reign over fifteen separate central bank divisions, one in each republic, created the perfect environment for institutional rivalry. It resulted in the so-called war of the banks, the long and successful attempt by the Central Bank of Russia to break free of Gosbank USSR. The war of the banks represented one of the first efforts by a republic-level institution to pull away

44. Association of Russian Banks, *Assotsiatsiia Rossiiskikh Bankov: Spravochnik*, 7.

from the center, as Gosbank and the newly formed Central Bank of Russia battled over which one would control the banks located on Russian territory. In the process, it led to the messy breakup of Agroprombank, Zhilsotsbank, and Promstroibank, with lasting consequences for the future Russian banking system. By September 1991, 1,215 commercial banks existed in the Russian Republic, with former spetsbanks comprising two-thirds of this number.[45]

From 1988 to 1990, the spetsbanks had uneasily existed alongside the new cooperative and commercial banks, dominating them in size and influence yet threatened by their relative flexibility and profitability (see Table 2.1). As Gosbank's Dmitri Tulin observed in July 1990, "It is clear that the present situation is not adequate and that the coexistence of old and new sectors is causing all sorts of conflicts that distort everything. It's a very dangerous phenomenon—like having two types of blood in the same body."[46] The persistence of the spetsbanks, which had little freedom to set their own interest rates or choose their own customers, alongside the small, lightly regulated cooperative and commercial banking sector led, as we have seen, to numerous opportunities for spontaneous privatization of spetsbank resources and uneven grounds for competition between the two kinds of banks.

Moreover, ambitious new commercial banks with money to burn had stolen the most talented staff from the spetsbanks. As one commercial banker stated in 1990, "Most of our employees come from the specialized banks. We select their best young staff—we never take long-serving people who have internalized the state sector's sluggish ways—and pay them up to three times the usual salary to come here. The state banks can't match that."[47] Vneshekonombank was particularly hard-hit, eviscerated by these recruiting efforts. As Soviet debts mounted, employees with any marketable skills at all fled the troubled foreign trade bank like rats from a sinking ship.

In this competitive environment, even as the central spetsbanks founded their own commercial banks, many of the spetsbank branches used their monopoly power in the regions to undermine other commercial banks. For example, when commercial banks needed to transfer payments in the early years of reform, they had to have spetsbank accounts in order to access the central clearing network. Yet as V. Zakharov, deputy director of Gosbank, notes, the spetsbanks "were not interested in sup-

45. Sergei Rodionov, "Nadeemsia na kollektivnyi razum," *Den'gi i kredit* 12 (December 1991): 3.
46. Quoted in David Fairlamb, "The Soviet Banking Brouhaha," *Institutional Investor*, July 1990, 189.
47. Ibid., 187–88.

Table 2.1. Overview of the Soviet banking system, September 1, 1990

	Loans outstanding to households and enterprises (in billions of U.S. dollars)					Employees (in thousands)
	Short-term	Long-term	Total	Capital	Branches	
Specialized banks	5.00	1.58	6.58	0.22	62,226	435.8
Promstroibank	1.90	0.45	2.35	0.05	1,466	68.6
Agroprombank	2.10	0.83	2.92	0.07	3,374	91.4
Zhilsotsbank	0.65	0.15	0.80	0.02	716	40.6
Sberbank	0.01	0.15	0.16	0.02	56,637	231.2
Vneshekonombank	0.35	0	0.35	0.06	33	4
Commercial and cooperative banks	0.30	0.08	0.38	0.09	400 (banks)	na
Gosbank				0.03	169	10.6

Source: Gosbank. Reported in IMF et al., *A Study of the Soviet Economy,* vol. 2 (Paris: IMF et al., 1991), 136. Dollar conversion by Jeffrey Abarbanell and Anna Meyendorff in "Bank Privatization in Post-Communist Russia: The Case of Zhilsotsbank," *Journal of Comparative Economics* 25 (1997). Conversion rate 52.2R = $1. Numbers may not add up because of rounding.

porting their competition."[48] Often they would simply refuse to open these accounts. For example, Neftekhimbank had serious problems with spetsbanks trying to sabotage its activities.[49] The spetsbankers also sometimes refused to transfer their clients' money to new commercial banks or froze the accounts of enterprises doing business with these banks. The drag this caused on the activities of the new banks gave the spetsbanks additional time in which to consolidate their positions in the regions. This ended, though, during the war of the banks in 1990–91 when the spetsbanks underwent "commercialization" in a rapid process that broke up the highly centralized system and gave shares in the resulting banks to their enterprise customers.

The USSR Council of Ministers fired the first salvo in the war of the banks. On July 10, 1990, the Council announced that it would reorganize two of the spetsbanks (Zhilsotsbank and Agroprombank) into commercial joint-stock banks, giving a controlling block of their shares to the USSR Ministry of Finance.[50] This was a clear attempt to keep the banks un-

48. Zakharov, "Stanovlenie sistemy," 26.

49. Yu. Korobov et al., *Bankovskii portfel'* #1, 201.

50. A joint-stock company is one in which the ownership has been divided into shares. It is different from a privatized company in that state-owned enterprises (or state government agencies themselves) may retain control over the shares in a joint-stock company.

der the control of the central Soviet rather than the Russian government. Three days later, the Supreme Soviet of the Russian Federation adopted a resolution calling for the creation of a two-tiered banking system in the Russian Republic headed by an independent Central Bank of Russia. The resolution declared all spetsbanks on Russian territory (save the overarching union-level governing boards) to be Russian property and provided for their rapid transformation into joint-stock banks. As a Russian official noted:

> The decision of the RSFSR Supreme Soviet was prompted largely by the Union government's indecision in restructuring the banking system and by its reluctance to surrender control of the USSR State Bank [Gosbank]. Through this largely political step, the Russian Supreme Soviet is saying, in effect, if you don't embark on reforms, we'll get along without you. All the necessary institutions have been created.[51]

Gosbank responded by sending a telegram to all Soviet banking institutions instructing them to ignore any legislation that conflicted with Soviet laws. On July 16, Gosbank's director Viktor Gerashchenko informed Russian banks that Gosbank's main computer center would assume direct control over their computer centers. Then, on July 18, Gerashchenko raised the battle to a higher pitch by appearing on television and threatening to nullify the Russian Republic's resolutions. The situation became so tense that on July 29 Gorbachev himself published a decree "recommending" that the republics "refrain from adopting and applying any legislative acts that destroy the existing financial and banking system" (Gerashchenko and the Gosbank staff actually composed the first draft of this decree, which was more harshly worded). Gorbachev followed this up with a stronger decree advising the spetsbanks to take active measures to protect themselves against attempts to commandeer their resources.

At this point, the battle moved from words to deeds. Russia took three fateful steps toward separating its banking system from Soviet control and solidifying Russian monetary sovereignty: it formed the Central Bank of Russia from the Russian Republic's branch of Gosbank, it founded Vneshtorgbank Russia to compete with Vneshekonombank USSR, and it took concrete measures to gain control over the spetsbank branches on Russian territory.

Although the bank as yet existed only on paper, Georgii Matiukhin, an academic, became the CBR's first director in July 1990. Matiukhin immediately busied himself with taking over the Gosbank and spetsbank

---

51. Quoted in Ivan Zhagel, "Don't Undercut the Ruble," *Izvestiia*, July 27, 1990, 2, trans. *Current Digest of the Soviet Press* 42, no. 38 (1990): 6.

branches on Russian territory through a mixture of coercion, persuasion, and bribery. As Matiukhin himself describes it:

> Then it was necessary to create the bank and find myself a place under the sun. The Russian Republic Bank of Gosbank USSR, with branches in all of the oblasts, was located in Moscow. I directed myself there. But, despite the promulgation of the resolution of the Presidium of the [Russian] Supreme Soviet . . . they simply didn't allow me into the building. V. Gerashchenko, the director of Gosbank USSR, announced that the decision of the Presidium wasn't a decree for him—he subordinated himself only to the decisions of the Union organs of power. . . . Then I decided to 'storm' [the bank] with a group of Russian deputies under the leadership of M.A. Bocharov. . . . Fortunately, our 'storm' succeeded, and Mikhail Aleksandrovich [Bocharov] introduced me to the staff at the bank, saying that in agreement with the resolution of the Supreme Soviet a Central Bank must be founded, and it would be desirable not to start from scratch but on the basis of the already existing bank. The collective supported this idea and we began to work.[52]

This represented the most direct challenge yet to Gosbank's authority, as renegade Russian leaders forcefully assumed control over its property, personnel, and responsibilities.

To further complicate matters, the Russian government founded Vneshtorgbank Russia, its own foreign trade bank, in October 1990 out of a Moscow Zhilsotsbank branch. As its director until August 1996 (and the previous head of Vneshekonombank) Yurii Poletaev observed, "In June 1990, the resolution of the First Congress of People's Deputies of the RSFSR on delimiting the powers between the USSR and the Russian Federation especially stressed the need to create a strong Russian bank that could serve the external economic ties of the new Russia."[53] The new bank officially started operations on January 2, 1991, and like Gosbank and the CBR, the two foreign trade banks worked side by side, carrying out almost identical functions.

Finally, Matiukhin administered the true coup-de-grace to the unified Soviet banking system. After he had ordered the spetsbanks on Russian territory to transfer their reserves to the CBR, he offered individual spetsbank branches the opportunity to become independent joint-stock banks registered with the CBR instead of with the overbearing Gosbank, promis-

52. Georgii Matiukhin, *Ya byl glavnym bankirom Rossii* (Moscow: Vyshaia shkola, 1993),
53. Bocharov was a respected member of the Russian Congress of People's Deputies from Moscow who had ties to the bank.
53. Yurii Poletaev, "Filosofiia banka—razumnyi konservatizm," *Den'gi i kredit* 10 (October 1995): 21.

ing them lighter regulation and more freedom if they switched loyalties. Too late, USSR banking legislation made the same provisions as a counterattack, despite Gerashchenko's statement just a few months earlier that "it is totally clear that the transition to a two-level banking system can take place as the socialist market develops, without any artificial acceleration of processes involved in converting specialized state banks into commercial banks."[54]

Seven other republics followed Russia's lead between July and October 1990, adopting sovereignty decrees that provided for independent central banks and control over their republics' spetsbanks. The political-legal battle resulted in Russia's adoption of the Law on the Central Bank and the Law on Banks and Banking Activity in December 1990, nine days before the USSR passed its own corresponding banking legislation. This Russian legislation, drawn up in haste to strike a blow against the Union, formalized the independence of the CBR as a major symbol of Russian sovereignty.

The war of the banks caused an extreme relaxation of already lax commercial bank regulatory requirements, because the CBR offered the spetsbanks increasingly better deals on reserves, capital requirements, and so on in order to get the banks to register with it. For example, in November 1990 the CBR established a reserve requirement of only 2 percent, as compared with Gosbank's 10 percent. The CBR further sweetened the pot for commercial banks by granting them large amounts of credits at interest rates between 2 and 9 percent (as opposed to Gosbank's 12 percent), leading to an inflationary increase in the money supply and exacerbating the shortage of cash money.[55] In addition, until the end of 1991, the former state banks kept their ability to draw extensive resources from the Soviet state, but had no reason to restrict the amounts now that no unified central plan descended upon them from above. The clearing system that existed until early 1992 facilitated this free lunch by, in effect, allowing these banks to accumulate unlimited overdrafts of their CBR accounts. The CBR had little capacity to monitor the use of these credits, and abuses were many and legendary. In fact, in 1991 credit issue rose by 36 percent, to 496 billion rubles.[56] This permissive approach by the CBR

54. Viktor Gerashchenko, quoted in A. Nikitin, V. Parfenov, and A. Fedotova, "Strategy and Tactics of the Economic Reform," *Pravda*, November 15, 1989, 1–2, trans. *Current Digest of the Soviet Press* 41, no. 47 (1989): 17.

55. V. Inozemtsev, "Monetary Emission Is Growing, but Will It Solve All Our Problems?" *Nezavisimaia gazeta*, May 6, 1992, 4, trans. FBIS Central Eurasia, June 1, 1992, 42.

56. Peter Rutland, "The Economy: The Rocky Road from Plan to Market," in Stephen White, Alex Pravda, and Zvi Gitelman, eds., *Developments in Russian and Soviet Politics* (Durham, N.C.: Duke University Press, 1994), 148.

did nothing to increase its authority in the eyes of commercial bankers. Tekhnobank president Garegin Tosunian remembered the atmosphere during these hectic months of commercialization:

> In practical activities . . . the Central Bank of Russia started to demonstrate its autonomy and independence [from Gosbank]. There was a distinct paradox in this, because until then the role of the Russian offices of Gosbank USSR [had been to carry out Gosbank's directives], and here the situation changed—90 percent of the units said 'I will now govern.' . . . It was a political moment . . . [Gosbank and the CBR] competed with each other . . . so banks had the opportunity to choose—if I prefer the instructions of Gosbank, I will place myself under its jurisdiction. If I prefer the instructions of the Central Bank, then I will choose it. . . . Gosbank spoke its language, the Central Bank spoke its language, and the commercial banks spoke their language. It was complete chaos.[57]

Moreover, when Russia commercialized the spetsbanks, the banks' enterprise-clients (at that point, almost exclusively state-owned enterprises) received most of the shares in exchange for nominal contributions to the banks' charter capital. This meant that the state enterprises that had worked with a particular bank in Soviet times now held shares in that bank and "owned" the bank's capital. During this process, the CBR temporarily transferred the assets and liabilities of Agroprombank, Promstroibank, and Zhilsotsbank to the local CBR offices while the managers of each individual spetsbank branch decided whether or not they wanted to join together with other branches or go it alone. In addition, Soviet ministries and agencies could funnel capital into the banks during this period. Once each "new" bank had gathered its shareholders and initial capital and registered with the CBR, the CBR transferred the assets and liabilities back to the bank.

The CBR did this in order to negate the potential influence of the central Soviet spetsbank offices in the commercialization process, inciting a "telegram war" that progressed quickly to the level of the individual spetsbanks. For example, the director of the main Russian branch of Promstroibank sent telegrams to his local subordinates ordering them to turn over their activities to their commercial successors by October 16, 1990. The chairman of USSR Promstroibank, Yakov Dubnetskii, responded by ordering Promstroibank branches to continue working according to USSR legislation. Matiukhin then sent a further telegram ordering banks not to carry out any instructions that conflicted with Russian legislation.

57. Garegin Tosunian, president, Tekhnobank, interview with author, July 14, 1995, Moscow.

As Dubnetskii complained, "the bank's branches are virtually being taken over by officials of Russia's State Bank."[58] Yet the central Soviet banks proved to be no match for the CBR. Russia began the spetsbank commercialization in September 1990, and the process was almost entirely completed by the end of that year. The spetsbanks, though, did not split themselves into uniform packages; commercialization created a few large remnant banks (primarily in Moscow) and hundreds of smaller banks, many of which became *de facto* pocket banks attached tightly to individual enterprises.

The biggest of the former state banks retained considerable political influence, inasmuch as they provided the conduits for state investment credits. Such banks included Promstroibank Russia, Promstroibank St. Petersburg, Unikombank, Agroprombank, Vozrozhdenie, Mosbiznesbank, and Tver'universalbank. Mosbiznesbank, with 26 branches, represented by far the largest remnant of Zhilsotsbank. The resourceful chairman of the board of Zhilsotsbank USSR, Viktor Bukato, used his power and connections to cut a deal with the Moscow city government and the CBR in 1990 that allowed him to transfer Moscow Zhilsotsbank's equipment and facilities directly to Mosbiznesbank. When he formed the bank during the commercialization process, Bukato called a meeting of certain regional Zhilsotsbank branches in order to persuade them to join with his new bank. Fifteen branches from seven regions concurred. The bank decided to distribute 10 percent of its shares to employees and 90 percent to the bank's clients, but Bukato controlled the process and chose which clients would be included. Major shareholders included the state insurance monopoly Gosstrakh (9.4 percent), the Moscow city government (6.9 percent), and the Board of Trade of the USSR Defense Ministry (6.3 percent). In all, the bank had 800 million rubles contributed as initial equity capital. The CBR, as usual, was not officially compensated for this transfer of ownership, but according to Mosbiznesbank officials, Zhilsotsbank sent between 70 and 80 million rubles to the CBR, money that never appeared on the CBR's books.[59] Bukato so effectively manipulated the CBR in part because he first registered Mosbiznesbank with Gosbank in order to protest what he considered to be "unfair" CBR policies. Considering the hot sovereignty battle and Bukato's long-standing connections with influential government officials, the CBR eventually relented to the bank's demands.

58. Ivan Zhagel, "They're Splitting Up the Country, Not the Banks," *Izvestiia*, November 13, 1990, 1, trans. *Current Digest of the Soviet Press* 42, no. 46 (1990): 27.

59. This paragraph is drawn from Jeffrey Abarbanell and Anna Meyendorff, "Bank Privatization in Post-Communist Russia: The Case of Zhilsotsbank," *Journal of Comparative Economics* 25 (1997).

Promstroibank Russia also wound up in the hands of its former director. Promstroibank USSR's head Yakov Dubnetskii resisted giving up the bank's ties to the Soviet government and to Gosbank for as long as possible. In the end, after much of Promstroibank's network had broken up, the CBR convinced the stubborn Dubnetskii to reorganize the bank's Soviet headquarters as Promstroibank Russia under the CBR's jurisdiction in November 1991. The CBR made this decision easier by agreeing to grant the bank a 700 million ruble interest-free loan.[60]

In another example, the large, centralized Agroprombank Russia emerged in Moscow out of the central portion of Agroprombank USSR. In January 1989, Agroprombank USSR had approximately twice as many clients as Zhilsotsbank USSR or Promstroibank USSR, and by far the most clients who subsisted on money from the state budget.[61] Since the agricultural sector in the Soviet Union continually lost money, the state agreed to write off 73 billion rubles of Agroprombank's nonperforming loans before its commercialization in 1990.[62] Agroprombank officials did not realize the future problems that this reliance on the state and on one poorly performing economic sector would cause, and waged pitched battles over who would get to control the pieces of the Agroprombank empire.[63] Originally the USSR Ministry of Finance itself "privatized" the top level of Agroprombank USSR (which it renamed Agrobank). It held one-third of the bank's initial share capital, while almost 4,000 farms and food-processing enterprises had the rest. In September 1991, after the attempted coup against Soviet leader Gorbachev, the RSFSR Supreme Soviet decreed the creation of Rossel'khozbank (the Russian Agricultural Bank) and demanded that Agrobank turn over its Russian assets to the new bank. The doomed Agrobank soon acquiesced to this liquidation, and its top management smoothly moved over to Rossel'khozbank (which was renamed Agroprombank in December 1993).[64]

However, these examples represented exceptional cases. The speedy commercialization process encouraged spetsbank managers at all levels to gain as much autonomy from the center as they possibly could. In most cases, this meant trying to form an independent, free-standing bank from their spetsbank branch. Spetsbank branches re-registering as autonomous units received little scrutiny. For example, Volgogradkredobank director Rosa Popova observed that:

60. Hellman, "Breaking the Bank," 214.
61. N. D. Barkovskii, ed., *Organizatsiia i planirovanie kredita* (Moscow: Financy i statistiki, 1990), 20.
62. IMF et al., *A Study of the Soviet Economy: Volume 2*, 111.
63. For example, see Agroprombank Deputy Director V. P. Arkhipov's article "Agroprombank nabiraet temp," *Den'gi i kredit* (September 1991): 3–10.
64. Hellman, "Breaking the Bank," 209–11.

Strangely, we were registered without any problem. The resolution 'On commercial banks' was passed in the beginning of October 1990, and on October 31 we had already received in Moscow all of the necessary documents and status of a commercial bank. I think that we were lucky, because the minimum charter capital for registration was five million [rubles], and we only had three. Maybe it helped that we had been a part of Zhilsotsbank.[65]

As the example of Volgogradkredobank demonstrates, even the modest requirements that existed on paper did not bind these banks in practice. When the spetsbanks were commercialized, most local branches succeeded, with the complicity of the CBR, in forming their own new banks rather than joining together with pieces of the old vertical hierarchy. As a result, practically three-quarters of the new "commercial" banks in existence in the Soviet Union by late 1991 had been created from these local offices. In turn, over half of these banks had been carved out of Agroprombank, financially the least stable spetsbank.

This decentralization strategy, although politically desirable for the Russian government, the CBR, and the branch managers of the spetsbanks, turned out to be counterproductive economically. In effect, it created a second layer of pocket banks—former spetsbank branches that had been "captured" by their enterprise client-shareholders, and were poorly capitalized and staffed. Interestingly, this phenomenon explains the surprising proliferation of banks in the Caucasus, because each Muslim leader in the region wanted to have his 'own' bank. In Dagestan, for example, the breakup of Agroprombank led to the creation of about 50 small banks.[66]

In Riazan' oblast', the commercialization process yielded eleven "new" banks created from Agroprombank, two from Promstroibank, and one from Zhilsotsbank. The commercialization experiences of two spetsbank branches in Riazan' illustrate the similarities between this process and the earlier creation of pocket banks. Stankobank was formed from a branch of Promstroibank that had served the Riazan' Machine-Tool Factory. This bank had twelve official founders (all industrial enterprises), but the Machine-Tool Factory represented its primary sponsor. As its directors described the bank's transformation, "[In 1990] we decided successfully to divorce ourselves from Promstroibank. . . . Arranging credit

65. Rosa Popova, director of Volgokredobank, interviewed by Valentina Reva, "Risk—roskosh' nepozvolitel'naia," *Delovye vesti*, August 6, 1993, 3.
66. V. V. Klimanov, "Territorial'naia organizatsiia bankovskoi sistemy Rossii" (ms, Moscow State University, Geography Department, 1997), 10 and 12.

is our primary activity, and we try to support our traditional clients. . . . Thirty people work here, and the average [employee] has been working here for 18–20 years."[67]

Similarly, Mesherabank was founded in December 1990 from two branch offices of Zhilsotsbank, with 23 shareholders and charter capital of 9 million rubles. Despite the seeming shareholder diversity, the largest shareholder gave the bank two million rubles, while the others gave only one to two hundred thousand each. Five years later, one of its directors emphasized the continuity with the past: "When we became a commercial bank, of course, our main clients remained . . . and in our bank practically everybody is an old employee of Gosbank. Even the youngest joined when we were still Zhilsotsbank."[68]

So, with the active encouragement of the CBR, the number of banks in the country exploded for the second time, as many individual spetsbank branches became free-standing banks, taking their clients, facilities, and ties to the CBR credit-granting machine with them. Zhilsotsbank officially disappeared altogether, and only the smaller central networks of Promstroibank and Agroprombank remained intact (see Table 2.2).

This decentralization had taken place rapidly, with central authorities exercising little control and without a market-oriented legal framework to guide it. Ironically, as a result, this increased autonomy led not to the coordination and flexibility necessary in a modern banking system, but to turf wars among and within banks and to the proliferation of undercapitalized banks. This politicized and poorly organized process simply encouraged the spetsbanks to strengthen their ability to use state connections for profit. Although not commonly realized, the commercialization of the spetsbanks represented the first formal step towards privatization in Russia. Since state-owned enterprises became the "owners" of the banks during commercialization, the banks had not technically been privatized; but as these state-owned enterprises were themselves privatized in the following years, the former spetsbanks also became privately owned.

As a result of this two-stage bank privatization process, Russia and the other former Soviet republics missed out on two important opportunities that had been available to East European countries. First, their governments received no payment in exchange for ceding control over these banks. For a deeply indebted country like Russia, this represented a potentially significant loss. Furthermore, the speedy, politicized commer-

---

67. Valentina Bidikova and Liudmila Krutova, chair and vice-chair of the board, Stankobank, interview with author, February 28, 1995, Riazan'.
68. Liudmila Komarova, Director of the Analysis Department, Mesherabank, interview with author, March 14, 1995, Riazan'.

Table 2.2. Commercial banks created from spetsbanks in the Russian Soviet Federated Socialist Republic (RSFSR), 1991

From branch offices:	
Promstroibank	126
Agroprombank	385
Zhilsotsbank	59
Total	570
From operational offices:	
Promstroibank	3
Agroprombank	3
Zhilsotsbank	3
Total	9
From management offices:	
Promstroibank	63
Agroprombank	68
Zhilsotsbank	65
Total	196
Percentage created from:	
Branch	73.5%
Management	25.3
Operational	1.2
Total Number of Banks:	775

Source: Kommercheskie banki Rossii: sprav-ochnik (Moscow: Inform-servis, 1991), reprinted in Joel Hellman, "Breaking the Bank: The Political Economy of Banking Reform in the Soviet Union (Ph.D. diss., Columbia University, 1993).

cialization process precluded the participation of foreign investors. Therefore, the former spetsbanks missed the chance to involve foreign banking professionals in their initial restructuring efforts.

The Banks and the Bankers

By late 1991, the basic shape of the future commercial banking system of the Russian Federation had already emerged. Russia would begin its statehood with 1,360 banks stratified by origin, location, and function: state banks, zero banks, ministry banks, new pocket banks, and the commercialized remnants of the spetsbanks (see Table 2.3).

Two of these large state banks, Vneshekonombank and Sberbank, bequeathed poison pills to the new Russian banking system. Vneshekonombank USSR, once a mighty monopoly foreign trade bank, was the most ex-

Table 2.3. Soviet banks in 1991

	Origin	Ownership	Size / Functions	Examples
State	1988 breakup of Gosbank USSR	State	Very large; function varied by specialization	Sberbank, Vneshtorgbank, Vneshekonombank, the five main Soviet foreign banks, and their majority-owned subsidiaries
Zero	1988 and after; formed with state funds from party organizations, spetsbanks, foreign banks, and cooperatives (not SOEs)	Diverse and / or bank itself; bank director maintained personal control over activities	Size varied; focused on short-term, speculative financial operations; bank-led FIGs emerged from zero banks	Menatep Inkombank Most Bank Stolichnii Bank Petrovskii Bank International Moscow Bank Dialog Bank
Ministry	1988 and after; formed mainly with state funds from central USSR ministries	Ministry and its associated enterprises	Often large; focused on loans to that sector	Avtobank Tokobank Neftekhimbank Zheldorbank
Pocket	1988 and after; formed by SOEs in same industry	Owned by founders	Usually very few branches; treasury and loan operations for owners	Lesprombank Avtovazbank Aeroflot Bank Dal'rybbank
Former Specialized	1990–91 commercialization of Agroprombank, Promstroibank, and Zhilsotsbank	Former SOEs in bank's specialization	Varied from numerous branches to only one branch; provided loans; in regions, many became de facto pocket banks	Mosbiznesbank Promstroibank Unikombank Zapsibbank Traktorobank Stankobank AvtoGAZbank

treme example of a state bank with an unfortunate specialization—namely, servicing the USSR's massive foreign debt. After Gorbachev began his economic reforms, this traditionally strong bank lost ground due to the Soviet Union's rising level of imports and public expenditures and its continued assistance to client states in developing countries. The country's falling level of exports (especially oil) also damaged Vneshekonom-bank. By 1989, this had resulted in a negative trade balance, which the USSR covered by accumulating massive amounts of foreign debt. The bank began exhibiting significant signs of trouble by late 1991, as Soviet enterprises that held their foreign currency reserves in Vneshekonom-bank found it nearly impossible to get their money back.[69] According to *The Economist:*

> By that time [December 1991], according to confidential bank documents, Vneshekonombank had already spent its commercial hard currency de-posits—$5.3 billion—servicing the debt. . . . The bank tried every trick in the book to prevent depositors from getting their hands on their money. It moved offices without telling its customers. It opened only one cash window at a time, causing huge queues and frustration. Sometimes it simply closed its doors. The bank also stopped paying letters of credit (a terrible sin in banking) . . . [70]

This had a devastating effect on the USSR's economic ties with the West, as companies started moving their money out of the country and Soviet and joint-venture firms defaulted on contracts that they had planned to fulfill with the inaccessible funds. Vneshekonombank de-clared a debt servicing moratorium in December 1991. In doing so, it de-faulted on about $65 billion in loans and completely froze the deposits of its Soviet customers. As a result, the Russian government and its banks en-tered the post-Soviet era burdened with problematic foreign debt that technically belonged to all of the former Soviet states, and found them-selves shut out of regular international credit markets.

Sberbank's existence as a state-owned, monopoly retail bank presented a different set of problems. Sberbank began its life in the newly indepen-dent Russia with massive advantages over other banks in the retail bank-ing sector because it held over 90 percent of all household deposits at the start of 1992. In Soviet times, people paid their telephone bills and picked up their pension payments at the corner Sberbank branch. Later,

---

69. In 1991, 80–90 percent of enterprises' foreign exchange earnings were either sur-rendered directly to the government or deposited in Vneshekonombank, with the small re-mainder held in authorized commercial banks. Baliño, Hoelscher, and Horder, "Evolution of Monetary Policy Instruments in Russia," 12.

70. *The Economist*, "Soviet Debt: Halfway There," March 21, 1992, 88. By other accounts, the frozen deposits equaled $7.89 billion (Geoff Winestock, "Russia Issues Bonds to Repay Trade Firms," *Journal of Commerce*, March 8, 1994, 1A); or $10 billion (Janet Guttsman, "New Bonds Designated as Makeup," Reuters, January 11, 1993). There were also widespread re-ports that much of the money had been stolen, or that frozen funds could be freed up for a "fee." See Duncan Robinson, "Frozen Foreign Funds: 8 Months and Waiting," *Moscow Times*, October 20, 1992.

Sberbank distributed Russia's privatization vouchers. Sberbank had existed for decades, and people were accustomed to going to their local Sberbank for their financial needs. Sberbank's extensive branch network made this possible. The bank had almost 40,000 branches and service counters in Russia, far more than any other bank, and in many smaller towns and villages Sberbank was the only game in town. Big factories and office buildings even had their own Sberbank branches. It is difficult to overstate the advantage that this network gave Sberbank in the competition for household deposits. Other banks could never hope to match the nationwide network that Sberbank inherited as the Soviet monopoly retail bank. Moreover, the government explicitly insured deposits only in Sberbank. Since Russia had no deposit insurance system for commercial banks, this made deposits in Sberbank much safer than those in other banks. As a result, Russian commercial banks ignored retail banking services at first, leaving individual depositors at the mercy of Sberbank. Without individual depositors, these banks depended upon deposits from enterprises and the government to beef up their liabilities, reinforcing their ties to these sectors.

By 1991, important differences had also emerged between regional banks and Moscow banks. Most regional banks were pocket banks or former spetsbank branches, and their founders typically used these banks as treasury departments and ready sources of cash. A small minority of banks, though, had formed a powerful new financial sector concentrated in Moscow. A list of the eighteen banks that had obtained general hard currency licenses by the end of 1991 provides a nice snapshot of this minority (see Table 2.4).

Although the list contains at least one representative of each type of bank, all shared a common trait—their connections to high-level state and party organizations. The stratum of elite banks proved remarkably stable over the next few years; 18 of the top 20 banks by assets in January 1996 could trace their origins to the Gorbachev era. Similarly, 81 percent of the commercial bankers listed in the 1996 edition of *Who's Who in the Russian Banking System* led banks founded before 1992.[71]

In short, although on the face of it banks in the Soviet Union seemed to appear from nowhere after 1987, their emergence directly reflected the way in which privileged, dynamic actors within the Soviet system managed to manipulate the changing economic situation by taking advantage of

71. Anvar Amirov, *Kto est' kto v bankovskoi sisteme Rossii* (Moscow: Panorama, 1996). My calculations are based on biographical information for 75 leading bankers. In these calculations, I included only those bankers whose primary job entailed running a commercial bank or commercial banking organization; this excludes central bankers and enterprise directors who happen to serve on the boards of leading banks.

Table 2.4. Banks with general hard currency licenses, December 1991 (of 234 with any hard currency license)

Bank	Type	Location
Aeroflot Bank	Pocket (air)	Moscow
AvtoVAZbank	Pocket (auto)	Togliatti
Evrasiia Bank	Former spetsbank	Izhevsk
Inkombank	Zero	Moscow
International Moscow Bank	Zero	Moscow
Konversbank	Ministry (atomic energy)	Moscow
Kredo Bank	Pocket (export)	Moscow
Kuzbassotsbank	Former spetsbank	Kemerovo
Mosbiznesbank	Former spetsbank	Moscow
Mosstroibank	Pocket (construction)	Moscow
Neftekhimbank	Ministry (oil)	Moscow
Promstroibank	Former spetsbank	Moscow
Rossel'khozbank	Former spetsbank	Moscow
Sberbank	State	Moscow
Stolichnii Bank	Zero	Moscow
Tokobank	Zero	Moscow
Vneshtorgbank	State	Moscow
Vserossiiskii Birzhevoi Bank (VBB)	Zero	Moscow

Source: Adapted from Sergei Yegorov, "Sistema kommercheskikh bankov Rossii," in Vladimir Vinogradov, ed., *Inkombank: Kratkaia entsiklopediia* (Moscow: Entsiklopedicheskaia tvorcheskaia assotsiatsiia, 1993).

their positions in and knowledge of the Soviet institutional context. Banks were crafted not from scratch, but from pieces of former state banks; from finance departments of enterprises; and with resources from Soviet state and party agencies, enterprises, and organizations. By the time that the failed reactionary coup of August 1991 sealed the imminent downfall of the Soviet Union, a significant (though difficult to measure) proportion of state assets had been transferred into private hands through the process of *nomenklatura* privatization. As Yegor Gaidar, Yeltsin's first prime minister and a prominent economist, observes, "officially, by January 1, 1992, 107 stores, 58 cafeterias and restaurants, and 36 service-oriented enterprises had been privatized in Russia. In reality . . . the *nomenklatura* had privatized practically every sphere of the economy."[72]

Although these banks could choose to act relatively autonomously from the legal system, the central government, and the central bank, their origins and interests still lay with the state. The increase in the autonomy of the banking system did not force the bankers to take commensurate economic responsibility for their actions. For the banks to operate as true

72. Yegor Gaidar, *Gosudarstvo i evoliutsiia* (Moscow: Evrasiia, 1995), 153.

banks rather than as funnels for the spontaneous privatization of state assets would have required profitable clients for the banks (meaning enterprises that operated on hard budget constraints), the complicated legal framework necessary to support a market-based economy, and trained bank personnel, among other criteria. Without this supporting institutional context, policies that increased the number and freedom of banks encouraged financial laxity and corruption.

However, just because the banks grew fat off the Soviet state does not necessarily mean that bank directors themselves had occupied the highest positions in the Soviet government and party apparatuses. As a general rule, these bankers came from the middle and lower strata of the Soviet hierarchy. Of the 75 commercial bankers listed in *Who's Who*, 45.2 percent had previously worked in Gosbank; 13.7 percent in a government ministry; and 19.2 percent in a university or institute. Confirming the prevalence of Gosbank veterans, a 1992 survey of 47 commercial bank directors found that 53 percent of them had been hired away from a spetsbank, while "the share of former spetsbank personnel was even higher among mid-level managers, *i.e.*, chief accountants, department heads, and credit managers."[73] In another study, David Lane found that of 118 leading financiers, 25.4 percent had previously held executive positions in the Party or Komsomol apparatus, while 56 percent had backgrounds in the Soviet government apparatus (including Gosbank; this represented a much higher proportion than any other economic sector).[74]

Bankers were also relatively young, especially compared to their Western counterparts or to Russian political and industrial leaders. In 1988, on average these bankers were only 37 years old. The difference becomes even more dramatic when we separate the bankers in zero banks from those in other kinds of banks. The twenty-five leading zero-bank founders averaged only 29 years old in 1988, while 84 percent were under 35. The oldest of the group, International Moscow Bank's then-director Vladislav Sudakov, was 41. These zero bankers, though well-connected, had not yet climbed to the top of the Soviet hierarchy. Similarly, the zero bankers had comparatively diverse backgrounds; only 28 percent had previously worked for the state bank.

In contrast, top bankers in ministry, pocket, and state banks averaged 41 years of age. Of these bankers, 54 percent had previously worked in Gosbank, 11 percent in ministries, and 25 percent in universities or institutes. This trend, not surprisingly, becomes magnified if we focus solely on the former spetsbanks. As a rule, the directors and upper-level man-

---

73. Hellman, "Breaking the Bank," 182.

74. David Lane, "The Role of Elite and Class in the Transition in Russia" (ms, University of Cambridge, January 1999).

agement in former spetsbanks remained the same as in the past. This led to an interesting disconnect between the practices and values of zero bankers and spetsbankers. While the zero bankers continually focused on making money and simply changed their strategies as new opportunities presented themselves, the spetsbankers began the transformation period with habits and beliefs aimed at supporting their affiliated enterprises. Former Finance Minister Boris Fedorov, for example, spoke in exasperation about such a banker from Tver': "He talks about personnel, about the harvest, about anything at all except money. Everything is turned upside-down."[75] A Riazan' banker remarked that "regarding the education that was received earlier in economics—everything is the other way now. Now the people who work best in banks are those with an engineering background, not finance. You can count about 10 specialists in banking in Riazan', not more, and practically none of them have financial educations."[76] The learning process would, of course, prove to be a long and painful one.

Moreover, female Gosbank veterans—80 percent of the state banking system's employees before the reforms—found it difficult to trade their former positions for better ones in the lucrative commercial banking sector. As banking became a prestigious, high-paying field, women, who had dominated banking in Soviet times, began to be edged out. Tellingly, of the 75 bankers in *Who's Who*, only four were women (and each headed a former spetsbank branch). Few women held executive positions at zero banks. Yurii Agapov, the director of Kredo Bank, justified the trend by observing that "banking in the West is a male profession."[77] The real reason for this change, of course, was the rise in the status and wealth of bankers in Russia. Russia had remained a patriarchal society, despite the occasional, half-hearted efforts of the Communist Party to change it, and few women had the respect or the connections necessary to prosper in the changing banking system. As Most Bank's Gusinskii argued when asked about the role of women in banking:

> I believe that the role of the woman should be to raise children. This is the most important role . . . although unfortunately, lots of women practice business. . . . Because of that, families are destroyed. . . . My personal opin-

75. Vladimir Gurevich, interview with Boris Fedorov, "Hand in Hand Along the Razor's Edge," *Moskovskie novosti*, February 7, 1993, trans. *Current Digest of the Post-Soviet Press* 45, no. 5 (1993): 2.

76. Boris Khitrov, director of Pereiaslavl' Bank, interview with author, September 2, 1994, Riazan'.

77. Yu. V. Agapov, "Osobennosti i problemy formirovaniia personala rossiiskikh kommercheskikh bankov," *Den'gi i kredit* 7 (July 1995): 12.

ion is that everyone should do what he is meant to do. This does not mean that women are any worse than men, but everyone has his own role.[78]

Overall, the vast majority of women who did keep high positions in the banking system were Gosbank veterans who stayed on to work in the CBR or in former spetsbanks. For example, Aleksandra Kozyreva began working at Stroibank as soon as she graduated from the Tver' Polytechnical Institute in 1971. By 1988 she had risen to direct Tver' oblast's main department of Zhilsotsbank, which she reincarnated as Tver'universalbank in 1990. Not surprisingly, Kozyreva realized that she would need significant political help to turn Tver'universalbank into a winner; to that end, after the USSR collapsed she convinced former Prime Minister Nikolai Ryzhkov to be chairman of the board.

The easiest way to estimate the rate of personnel turnover in a former spetsbank is to look at the number of women employed in the bank. For example, Moscow Sberbank lost comparatively little of its pre-reform staff. At the beginning of reforms in 1987, it had a staff of almost 100 percent women; in 1992 90 percent of its staff were women; and by 1995 only 80 percent were women.[79] As a rule, the spoils of the Soviet Union went to young, well-connected, ambitious men.

The CBR Swallows Gosbank

While commercialization destroyed the Soviet spetsbank network from within, Gosbank and the CBR entered the last phase of their high-level struggle for control over the ruble. As a response to Russia's passage of its fundamental sovereign banking laws in December 1990, Soviet Prime Minister Valentin Pavlov and Gosbank director Gerashchenko invalidated all 50 and 100 ruble notes in circulation in January 1991 without informing the CBR of its plans. Pavlov claimed publicly that they took this action to forestall a "financial war" against the USSR by foreign agents who planned to release a massive number of high-denomination ruble notes into the economy.[80] But, as a top CPSU official observed with relish, "for those who would like to continue their separatist games with the

---

78. Vladimir Gusinskii, public lecture, Georgetown University, September 26, 1995.
79. Svetlana Klimova, assistant director, hard currency division, Moscow Sberbank, interview with author, July 7, 1995, Moscow.
80. V. Pavlov, "Let's Be Realists," *Trud*, February 12, 1991, 1–2, trans. *Current Digest of the Soviet Press* 43, no. 6 (1991): 1. Viktor Gerashchenko, however, stated that "the entire operation confirmed specialists' earlier estimates of the insignificant amount of paper rubles circulating abroad." *Izvestiia*, February 13, 1991, 2.

USSR, it has turned out to be a difficult measure to block."[81] This politically motivated move severely damaged the public's trust in the financial system. The lesson the CBR learned, though, was that it needed to gain control of the printing presses.

During this battle, the decentralizing forces in the Soviet economy spun completely out of the center's control. Republics stopped paying most taxes to the Soviet government, retail prices rose by 103 percent, and the deficit grew to 20 percent of GDP.[82] By March 1991, Gosbank estimated that only 7 billion of the 23.4 billion rubles of expected tax revenues had been remitted to the center by union republics.[83] Large wage increases "compensated" for the slight price hikes that the state allowed to occur, a steep fall in production began, and the ruble-dollar exchange rate fell rapidly at controlled foreign currency auctions. As a *Pravda* reporter observed, "one gets the feeling that our economy is switching from the production of things that people need to the production of 10–ruble bills."[84] The elite-level debates over grandiose economic restructuring programs like the 500 Days Plan masked a lack of real action and direction from the top, as in practice the Soviet government ceded day-to-day control over the economy to lower-level institutions. Actors within those institutions responded by using the opportunity to consolidate their *de facto* property rights over banks, enterprises, and other economic and political structures; and in general to appropriate as many state resources as possible for themselves. As we have seen, the CPSU then added fuel to the fire by consciously encouraging its affiliated bodies to channel their endangered resources into banks and enterprises.

The CBR and Gosbank continued to operate in parallel until after the failed coup attempt in August 1991, when the Soviet governing bodies lost their hold on power. On August 23, Yeltsin ordered the USSR Council of Ministers to complete the transfer of Union-level organizations on Russian territory to the custody of the Russian state by the end of the year. The Russian government appointed Andrei Zverov, the Russian Republic's deputy minister of finance, as temporary director of Gosbank (although Gerashchenko, awkwardly, refused to leave his post and did not submit his resignation until December 26). On November 15, 1991, Yeltsin took over the USSR Ministry of Finance and the USSR Chief Ad-

81. Yu. Liubimtsev, "The Power of the Ruble," *Ekonomika i zhizn'*, January 5, 1991, trans. *Current Digest of the Soviet Press* 43, no. 4 (1991): 7.

82. Rutland, "The Economy: The Rocky Road from Plan to Market," 147.

83. A. Stepovoi and S. Chugaev, "How to Get the Budget Out of Crisis," *Izvestiia*, April 5, 1991, 2, trans. *Current Digest of the Soviet Press* 43, no. 14 (1991): 6.

84. Aleksandr Nikitin, "Invasion of the 10–Ruble Bills," *Pravda*, October 20, 1990, 1, trans. *Current Digest of the Soviet Press* 42, no. 42 (1990): 27.

ministration for the Production of State Bank Notes, Coins, and Medals by decree.

In early December, Yeltsin, Ukrainian leader Leonid Kravchuk, and Belorussian leader Stanislav Shuskevich signed the Belovezh Accord, the Soviet Union's death warrant. Meeting at a hunting lodge in the Belorussian woods, they agreed to dissolve the USSR and create a Commonwealth of Independent States in its place. Days later, the Central Asian states expressed their desire to join the new Commonwealth. As a result, Gorbachev found himself the president of a country that no longer existed. This secretive and hastily conceived decision by the three leaders epitomized the character of the entire decentralization process, and completed the political and economic disempowerment of the central Soviet government.

The end of the USSR meant the end of Gosbank, too. Preempting a meeting of Soviet republic leaders in Alma-Ata that was called to discuss transitional economic and political arrangements, the Presidium of the Russian Supreme Soviet unilaterally passed a resolution dissolving Gosbank and transferring its "facilities, documents, and specialists" to the CBR. On January 1, 1992, the CBR took over the rest of Gosbank's resources in Russia, and Gosbank officially ceased to exist. The lengthy period of coexistence for the two central banks, culminating in the CBR's absorption of Gosbank, had allowed the CBR to assert its own political authority yet did not provide it with additional technical tools with which to wield its growing power. These mixed institutional legacies set the stage for the battle between Yeltsin and the CBR that began in 1992.

CHAPTER THREE

The Central Bank of Russia

The problem with the Central Bank is that there are practically no
central bankers over there.

—Finance Minister Boris Fedorov, 1993

I n February 1999, Russian prosecutor general Yurii Skuratov
revealed that over a six-year period the Central Bank of Russia had secretly funneled more than $50 billion of Russia's
hard currency reserves through a tiny offshore bank called FIMACO (Financial Management Company Ltd.). The resulting scandal illuminated
the bold, unusual way in which the CBR has wielded political and economic power since the collapse of the USSR. The FIMACO tale dates back
to November 1990, when Eurobank (the Paris subsidiary of Gosbank) created FIMACO on the Isle of Jersey to help handle Soviet era debt (and, allegedly, to spirit CPSU funds out of the country). When the CBR took
over Gosbank, it also acquired FIMACO. By 1993, the Central Bank had
started to move significant funds offshore to FIMACO, including funds received as a part of Russia's first standby agreements with the IMF. Following Skuratov's accusations, the CBR admitted that it used its financial
haven to hide reserves from foreign creditors, particularly during its debt
negotiations with the London and Paris Clubs; that it had sent IMF money
through FIMACO; and that, via Eurobank-controlled FIMACO and Evrofinans, it had invested heavily in the Russian treasury bill (GKO) market
and in other domestic securities.[1]

1. The CBR owned 78.9 percent of Eurobank, and Eurobank owned 100 percent of FI-
MACO. Eurobank also owned the Moscow-based bank Evrofinans (rated Russia's sixteenth

Foreign central bankers expressed outrage at the FIMACO revelations, condemning the irregularity of such practices. These autonomous underground activities compromised the ability of the Central Bank to act as an impartial arbiter of monetary policy, and may have contributed to its imprudent defense of the ruble in the face of impending crisis in 1998. Yet CBR directors as diverse as Viktor Gerashchenko and Sergei Dubinin had used and excused FIMACO. As former CBR deputy director Sergei Aleksashenko lamented after Skuratov blew the whistle, FIMACO "was an essential measure to protect the economic safety of the country—and now that mechanism is ruined."[2]

Understanding events like the FIMACO scandal, surprising to the West yet standard practice for the Central Bank of Russia, requires an analysis of the CBR's institutional development since 1991. It also raises broader questions about the proper role of central banks in post-communist democracies, and about the policy choices that contributed to such unexpected outcomes.

Post-communist policymakers and their Western advisors concerned themselves early on with how best to transform the central banks of these command economies—banks that were created to be no more than the state's lowly accountants—into modern, technically sophisticated central banks. One particular recommendation met with widespread approval from the West—post-communist democracies required the monetary discipline of an independent central bank. Russia's experience, however, confounded this conventional wisdom. The CBR's freedom to maneuver in the political arena did not encourage it to behave like an "independent," Western-style central bank. Far from it. Instead of a cautious CBR restraining the government, in the early 1990s Yeltsin's more monetarist executive branch attempted in vain to rein in the profligate, powerful central bank. This surprising behavior convinced many Western observers that the CBR could not actually be politically autonomous, since, *ipso facto*, no self-respecting central bank would act that way.[3] Others knew bet-

---

largest bank by assets in January 1999). It is no coincidence that in 1996 Evrofinans received one of the first licenses to work with nonresident investors and became a primary dealer on the bond market, accounting for over 40 percent of nonresident GKO activities in 1996. Central Bank of Russia, "Annual Report, 1997"; Bill Powell and Yevgenia Albats, "Follow the Money," *Newsweek*, March 29, 1999, 38; Rating, "Spisok 100 krupneishikh bankov Rossii po sostoianiiu na 01.01.99," http://www.rating.ru/RUS/100; Evgenii Vittenberg, ed., *Banki Moskvy* (Moscow: Intelbridge Plus, 1997); and Gary Peach, "The Central Bank Subsidiary Shuffle," *The Moscow Times*, March 12, 1999.

2. Quoted in Bloomberg, "Russian Central Bank Officials Defend Moving Assets to Haven," February 12, 1999.

3. For example, see Annelise Anderson, "Reforming the Money and Banking Systems in Formerly Communist Countries," paper presented at the Conference on Monetary Reform in the Former Soviet Union, Claremont, California, April 2, 1993; Gail Buyske, "A Tough

ter. As Matiukhin himself put it: "despite the widely stated suspicion of parliament that I was subordinate to the executive and of the executive that I was subordinate to the parliament . . . the Central Bank was in actuality independent."[4] The policy standoff between the CBR and the executive, exacerbated by Soviet-era institutional legacies plaguing the CBR, resulted in an uncoordinated, rancorous policy-making process. Most importantly, it doomed Russia's shock therapy attempt in 1992 and led to the messy breakup of the ruble zone in 1993.

Furthermore, when the CBR's political freedom began to erode after Yeltsin's dissolution of parliament in late 1993 (at the same time that the Bank's technical capabilities began to improve), its increasingly conservative monetary policies appeared more typical of an "independent" central bank. These more conservative policies, in turn, proved unable to transform enterprises and banks in the face of persistent institutional legacies and political uncertainty. While the CBR did temporarily bring inflation under control, this unexpectedly contributed to the rise of a barter-based industrial economy in Russia. The economy was destroyed in order to save it.

Advocates of central bank independence failed to predict Russia's combination of political autonomy for the Central Bank with loose monetary policy, and vice-versa, because of assumptions that inadvertently obscure our understanding of the CBR's role in Russian economic policy-making. Although the CBR had achieved a great deal of political autonomy by 1992, it had also inherited from its Soviet predecessor command-era values and technical capabilities. These characteristics naturally take much longer to change. For the CBR, this meant that its increasing political autonomy was not matched either by technical competence or by an internal or external consensus on its economic goals. A politically powerful central bank could not ensure stable monetary policy during Russia's transformation; nor could stable monetary policy engender deeper structural changes in the Russian economy. Moreover, throughout the transformation period the CBR remained a contentious, secretive bank not effectively bound by the rule of law nor accountable to representative institutions. As a result, rather than stabilizing Russia's fragile democratic institutions, the politics and policies of the CBR during the 1990s exacerbated the ongoing conflicts between the executive and the parliament.

Task for Russia's Central Bank," *The Wall Street Journal Europe,* December 1–2, 1995; and Stephen Lewarne, "The Russian Central Bank and the Conduct of Monetary Policy," in *Establishing Monetary Stability in Emerging Market Economies,* ed. Thomas Willett et al. (Boulder, Colo.: Westview Press, 1995). For an excellent article that confirms this analysis of the CBR's relative independence, see William Tompson, "The Politics of Central Bank Independence in Russia," *Europe-Asia Studies* 50, no. 7 (1998): 1157–82.

4. Georgii Matiukhin, *Ya byl glavnym bankirom Rossii* (Moscow: Vyshaia shkola, 1993), 71.

Independence and Intransigence

In order to understand the CBR's unusual policy-making during the transformation period following the dissolution of the Soviet Union, we must unpack and reevaluate traditional definitions of central bank independence.[5] The key components of central bank independence include formal autonomy (the bank's independent legal status), political autonomy (the bank's freedom to set its own goals and to implement its desired policies despite external pressures), and technical capability (its internal, practical ability to act on the goals it sets). An examination of the CBR's evolution on all three levels reveals that the development of its technical capabilities lagged behind its legal and political autonomy, engendering a powerful yet heavy-handed Central Bank.

The Central Bank of Russia enjoyed significant formal autonomy at the beginning of the transformation period, autonomy that grew steadily as the decade wore on. By 1995 its formal autonomy compared favorably with the German Bundesbank, then widely considered the most independent central bank in the world (see Table 3.1).

The Russian government enshrined the CBR's formal autonomy in the brief 1990 RSFSR Law on the Central Bank, enhanced it in the Russian Constitution of December 1993, and further confirmed it in the April 1995 revised Law on the Central Bank. The revised law stated that "The Bank of Russia . . . is independent in its activities. Federal organs of state power, organs of state power of the subjects of the Russian Federation, and organs of local self-government do not have the right to interfere in the activities of the Bank of Russia."[6] This detailed legislation gives the CBR additional powers and makes it illegal for the Central Bank to finance the budget deficit directly. According to the law, the CBR director

5. While the term "independence" is in itself problematic (since no governmental institution is ever really independent from all of the others), I use it and attempt to clarify its meaning because it is the term that central bankers themselves use to describe their desired relationship with the government. For works on measuring central bank independence, see Alex Cukierman, *Central Bank Strategy, Credibility, and Independence* (Cambridge, Mass.: MIT Press, 1992); Alberto Alesina and Lawrence Summers, "Central Bank Independence and Macroeconomic Performance: Some Comparative Evidence," *Journal of Money, Credit, and Banking* 25, no. 2 (May 1993): 151–62; Mark Swinburne and Marta Castello-Branco, "Central Bank Independence and Central Bank Functions," in *The Evolving Role of Central Banks*, ed. P. Downes and R. Vaez-Zadeh (Washington, D.C.: IMF, 1991); Alex Cukierman, Steven Webb, and Bilin Neyapti, "Measuring the Independence of Central Banks and Its Effect on Policy Outcomes," *The World Bank Economic Review* 6, no. 3 (1992): 353–98; and Eugenia Froedge Toma and Mark Toma, *Central Bankers, Bureaucratic Incentives, and Monetary Policy* (Boston: Kluwer Academic Publishers, 1986).

6. Law of the Russian Federation "O vnesenii izmenenii i dopolnenii v Zakon RSFSR 'O tsentral'nom banke RSFSR (Banke Rossii)'," April 12, 1995, st. 5.

Table 3.1. Formal legal measures of central bank independence

	CBR 1992–1995	CBR 1995–1999	Bundesbank 1995
CB director's term of office	5 years	4 years	8 years
Who appoints director?	President presents candidate; Parliament must confirm	President presents candidate; Parliament must confirm	Council of CB board, executive, and legislative branches
Number of central bank board members appointed by government?	Zero of 10–12 (number not fixed). Members all drawn from within CBR itself; Parliament confirms director's choices	Zero of 12 (number not fixed). Members all drawn from within CBR itself; Parliament confirms director's choices	10 of 21
Who dismisses director?	Supreme Soviet of the RSFSR	President and Parliament must both approve dismissal; permitted only if director breaks the law	No provision for dismissal
Can director hold other offices?	No rule against holding other office	Not allowed	No rule against holding other office
Who formulates monetary policy?	Primarily bank, in consultation with government	Primarily bank, in consultation with government	Primarily bank, in consultation with government
Who has the final word in conflict resolution?	No institution for conflict resolution, but CBR has right to appeal to courts if a law violates CB legislation	No institution for conflict resolution, but CBR has right to appeal to courts if a law violates CB legislation	Bank, on issues clearly defined in the law as its objectives
CB role in government budgetary process?	Consulting role	Consulting role	No influence
Limitations on lending to the government?	Yes, can lend to the Ministry of Finance for defined terms up to 6 months but cannot print money at government's request	Yes, forbidden to loan money to the government to fund deficit or to purchase securities directly from government	Yes, but can advance loans to government and engage in securitized lending within limits

Sources: Primarily Cukierman, Webb, and Neyapti, "Measuring the Independence of Central Banks and Its Effect on Policy Outcomes," *World Bank Economic Review* 6, no. 3 (1992); John Goodman, *Monetary Sovereignty* (Ithaca, NY: Cornell University Press, 1992); Law of the Russian Federation, "O tsentral'nom banke RSFSR (Banke Rossii)," 2 December 1990; and Law of the Russian Federation, "O vnesenii izmenenii i dopolnenii v Zakon RSFSR 'O tsentral'nom banke RSFSR (Banke Rossii)'," 12 April 1995.

(who must be nominated by the president and confirmed by parliament) controls the board of the bank and makes many decisions autonomously.

In addition, the CBR has legal jurisdiction over a wide array of areas. For example, it controlled the exchange rate regime directly until late 1995, then introduced a ruble corridor in cooperation with the government; most governments reserve control over the exchange rate regime for themselves. The CBR decides on most emission levels for cash and credit, and sets the refinancing and reserve rates. It also regulates commercial bank activities, including some securities operations, and has total responsibility for supervising, licensing, and shutting down commercial banks. By contrast, many Western central banks (such as those in Switzerland, Chile, and Germany) do not regulate commercial banks at all; separate banking supervisory institutions have this power.

In developing countries, though, formal autonomy often proves to be a poor measure of a central bank's actual behavior.[7] Where the court system and the rule of law have not traditionally been strong, where corruption and clientelism reign, and where the political and economic framework of a society is undergoing upheaval, autonomy granted on paper provides little comfort to central bankers. Granting a post-communist central bank formal legal autonomy is a necessary but not sufficient condition for insulating the bank from government interference. Therefore, to fully understand the CBR's role in the Russian economy, we need to evaluate the development of the Bank's political autonomy.

Political Autonomy

Measuring a central bank's political autonomy can be difficult, because it involves tracing informal channels of authority. This problem becomes even more severe in transitional economies, where alliances, preferences, and the relative power of actors can change fairly quickly. In addition, because post-communist economies have only recently created true central banks, measures of informal autonomy based on time-sensitive data such as the rate of turnover for bank directors prove unhelpful. For this reason, my analysis of the CBR's political autonomy relies on a deeper, case-specific look at its informal exercise of power.

Put simply, the executive, parliament, and commercial banks all continually and vociferously complained that the CBR ignored their wishes and directives. The Central Bank's political autonomy, born during the course of its struggle with Gosbank, continued to increase throughout 1992 due to the ongoing duel over economic policy between Boris Yeltsin

7. Sylvia Maxfield, "Financial Incentives and Central Bank Authority in Industrializing Nations," *World Politics* 46 (July 1994): 556–88.

and the Supreme Soviet. The CBR found itself at the nexus of many of the battles between president and parliament for two reasons. First, in practice, the CBR did not have to answer to or cooperate with the executive or parliament (or any other policy-making institution, for that matter), which heightened the tension between these groups. With the limited exception of a Credit Commission created in 1992, no coordinating institution to resolve conflicts over high-level macroeconomic policy existed, despite the government's numerous decrees, resolutions, and laws calling for the creation of such bodies. Indeed, even though the revised 1995 Law on the Central Bank explicitly required the creation of a National Banking Council, this institution did not appear until 1997.

But more importantly, the president and the parliament held deeply conflicting ideas about the proper conduct of monetary policy, with the parliament preferring a looser policy and the executive a tighter one. Both sides realized that the CBR represented the key to Russian macroeconomic policy-making. As former Finance Minister Boris Fedorov put it during his own unsuccessful campaign to be named CBR director, "If you can control the Central Bank, you can control a dozen other things."[8] Neither president nor parliament could allow the other to gain control over the Bank. For example, the parliament firmly blocked Yegor Gaidar's November 1991 attempt to subordinate the CBR to the executive. Gaidar and Yeltsin chose Gerashchenko to head the CBR after Matiukhin's firing in July 1992, but might have chosen a more partisan candidate if the Supreme Soviet had not held the power to reject the executive's nominee. This standoff led to a string of initiatives on the part of both president and parliament to further formalize the Central Bank's institutional independence, even as each tried (and usually failed) to undermine the CBR regarding specific policies. This conflictual relationship between the equally powerful president and parliament gave the CBR wide latitude in implementing its own preferred policies in the face of political opposition, only undermined when Yeltsin upset the balance of power by disbanding the Supreme Soviet in late 1993.

The Central Bank often battled with the executive, most notably over credit emissions in July–August 1992 and the introduction of new ruble notes in July 1993. (These issues are discussed extensively in the next section.) Just as regularly, the CBR defied the wishes of parliament.[9] For example, from 1990 to 1992, the Russian Supreme Soviet had the legal

8. Boris Fedorov, quoted in Terence Roth, "Fedorov Aims for Top Post at Russia's Bank," *Wall Street Journal,* November 1, 1993, A13.

9. On this general point, see Inna Vysman, "The New Banking Legislation in Russia: Theoretical Adequacy, Practical Difficulties, and Potential Solutions," *Fordham Law Review* 62 (October 1993): 265–86.

right to confirm members of the CBR board, but then-director Matiukhin ignored this law and appointed members personally without seeking confirmation.[10] A May 1992 Supreme Soviet memorandum criticized Matiukhin for arbitrary, autonomous, and dangerous actions in the areas of monetary and credit policy, clearing, budget operations, and relations with commercial banks.[11] In 1992, parliament could not get reports on the CBR's balance sheet or on its monetary and credit principles, and complained that "the leadership of the Central Bank of Russia systematically refuses to fulfill the decisions of the Russian Federation Supreme Soviet and its Presidium."[12] In January 1993, well after the CBR directorship had passed to Viktor Gerashchenko, experts with the parliament's subcommittee on banking affairs published an extensive article in the influential journal *Den'gi i kredit* (*Money and Banking*) again charging that the CBR was accountable to the parliament in name only. Among the Bank's offenses: not providing information on its operations, strategizing and making decisions without the input of parliament, regularly violating the Law on the Central Bank of Russia, and not allowing the parliament to confirm members of the board of directors.[13] In addition, under Gerashchenko the Bank's board did not meet regularly and Gerashchenko often made decisions without consulting it.[14] The CBR deftly manipulated the antagonistic relationship between the executive and the parliament to further expand its own authority.

In this respect, the CBR is an unusual case. Scholars commonly argue that central banks gain independence primarily through the support of domestic financial institutions, which prefer stable and conservative monetary policies.[15] Russian commercial banks, by contrast, have consistently and regularly opposed the CBR's activities for two reasons. First, commercial bankers often have disagreed with the CBR's monetary policy. Many

10. Sergei Chugaev, "Central Bank Scored for Arbitrary Actions," *Izvestiia*, May 15, 1992, trans. *Current Digest of the Post-Soviet Press* 44, no. 20 (1992): 6.
11. "Explanatory Memorandum on the Agenda Item of the Meeting of the Presidium of the Russian Federation Supreme Soviet 'On the Chairman of the Russian Federation Central Bank'," published in *Nezavisimaia gazeta*, May 19, 1992, 4, trans. *FBIS Central Eurasia* (June 5, 1992): 34–36.
12. Document of the Presidium of the Supreme Soviet, published in *Nezavisimaia gazeta*, May 19, 1992, trans. *Current Digest of the Post-Soviet Press* 44, no. 20 (1992): 8.
13. O. I. Lavrushin and Y. M. Mirkin, "Dolgosrochnaia konseptsiia razvitiia denezhno-kreditnoi sistemy Rossii," *Den'gi i kredit* 1 (1993): 6.
14. Joshua Chadajo, "The Independence of the Central Bank of Russia," *RFE / RL Research Report* 3, no. 27 (July 8, 1994): 27.
15. Adam Posen, "Why Central Bank Independence Does Not Cause Low Inflation: There Is No Institutional Fix for Politics," *AMEX Bank Review: Finance and the International Economy* 7 (1994): 41–54; John Goodman, "The Politics of Central Bank Independence," *Comparative Politics* 23, no. 3 (April 1991): 329–49; and Sylvia Maxfield, "Financial Incentives."

banks profited during the inflationary period from 1991 through 1993, and found the subsequent, erratic stabilization process threatening. Moreover, the CBR's stabilization efforts often have come at the direct expense of the banks, since it has freely used reserve requirements and the refinance rate as its chief instruments of monetary policy. As the assistant director of a leading Riazan' bank complained, "the Central Bank's interest rates have changed many times. How can a bank come up with its own credit policies under these circumstances? Today the Bank gives credit at 150 percent, so we give out credits at 160 percent. After a week the Central Bank rate goes up to 160 percent, but we have already made a one-month contract for that rate. After a month, it might not be 160 percent but 130 percent. It can be profitable, but it is bad economic politics."[16] In another example, the CBR's refinance rate plummeted from 210 percent in the second quarter of 1994 to 130 percent by the end of August, even though there had been a far smaller decrease in the inflation rate. Commercial bankers, in short, have felt that the CBR carried out dangerous, destabilizing monetary policies and have loudly voiced this opinion.

Second, commercial bankers have found the CBR's regulatory policies to be exceedingly and persistently heavy handed. The CBR has a long history of establishing confusing regulations, unevenly enforcing them, and allowing commercial banks little time to adjust to new requirements. As early as 1992, Sergei Yegorov, the president of the Association of Russian Banks (ARB), observed that:

> The Central Bank has pursued a policy of genocide in the full sense of the word. There are a host of obstacles in the way of opening a new bank, from countless petitions to items on the application for would-be bankers concerning their nationality and party membership. Meeting with the Central Bank's management, I once asked: 'Why do you need all this?' and heard in reply, 'We must know to whom the banks are being given.' I then suggested in a fit of anger that they should also check on my criminal record. And what do you know? A new application form immediately appeared with an item: 'Do you have any previous convictions?'[17]

Although the commercial bankers' complaints do seem self-serving, they argued fairly that the Bank's efforts often have borne more resemblance to Gosbank-style administrative commands than to market-oriented regulatory decisions. When faced with cash shortages, for example, the CBR

16. Liudmila Khrutova, assistant director, Stankobank, interview with author, February 28, 1995, Riazan'.
17. Sergei Yegorov in "Roundtable Discussion on the State of Russian Banking," *Moscow News*, June 7–14, 1992, 10.

would order commercial banks to keep more cash on reserve, require enterprises to deposit more of their cash proceeds into their banks, and forbid enterprises to conduct large transactions in cash. Nor did this antagonistic relationship seem likely to change. Seventy-five percent of bankers polled at the May 1995 ARB convention stated that in "recent times" the Central Bank's relationship with commercial banks had worsened.[18]

This antagonism has encouraged commercial bankers to evade and undercut the CBR instead of supporting it. Whenever I asked commercial bankers about their attitudes towards the Central Bank of Russia, many just shrugged their shoulders and gestured towards impressive mounds of CBR directives piling up on their desks. Commercial banks regularly and consistently have violated CBR norms and directives. An ironic numerical coincidence illustrates the point. In 1992, the CBR charged 1,064 banks (over 60 percent of all banks) with violating prudential norms. In 1997, the CBR's own annual report admitted that 1,064 banks had outright falsified their required financial documentation.[19] Since the CBR could not rely on the commercial banks for support, its post-Soviet political freedom has rested not on domestic societal or interest group backing, but on its own ability to concentrate its power and responsibilities, on the continued antagonism of president and parliament, and on increasing international support for independent central banks.

Autonomy, Ideology, and Secrecy

Western central banks make headlines by adjusting interest rates by fractions of a percentage point. Indeed, even inaction attracts attention. For example, a prominent headline in the *Washington Post* on October 6, 1999, declared: "Fed Leaves Rates As Is."[20] The CBR, in contrast, introduced a new currency without informing the Ministry of Finance or parliament, attempted to save and then destroyed the ruble zone, introduced an unpopular payments system, cleared the interenterprise debts of thousands of state enterprises, and printed money almost at will. In short, the CBR often has formulated and carried out its own policies, and in doing so has demonstrated the capacity to act much more radically than almost any other central bank in the world.

18. Survey of 396 bankers by Cassandra research service carried out at the Fifth Annual Conference of the Association of Russian Banks, May 24, 1995.

19. The 1992 figure comes from L. G. Efimova, *Bankovskoe pravo* (Moscow: Izdatel'stvo vek, 1994): 13. The 1997 figures are from the CBR's "Annual Report, 1997," 89. In 1997, 1,319 credit institutions "failed to comply with economic standards," and 1,326 committed "other" violations.

20. John M. Barry, "Fed Leaves Rates As Is," *Washington Post*, October 6, 1999, E1.

Why did this autonomy lead to unexpected and uncoordinated policy outcomes? This occurred in part because in the early 1990s Russia's central bankers held conflicting beliefs about what central banks should do. Moreover, many of these beliefs differed significantly from those typical of central bankers in established market economies. Gosbank had disbursed centralized credits and maintained strict monetary control over the territory of the USSR, and after Russia became independent, the first CBR leaders continued to see these tasks as vital in order to shore up Russia's failing industrial and agricultural enterprises. Gerashchenko, the longest-serving and most influential CBR director, particularly supported an active role in enterprise policy and became infamous for claiming that it was "impossible to apply economic theory to Russia."[21] As late as September 1994, Gerashchenko stated that the fall in production and the related catastrophic drop in long-term investment by commercial banks could not be solved by monetary-credit methods and that the government should impose a state investment policy in order to turn the economy around.[22] These policy preferences prioritizing employment and production over lowering inflation strongly affected the CBR's early actions. On the other hand, CBR officials such as Dmitri Tulin, Andrei Kozlov, and Tat'iana Paramonova, who were more influenced by Western economic theories and advisors, gradually began to express more monetarist viewpoints. No consensus existed on the proper role of the Central Bank even within the Bank itself. As a result, the CBR adopted a multiplicity of policy preferences over time that were not all compatible. This internal confusion paralleled the lack of consensus in wider Russian political circles over the CBR's proper mission.

Perhaps more importantly for the CBR's long-term development, though, this political autonomy also permitted it to shield its activities from the prying eyes of elected officials, bureaucrats, and commercial bankers. As one Moscow banker observed:

> [the CBR] is a very typical Soviet—not Russian, Soviet—type of institution. Very rarely do they answer your letters. Very rarely do they return your calls. . . . All decisions recently came as a surprise . . . they are independent from the government, but I doubt that they use this independence properly because their mentality is the same.[23]

21. Quoted in Claudia Rosett, "Obstacle to Reform: Rooted in Soviet Past, Russia's Central Bank Lacks Grasp of Basics," *Wall Street Journal*, September 23, 1993, A1.

22. Viktor Gerashchenko, "Denezhno-kreditnaia sistema v Rossii v perekhodnyi period," *Biznes i banki*, September 1994, 2. Also, see his address to the Fourth Annual Congress of the Association of Russian Banks on April 29, 1994, printed in *Biznes i banki*, May 1994, 7–8.

23. Anonymous banker, interview with author, winter 1995, Moscow. Also, see various comments criticizing the "monopolism" of the CBR in Garegin Tosunian, *Bankovskoe delo i*

Table 3.2. Directors of the Central Bank of Russia

	Hired	*Left*
Georgii Matiukhin	July 1990 Had taught at Academy of Foreign Trade	July 1992 Returned to academe
Viktor Gerashchenko	July 1992 Previously head of Gosbank USSR	October 1994 Became Chairman of Board, International Moscow Bank
Tat'iana Paramonova (acting director)	October 1994 Previously CBR deputy director	November 1995 Became CBR deputy director again; in 1997, became deputy director of Elbim Bank
Sergei Dubinin	November 1995 Previously acting finance minister, official at Imperial Bank	September 1998 Became vice-president of Gazprom
Viktor Gerashchenko	September 1998	

Reflecting its heritage, and in defiance of the 1990 Law on the Central Bank, the CBR reluctantly published its first consolidated balance sheet only in February 1992, under extreme pressure to increase the transparency of its activities. As late as 1995, "Other" represented the fourth largest asset and the largest liability on the CBR's published balance sheet. By 1998, "Other" still represented a significant, but less alarming, figure (see Table 3.3). The CBR rarely circulated its draft policies for commentary and gave out as little information on its internal workings as possible. As we have seen, it also regularly refused to submit legally mandated information to the parliament.

The attitudes of the CBR toward researchers reflected this concern for secrecy, as my own experience with the Bank's headquarters in Volgograd oblast' illustrates. After speaking to numerous CBR officials on the phone, submitting a list of my questions on official university stationery, and visiting the headquarters building in person three times, I had gotten no further than meeting with a CBR public affairs officer on the front steps. According to one official, I could not go into the building itself because it was "under renovation." After I had shown my academic credentials to several CBR employees, yet another screamed at me over the phone, say-

bankovskoe zakonadatel'stvo v Rossii (Moscow: Akademiia narodnogo khoziaistva pri pravitel'stve RF, 1995).

Table 3.3. Consolidated Central Bank of Russia balance sheet as of January 1, 1998 (in millions of rubles)

Assets		Liabilities	
Gold	36,210,064	Authorized capital	3,000
Foreign exchange	85,856,036	Reserves and funds	47,918,511
Cash	45,022	Cash in circulation	137,042,262
Loans to the Ministry of Finance	260,634	Foreign currency accounts	2,627,927
Credits	13,049,448	Funds of credit institutions	66,970,977
Securities	159,830,999	Budget and customer funds	26,986,584
Interstate settlements	4,005,004	Funds in settlements	2,611,798
Other	36,114,574	Other	51,210,722
Balance	335,371,781	Balance	335,371,781

Source: CBR, *Annual Report 1997*

ing "How do we know you are really a scholar? We have no proof!" Still another said that I should have brought a letter from CBR headquarters in Moscow allowing me to do such an interview. Then the public affairs officer said that he would have liked to set up an interview for me, but that the person I ought to meet was out of town and would not return until after I had left. Finally, in the face of my persistence, I was told that I would have to get permission from the head of the Volgograd CBR himself in order to speak to anyone at the bank. Unfortunately, however, getting such permission would be impossible. The director had gone on an extended business trip to Moscow.

Not surprisingly, such secrecy provided numerous opportunities for financial shenanigans like the FIMACO scandal. A 1993 Coopers and Lybrand audit of the Central Bank of Russia found that its 1991 and 1992 accounts could not be reconciled and that there were "abuses connected with a very high level of unaccounted-for sums, both for accounts within Russia and between members of the Commonwealth of Independent States, in rubles and in foreign currency."[24] Commercial bankers complained that they sometimes had to make payoffs to ensure the timely completion of interbank transfers, payoffs that economist Anders Åslund estimated at about 15 percent of the transaction's value.[25]

This pervasive, corrupting secrecy landed CBR officials squarely in the middle of the first big scandal to face the new Russian banking system, the so-called "Chechen affair" of May 1992. The Chechen affair, the most serious attempt at a new kind of financial crime that swept Russia from 1991

24. Rosset, "Obstacle to Reform."
25. Anders Åslund, "Russian Banking: Crisis or Rent-Seeking?" *Post-Soviet Geography and Economics* 37, no. 8 (October 1996): 495–502.

to 1993, took advantage of institutional inadequacies within the CBR. Swindlers would make forged copies of CBR promissory notes, present them for payment at commercial banks, and make off with the money. Credulous or corrupt commercial bankers often did not question the authenticity of the documents and were "shocked" when they presented the notes to the CBR for payment, only to be told that the documents should not exist. The Chechen affair attempted to carry out such an embezzlement on a grand scale—if it had succeeded, the criminals would have received over sixty billion rubles. The affair required insider participation, and four CBR officials were eventually arrested and charged with conspiracy, "accused of accepting bribes of millions of rubles and tens of thousands of dollars to assist in distributing the forged promissory notes."[26] Although the CBR fixed the technical loopholes that facilitated this scam, it did not learn the broader lesson about the inverse relationship between transparency and corruption. As the FIMACO scandal later made clear, a lack of democratic accountability combined with Soviet-era predilections for secrecy proved problematic for the CBR and for Russia time and again.

Technical Difficulties

Despite its legal and political autonomy, the CBR began the transformation period suffering from severe handicaps because of its constrained responsibilities under the Soviet system and the subsequent lack of attention paid to restructuring the bank during the political battles of 1990–91. Thus, it started 1992 with essentially the same command-oriented technical capabilities that Gosbank had enjoyed, even though its fundamental responsibilities had changed dramatically. The state's focus on trickle-down liberalization and privatization policies meant that it continued to neglect the CBR's technical development in the first few years after the Soviet breakup. Soviet-era legacies restricted the CBR's policy choices, making it difficult for the Bank to carry out many market-oriented policies and encouraging it to rely heavily on old, increasingly inappropriate practices to get things done. While the CBR faced a wide range of such problems, the existence of the ruble zone, a command-era staff, limited tools of monetary policy, and an extremely weak payments system proved to be the most detrimental.

The ruble zone was a particularly troubling Soviet-era legacy. When the USSR broke up at the end of 1991, the CBR found itself saddled with many of the problems but none of the all-Union power of Gosbank. Sud-

26. Stephen Handelman, *Comrade Criminal: Russia's New Mafiya* (New Haven: Yale University Press, 1995), 133.

denly, the CBR faced fourteen other "independent" central banks, all using the ruble as their sole currency. Although only the CBR could print rubles (since all of the printing presses were on Russian territory), many of the central banks could and did emit large quantities of ruble credits (*beznalichnye*) to local enterprises, dramatically increasing the money supply. For example, in 1992 Ukraine issued credits totaling 1.3 trillion rubles, which led to 2,000 percent inflation and adversely affected other states in the ruble zone.[27] All of this occurred amid an atmosphere of legal and regulatory confusion due to the initial ambiguity and inconsistency among the laws of the ruble zone members. Ruble zone members took their time updating their own banking legislation, and therefore their laws referred to Gosbank policy long after Gosbank itself had been defunct. Legally, therefore, these central banks were required to take direction from another central bank that no longer existed.[28]

A lack of coordination also snarled the payments systems among the former republics, because clearing a transaction required it to be routed through two central banks instead of one. To further complicate matters, the Russian Federation had always subsidized the other republics, and the other republics naturally preferred to continue that arrangement for as long as they could (see Table 3.4). As long as the ruble zone existed, the CBR could not control its own money supply. This transitional legacy put the Central Bank of Russia in a unique position compared to the post-communist central banks of Eastern Europe—a situation which Yeltsin's economic policy team failed to take into account.

The central bankers who were forced to deal with these issues, however, proved ill-equipped to do so. The Soviet central bank lived on, despite the demise of the Soviet system. Even as late as 1997, almost one third of the CBR's employees had worked directly for the central bank for ten years or more; that is, they had worked in the pre-reform Gosbank.[29] Yet the skills that central bankers had developed in Soviet times differed dramatically from those necessary to function within a market-oriented central bank. Georgii Matiukhin himself flatly stated that "the problem of cadres was and remains to this day one of the main problems for the Central Bank of Russia."[30] In Soviet times, Gosbank staffers shuffled papers and kept accounting books in fulfillment of orders from above. When Matiukhin took over the Russian Republic branch of Gosbank in 1990, he noted that only 17.4 percent of the employees had any higher education at all.[31] CBR

27. "Ukraine: Tough Enough," *The Economist*, March 13, 1993, 56.
28. Stephen Lewarne, "Legal Aspects of Monetary Policy in the Former Soviet Union," *Europe-Asia Studies* 45, no. 2 (1993): 195.
29. Central Bank of Russia, "Annual Report, 1997," 174.
30. Matiukhin, *Ya byl glavnym bankirom*, 67.
31. Ibid., 67.

Table 3.4. Central Bank of Russia financing of other former Soviet Union states in 1992 (Year-end Central Bank of Russia correspondent account position)

	Billions of rubles	% of GDP financed by Russian Federation
Russia	-2,109	-11.7
Tajikistan	36	90.7
Uzbekistan	292	69.9
Turkmenistan	172	53.3
Georgia	69	51.5
Armenia	34	49.0
Azerbaijan	51	25.8
Kazakhstan	407	25.5
Kyrgyzstan	42	22.9
Ukraine	862	21.7
Moldova	27	11.3
Belarus	102	10.7
Estonia	4	4.0
Lithuania	9	3.2
Latvia	2	1.0

Source: IMF, *Economic Review: Financial Relations among Countries of the Former Soviet Union* (Washington, D.C.: IMF, 1994).

staff, with only a few exceptions, did not know how they might use different tools of monetary policy to affect the money supply and inflation rate, did not know how commercial banks ought to be licensed and regulated, and did not understand how security markets worked. Moreover, some central bankers, especially in the early years of reform, had a poor understanding of market economics. They saw, for example, no inherent incompatibility between controlling inflation and supporting enterprises with subsidized credits.[32] As a central banker in Riazan' admitted, "problems arise that no one can solve. Our work used to be easier."[33]

The early 1990s gave Russia's central bankers a painful crash course in financial policy-making and market economics. They had to learn their new roles while on the job, through trial and error. Many took classes at one of the numerous new financial academies that sprouted up around the country or visited banks overseas. As early as 1991, Matiukhin opened

32. Ernesto Hernandez-Cata, "Russia and the IMF: The Political Economy of Macro-Stabilization," *Problems of Post-Communism* (May / June 1995): 20.

33. Elena Morozova, head economist, Department of Analysis and Regulation of the Activities of Commercial Banks, CBR Riazan', interview with author, September 2, 1994, Riazan'.

a training center in the CBR and sent many of his staffers abroad for training.[34] Nevertheless, such skills take time to acquire, and most central bankers only gradually began to feel comfortable in their positions. In the interim, experimentation and on-the-job training lent a large degree of unpredictability to the CBR's policy decisions and implementation, from top-level judgements on credit disbursement to local-level decisions on how to sanction commercial banks for infractions of CBR regulations.

The limited tools of monetary policy in the CBR's arsenal further constrained its policy options. The Central Bank never needed such tools under the command economy, when monetary output, exchange rates, and so on were determined by the government. For example, instead of using the refinance rate as an expensive source of short-term liquidity for the commercial banking system, the CBR consistently disbursed centralized credit at negative real interest rates until October 1993. Directed credits from the CBR or the federal budget still formed about half of all commercial bank loans granted in 1992, and their level remained high through 1994.[35] Neither Matiukhin nor Gerashchenko wanted to cut off credits to industry or shock industrialists by raising rates to what would appear to be, in nominal terms, extremely high levels in order to compensate for the over 2,500 percent inflation in 1992. As then-Deputy Prime Minister Boris Fedorov exclaimed in March 1993, "[because of the] abyss between [commercial bank rates] and the Central Bank's rates . . . seekers of free credit are flocking to Moscow."[36] Therefore, during this period the banking system continued to act as an allocator of resources, not as a guardian of money.

To make matters worse, the CBR's most important late-Soviet-era tool of monetary policy—reserve requirements—initially proved ineffective in the post-Soviet environment. As IMF economists Tomás Baliño, David Hoelscher, and Jakob Horder have argued, structural factors, legal loopholes, and poor enforcement made increasing reserve requirements a poor tool with which to battle inflation.[37] Structurally, uneven liquidity distribution among banks and the unreliable payments system meant that significantly changing reserve requirements would have had uncertain and inequitable effects upon commercial banks. Legal loopholes such as

34. Matiukhin, *Ya byl glavnym bankirom*, 54–55. In fact, he was widely criticized in Russia for sending so many staffers abroad, which was viewed as a suspicious, money-wasting activity.

35. Ruben Lamdany, ed., *Russia: The Banking System During the Transition* (Washington, D. C.: The World Bank, 1993), 4.

36. Boris Fedorov, "Fedorov Confronts Gerashchenko on Credits," *Segodnia*, March 16, 1993, trans. *Current Digest of the Post-Soviet Press* 45, no. 13 (1993): 14.

37. Tomás J.T. Baliño, David S. Hoelscher, and Jakob Horder, "Evolution of Monetary Policy Instruments in Russia," *Working Paper of the International Monetary Fund*, December 1997, 19.

the initial exemption of foreign exchange deposits from reserve requirements and automatic reductions in required reserves for banks with falling deposits added to the confusion. Finally, commercial banks easily evaded the reserve requirements, and did not fear the potential consequences because of the minimal financial penalties for holding insufficient reserves.

The CBR's inability to use open market operations represented another potentially serious problem. The U.S. Federal Reserve, for example, can buy or sell U.S. Treasury Bills on the secondary market in order to raise or lower liquidity in the banking system, which is a more flexible instrument of control than simply printing (or not printing) money or adjusting reserve requirements and the refinance rate. Moreover, because the Russian government could not raise money by selling treasury bills, it had little choice but to turn to the CBR for deficit financing. During 1993, the CBR loaned over 10 trillion rubles to the Ministry of Finance, more than it lent to all commercial banks during that same year.[38]

Instead of slowing down, this trend of government borrowing increased markedly in 1994 just when centralized credit disbursements to enterprises dramatically decreased.[39] In 1994 the CBR gave the government 43.7 trillion rubles, covering 66.9 percent of the budget deficit. This occurred not simply because the government or the CBR lacked the will to restrain spending, but because the government had few other financial resources available to it. It had lost many of its traditional revenue sources through privatization, upheaval in the tax system, exchange rate liberalization, and the falling value of household deposits in Sberbank. Yet treasury bill sales require time to prepare, a certain level of economic and political stability to carry out, and a domestic financial sector with the desire and wherewithal to support the market, conditions which are often difficult to fulfill. Indeed, 47 percent of government debt in developing countries and 12 percent in developed countries is financed by direct borrowing from central banks because of shallow domestic financial markets.[40] Russia did not carry out its first experimental treasury bill auction until March 1993, and it took the market well over a year to develop.

At the same time, Russia could not instantaneously develop the other tools that governments in market economies use to acquire revenue. It had a poor institutional infrastructure for collecting taxes—no equivalent of the U.S. Internal Revenue Service, no modern tax code, and a legal system poorly equipped to punish tax offenders. Russian enterprises and cit-

38. Central Bank of Russia, *Tekushie tendentsii v denezhno-kreditnoi sfere* 3 (1994), 18–19.
39. Credits to the Ministry of Finance represented the great majority of the increase in CBR credit dispersals. See *Russian Economic Trends* 4, no. 1 (1995) for detailed figures.
40. World Bank, *World Development Report* (Washington, D.C.: World Bank, 1989), 62.

izens, who had not previously paid direct taxes and who had become quite adept at getting around officialdom in Soviet times, felt little moral compunction to pay up. Furthermore, the Soviet Union had a disastrous international credit rating by the end of 1991, and the dissolution of the Soviet Union had left the former republics with the knotty problem of dividing up the debt of the USSR. These debts were completely unrecoverable until December 1994, when the last holdout—Ukraine—agreed to give up its claims on Soviet foreign assets in exchange for Russia's pledge to service the Soviet debt.[41] This unresolved Soviet-era legacy meant that the Russian government could not finance itself through noninflationary means by borrowing on international commercial debt markets, a common procedure for most nations. Only after long negotiations did Russia agree to a debt rescheduling with the London Club of commercial banks in November 1995 and with the Paris Club of sovereign creditors in April 1996, freeing Russia to borrow on international markets once again.

Finally, the Soviet-era payments and clearing system proved to be another nearly catastrophic institutional legacy for the CBR.[42] This is the mechanism through which domestic banks transfer money among each other. So, for example, instead of physically transporting a sack of money from an account in one bank to an account in another whenever a client orders a payments transfer, a country's central bank coordinates a system by which all commercial banks match up the debts and credits they have accrued over a specified period of time and then balance out their mutual accounts. The paper-based Soviet-era payments system, however, could not handle the hundreds of thousands of payments transfers being routed through the CBR by the numerous new commercial banks, and such transfers often took weeks to complete. Moreover, the separation of rubles into *nalichnye* and *beznalichnye* in effect necessitated two kinds of payments systems and created a relaxed attitude on all sides towards completing timely payments transfers.[43] The old payments system transferred money from one bank to the next, and, as Inkombank founder Vladimir Vinogradov has pointed out, "it did not matter in particular to whom the money belonged. It belonged to the state."[44] As we have seen, though, in 1988 cooperatives began to turn noncash rubles into cash by, for ex-

41. "Russia, Ukraine Sign Zero-Option Debt Deal," Reuters, December 9, 1994.

42. For the most detailed information available on the development of the Russian payments and clearing system, see M. P. Berezina and Yu. S. Krupnov, *Mezhbankovskie raschety* (Moscow: Finstatinform, 1994).

43. For more on the separation of rubles into "cash" (nalichnye) and "noncash" (beznalichnye), see chapter 2.

44. Vladimir Vinogradov, quoted in "Payments Crisis Tied to Central Bank," *Moskovskaia pravda* (May 8, 1992): 1–2, trans. *FBIS Central Eurasia* (June 5, 1992): 33.

ample, purchasing goods from state enterprises for low, noncash payments and then turning around and selling these goods at market value for cash. As inflation began to rise and cash (but not credits) became scarce in early 1992, the CBR came under increasing pressure to streamline the payments system, unify the dual monetary circuit, and expedite the increasing volume of credit transfers.

So on April 1, 1992, in an effort to increase its control over payments transfers, the CBR began to require that all commercial bank payments be processed through the CBR's payments-cash centers (*raschetno-kassovykh tsentr,* or RKTs). The RKTs system, originally designed to transfer tax money from the Russian Federation to the Soviet budget, proved inadequate to the task. This unpopular move caused incredible backlogs, contributing to the parliament's May 1992 decision to call for a vote of no confidence in CBR director Georgii Matiukhin and to his subsequent resignation.[45] Payments became especially backed up in July and August 1992. At that time, as former acting CBR director Tat'iana Paramonova "remembers with terror," mountains of sacks filled with bank payments documents piled up in the CBR.[46] Some people in commercial banks worked full-time just to find out to whom in the RKTs they were supposed to give documents and payments, while bank employees could stand in line for weeks to get cash money.[47] In a 1993 survey of commercial bankers, 77 percent named the payments system as the problem most in need of immediate resolution for the successful development of the banking system.[48]

The CBR's secrecy combined with these problems in the payments system yielded tempting opportunities for corruption. Commercial bankers, politicians, and entrepreneurs alike accused the CBR of delaying transfers

45. Conventional wisdom holds that Matiukhin was asked to resign by the Supreme Soviet because of his unacceptably tight monetary policy, but this was only one of many reasons. In fact, Matiukhin's monetary policies were tight only in comparison with Gerashchenko's, and he had previously enjoyed a good relationship with the Supreme Soviet. Matiukhin had been a long-time friend of Supreme Soviet speaker Ruslan Khasbulatov, who championed his initial appointment and cut him loose only reluctantly. Many of the Supreme Soviet's complaints about Matiukhin focused on issues of competence, including the CBR's secrecy, its continual flaunting of the Law on the Central Bank, the payments system fiasco, its "interference" in the work of commercial banks, and late wage payments. See the summary of Supreme Soviet complaints published in *Nezavisimaia gazeta,* May 19, 1992, 4.

46. Tat'iana Paramonova, remarks, Plenary Session of the Russian-American Bankers' Forum, June 30, 1995, St. Petersburg, Russia.

47. Mkrtich Kirakossian, co-chair of the board, OPM bank, interview with author, July 17, 1995, Moscow.

48. Survey by Cassandra research service. Results reported in the *ARB Informatsionnyi bulletin #6,* 1994.

for speculative purposes, while the CBR admitted to holding up payments often for 30 days and occasionally for several months.[49] At that time, a commercial banker in Volgograd commented, "The Central Bank is not interested in speeding up payments. Money takes 15–20 days to be processed through Moscow."[50] This easy source of profits encouraged the CBR to resist making changes to the payments system, despite the vociferous complaints of commercial bankers, until it began to face competition from commercial bank payments networks.

Eventually, with the help of international financial organizations and advisors, the CBR began to revamp its payments system. In 1993, the CBR established a National Steering Committee to develop the payments system, and by 1995 its main RKTs offices reliably transferred money on a same-day basis within Moscow.[51] However, smaller banks had trouble getting access to the two main RKTs branches in Moscow that did electronic same-day clearing. Of the approximately 600 bank-members of the Moscow RKTs network in 1995, about 130 still needed to present paper documents in person to their designated RKTs affiliates for official clearing.[52] Regional banks, except in those areas chosen for initial payments system improvements, had still more serious problems. Riazan' was one of the lucky regions; an experiment with electronic RKTs transfers introduced in June 1994 increased transfer speed by five times, and over 70 percent of transfers within Riazan' oblast' then took place electronically.[53] In Siberia, by contrast, most banks avoided routing payments through the RKTs altogether, preferring to use correspondent networks (accounts opened directly between individual commercial banks).[54] According to the CBR's own figures, in 1997, despite reform efforts, 77.8 percent of all settlements (by sum) still took four days or more to clear (actually a slight *increase* from 1996), and many settlements continued to be processed

49. See Sergei Yegorov's comments in "Roundtable Discussion on the State of Russian Banking," *Moscow News*, June 7–14, 1992, 10 ("After all it's an open secret: if a remittance exceeds five million rubles it is bound to be 'lost' at the Central Bank"); Ivan Zhagel, "We're Not Going to Rescind the Central Bank's Telegram," *Izvestiia*, August 4, 1992, trans. *Current Digest of the Post-Soviet Press* 44, no. 31 (1992): 4; and "Explanatory Memorandum on the Agenda Item of the Meeting of the Presidium of the Russian Federation Supreme Soviet 'On the Chairman of the Russian Federation Central Bank'," published in *Nezavisimaia gazeta*, May 19, 1992, 4, trans. *FBIS Central Eurasia* (June 5, 1992): 34–36.

50. Liudmila Khomutetskaia, director of Slavianin Bank, quoted in Anna Stepanova and Vladimir Teplitskii, "Pri slaboi ekonomike ne budet sil'nykh bankov," *Delovoe povolzh'e* 14 (April 1994): 1.

51. Christine Grzesiak-Seliansky, Legal Counsel, Citibank Moscow, interview with author, June 22, 1995, Moscow.

52. Mkrtich Kirakossian, interview.

53. Stanislav Yushkovskii, "V rezhim real'nogo vremeni," *Priokskaia gazeta* (June 10, 1994): 2.

54. Jeffrey Millikan, banking consultant, interview with author, June 26, 1995, Moscow.

through the mail.[55] The burden of an inappropriate payments system left over from Gosbank, a lack of technology and expertise for improving it, plus financial incentives for the CBR to slow up payments limited speedy development in this area.

Policy Consequences

The CBR's political autonomy and technical incapacity combined to yield undesirable policy outcomes during Russia's shock therapy attempt in 1992 and during the breakup of the ruble zone in 1993—with major consequences for Russia's political and economic transition. These events point out the lack of coordination among different Russian organizations, the problems created by the CBR's policy autonomy, and the institutional barriers to the implementation of rapid economic reform programs in the post-communist context. Instead of stabilizing Russia's economy and protecting Russian democracy, the Central Bank's actions made matters worse.

The Unpredictable Money Supply

On October 29, 1991, before the breakup of the USSR, Yeltsin announced that he planned to "shock" the Russian economy into modernity by liberalizing prices and trade, eliminating the budget deficit, and rapidly privatizing state enterprises. Directed by economist Yegor Gaidar and supported by the IMF and Western economic advisors, shock therapy in Russia represented an ill-defined economic program with an explicit political strategy. Yeltsin and Gaidar hoped to take advantage of the purported window of opportunity that existed after the failed August coup had discredited old Soviet institutions. In effect, they replaced the utopian proclamations of communism with those of capitalism, with the concomitant faith that decentralizing measures taken from above could restructure the economy in a predictable way. Yeltsin promised that this decisive blow, although causing some brief economic pain, would tame inflation rapidly and restore the productive power of the Russian economy.[56] After much debate, the Russian parliament granted Yeltsin emer-

---

55. CBR, "Annual Report, 1997," 104.

56. On this point, see Gaidar and Matiukhin, "Memorandum ob ekonomicheskoi politike Rossiiskoi Federatsii," *Ekonomika i zhizn'* 10 (March 1992): 4–5. In three separate places, including at the beginning and end of the memorandum, Gaidar and Matiukhin make clear that the success of the program depended upon significant external financing from the international community. Although much of the expected support did not materialize, Gaidar and his reform team now blame institutional constraints rather than the IMF for the failure of shock therapy in Russia.

gency decree powers for one year to allow him to whip the economy into shape.

Accordingly, on January 2, 1992, Russia set the wheels of shock therapy into motion. Prices were liberalized, while CBR credits to the government fell by 31 percent in the first quarter of 1992 as a result of drastic spending cuts. The government had laid little institutional groundwork for this plan, however, and it immediately began to fall apart as a result of institutional barriers. In order for shock therapy to work, the CBR had to gain control over Russia's money supply and restrict both cash and credit emissions. The CBR, though, was neither willing nor able to carry out either task. The outcome proved to be disastrous, as high inflation wiped out people's life savings, cash became scarce, capital flight and the dollarization of the economy both skyrocketed, the ruble's value plummeted, and the level of mutual debt among enterprises reached billions of rubles. As ARB president Yegorov bitterly observed, "The idea was great: to beat inflation and minimize the budget deficit. How was it realized? To reduce the fever the patient was taken outside and exposed to freezing temperatures."[57]

Why did the CBR prove unwilling to try to restrict the money supply during the shock therapy attempt? First, the Central Bank's two directors during this period, the agents upon whom tight monetary policy depended, had differences with the Yeltsin plan. They believed that the CBR should support production, and regarded shock therapy as a threat to that goal. Matiukhin had said in January 1992 that "an evolutionary way is better for us."[58] Gerashchenko thought that the rise in interenterprise debt had occurred because not enough money circulated in the economy as a result of the huge price rises after liberalization.[59] He stated later in 1992 that complying with IMF monetary and credit targets could destroy Russia's industrial base and crush the financial system, and saw no alternative to releasing credits to cover interenterprise debts.[60] Not only did the two CBR directors disagree with the executive's policy—they had the political power to act on their views. To attempt to deal with the cash

57. Andrei Borodenkov interview with Sergei Yegorov, "A Poisonous Overdose," *Moscow News*, April 26, 1992, 11.

58. Quoted in Fred Hiatt, "Pro-Reform Russian Quits Top Bank Post," *Washington Post*, July 17, 1992, A14.

59. Anders Åslund, *How Russia Became a Market Economy* (Washington, D.C.: Brookings Institution, 1995), 210. Although Åslund argues that Gerashchenko was mistaken in his views, the important point here is that Gerashchenko believed that expansion of the money supply was a rational response to the unintended consequences of price liberalization, and took action accordingly.

60. Michael Dobbs, "Russian Banker Urges Renegotiation of Economic Reform Plan," *Washington Post*, August 21, 1992, A16.

shortage, Matiukhin printed money as fast as possible, day and night.[61] He introduced higher denomination notes, increased the capacity of the printing presses, and did away with the lowly kopeck. This failed to stem the tide. Adding insult to injury, the IMF's refusal to provide a promised ruble stabilization fund for Russia made it clear that the CBR could not rely on significant Western financial assistance to support the shock therapy program in 1992. Therefore, with ruble zone members emitting credits and parallel currencies, and the volume of interenterprise debt rising by eighty times from January to July 1992 (reaching 70 percent of GDP at its height), the CBR used its political autonomy to carry out its own preferred, traditional policies aimed at supporting production, centralizing control over financial transactions, and maintaining the ruble zone. Gerashchenko issued a telegram on July 28, 1992, authorizing the emission of 1.2 trillion rubles in credits to clear the interenterprise debt. After protests from the government, he rescinded the telegram and worked out a compromise with Gaidar that remained quite favorable to CBR preferences.[62] The Central Bank organized the offset of all interenterprise debts accumulated by July 1, 1992, and allowed enterprises to use positive balances in these offset accounts to pay their tax bills. This, as political scientist David Woodruff has observed, was tantamount to permitting enterprises to print their own money.[63] The CBR continued to issue new credits to enterprises throughout the summer and fall. The shock therapy attempt had ended.

Importantly, though, the CBR's willfulness cannot adequately explain the failure of shock therapy. Indeed, even if the CBR had wanted to cooperate with the executive's plans, in January 1992 it could not have done so. Simply put, the Central Bank of Russia did not control Russia's money supply. The ruble zone prevented the CBR from immediately restraining ruble-denominated credit disbursement outside of Russian territory. Moreover, few of the other former republics had any interest in undertaking shock therapy, and refused to coordinate their monetary and fiscal policies with Russia's. Along with continuing to emit large amounts of credits to their domestic enterprises, some ruble zone members also began to issue parallel currencies to supplement the dwindling supply of

61. "Russian Congress Opens on Note of Discord," *Rossiiskaia gazeta*, April 8, 1992, 4–6, trans. *Current Digest of the Post-Soviet Press* 44, no. 14 (1992): 4; and Ivan Zhagel, "5,000 Ruble Notes Will Be Russian," *Izvestiia*, April 21, 1992, 2, trans. *Current Digest of the Post-Soviet Press* 44, no. 16 (1992): 25.

62. Barry Ickes and Randi Ryterman, "Roadblock to Economic Reform: Inter-Enterprise Debt and the Transition to Markets," *Post-Soviet Affairs* 9, no. 3 (1993): 231–52.

63. David Woodruff, *Money Unmade: Barter and the Fate of Russian Capitalism* (Ithaca, N.Y.: Cornell University Press, 1999), 98.

cash rubles. This cash and credit emission by the former Soviet republics amounted to issuing new rubles in defiance of the shock therapy plan, and contributed to its ultimate failure.

More surprisingly, the CBR could not even control the domestic money supply, as the 1992 interenterprise debt crisis made painfully clear. The inflation that followed price liberalization led to a cash shortage in Russia. Instead of responding by restructuring and operating on a transparent, for-profit basis, enterprises chose to raise prices to levels well above expected inflation, and then to continue delivering goods to each other without receiving payment. This practice hid the true financial viability of enterprises in a labyrinthine tangle of debt. The crisis resulted from a combination of Soviet-era technical difficulties (backups in the payments system and the exigencies of the dual monetary circuit) and a lack of policy credibility. As we have seen, these technical difficulties made it all but impossible for enterprises to conduct financial transactions quickly in the inflationary environment. Most soon refused to deposit cash in the banking system at all, and wage arrears began to skyrocket as enterprises ran out of cash with which to pay workers.

At the same time, enterprises remained confident that the government would be forced to cancel or cover these debts and to release more cash into the economy. For years, enterprises without enough money to pay their debts had these arrears thrown into "card-file number two" at the CBR and covered, a system that the CBR did not dismantle until July 1992.[64] In addition, Gorbachev's reform programs of "self-financing" for enterprises had not led to bankruptcies or significant reductions in credits, while the CBR's generosity during the war of the banks had undermined the credibility of Yeltsin's forces. The vocal lack of consensus on economic policy at the highest levels of power, the technical problems inherent in implementing strict policies throughout the country, the difficulty of untangling the debt chain, and the political impossibility of shutting down thousands of state enterprises combined to force the hand of the government and the CBR.

Shock therapy proved impossible to implement in Russia not because of a lack of political will on the part of Russia's leaders, but because it assumed that micro-level economic practices could be changed rapidly by making a few macro-level economic policy adjustments. Instead, shock therapy led to a breakdown in Russia's monetary system. Without CBR support, and without previous reform in the payments system, the ruble zone, and the accounting relationships between the CBR and enterprises, shock therapy could not have worked in Russia. With the executive branch and the CBR working at cross-purposes, Russia had no consistent

64. "Russian Congress Opens on Note of Discord," 62–63.

macroeconomic policy throughout this entire period. Instead, the painful results of this abortive shock therapy attempt exacerbated hostilities between the formerly agreeable president and parliament, and led to Gaidar's removal as prime minister in December 1992.

Razing the Ruble Zone

The breakup of the ruble zone demonstrated once again how the CBR's political autonomy and technical incapacity combined to cause problems for the Russian Federation. In early 1993, no consensus existed on what should happen to the ruble zone. Gerashchenko's CBR preferred to retain the ruble zone, but only if the Central Bank itself assumed complete control over monetary and regulatory policy within the zone. The IMF concurred that the ruble zone should be maintained, but thought it could be directed by an overarching interstate bank or a federal-reserve-style system. The Russian government held mixed views. Parliament, influenced by the industrial lobby, favored preserving the ruble zone at all costs. Yeltsin and his economic team, on the other hand, increasingly began to regard the ruble zone as an economic liability, as it became clear that most other ruble zone members preferred to reform their economies at a relatively slower pace. The executive and the CBR quickly clashed over this issue, undermining each other's efforts and creating a policy debacle.

In order to keep the ruble zone together, the CBR maintained its traditionally high levels of financial support for the economies of the other former republics. Despite numerous presidential decrees attempting to limit their access to Russian financing, the CBR managed to find ways to undercut Yeltsin. The president would set limits on technical credits to the former republics, and the CBR would regularly exceed them. For example, in late 1992, the CBR gave 1.5 trillion rubles ($7 billion) in credit to CIS states—in defiance of the July agreement between the executive and CBR limiting the extent of these credits. The CBR continued to credit the CIS states until the Russian government, under pressure from the IMF, shut such credits down completely in April 1993. In order to soften this blow, in 1993 the CBR delivered 1.5 trillion rubles in cash to the former republics, an unpopular move in increasingly nationalistic Russia.[65]

However, the CBR did not deliver cash to just any state: it used cash disbursement to reward and punish ruble zone members. For example, Ukraine's refusal to control its credit and coupon emissions led the CBR to cut off its cash supply completely, while more compliant states like

---

65. Andrei Illarionov, "What Is the Price of Friendship?" *Izvestiia*, September 16, 1993, trans. *Current Digest of the Post-Soviet Press* 45, no. 37 (1993): 23.

Kazakhstan "earned" additional ruble shipments that eased the ubiquitous liquidity crunch.

The CBR continued its efforts to increase its control over fiscal flows within the ruble zone. As we have seen, the dual monetary circuit let the other central banks release credits to their own national enterprises without CBR coordination or approval. Therefore, the CBR announced in mid-1992 that in order to import or export within the ruble zone, an enterprise had to be able to pay or receive payment in the *beznalichnye* ruble of the region. *Beznalichnye* rubles lent by the Central Bank of Ukraine, for example, were Ukrainian rubles, with which an enterprise could not buy Russian goods. Naturally, a market in which to trade these ruble credits grew and the differentials among the rates of exchange began to widen. For example, during Ukraine's 1992 credit expansion, its *beznalichnye* ruble was worth only 30 percent of the Russian ruble.[66] This effort allowed the CBR to gain control over the external circulation of *beznalichnye* rubles, but did not affect the parallel cash currencies that some republics had introduced during Russia's shock therapy attempt.

The CBR had another plan for dealing with these parallel currencies. It began to print Russian ruble notes that circulated at equivalency with the old Soviet ones, but did not send these new rubles to the other states; they received their cash shipments solely in old rubles. The crafty CBR had boxed in the other ruble zone members. In an effort to force these states to submit to complete CBR control, in July 1993 the Central Bank announced that within one week all pre-1993 ruble notes would become invalid in Russia. If ruble zone members would not accept the Central Bank of Russia as the sole monetary authority, they could get out. This action took the Russian Ministry of Finance, the parliament, and the other ruble zone members by surprise. Rather than negotiating or ceding some of its authority, the CBR adopted a policy straight out of the Gosbank handbook—administrative, confiscatory, and secretive. Indeed, it explicitly broke agreements that the CBR had previously made with the other former republics, agreements that required the CBR to inform them before adopting any currency reforms. The Russian parliament and executive, the former republics, and international organizations all decried the move as illegitimate but were powerless to stop it. All Yeltsin could do was extend the length of the original three-day period in which individuals and organizations could exchange a limited amount of old rubles for new ones.

Ironically, however, the CBR had misjudged the remaining ruble zone members. It underestimated both their reluctance to accelerate their economic reform programs and their willingness to cede monetary sover-

66. "The Rouble Zone: Behind the Facade," *The Economist*, April 10, 1993, 51.

Table 3.5. Currency reforms in the former Soviet Union

Country	Currency	Introduction	Sole Legal Tender
Armenia	Dram	November 22, 1993	November 22, 1993
Azerbaijan	Manat	August 15, 1992	January 1, 1994
Belarus	Belarussian ruble	May 25, 1992	May 18, 1994
	Rubel	August 20, 1994	October 21, 1994
Estonia	Kroon	June 20, 1992	June 20, 1992
Georgia	Coupon	April 5, 1993	August 3, 1993
	Lari	September 25, 1995	October 2, 1995
Kazakhstan	Tenge	November 15, 1993	November 18, 1993
Kyrgyzstan	Som	May 10, 1993	May 15, 1993
Latvia	Latvian ruble	May 7, 1992	July 20, 1992
	Lat	March 5, 1993	October 18, 1993
Lithuania	Talonas	May 1, 1992	October 1, 1992
	Litas	June 25, 1993	August 1, 1993
Moldova	Moldovian coupons	June 20, 1992	July 25, 1993
	Leu	November 29, 1993	November 29, 1993
Russia	Russian ruble (1993)	July 24, 1993	July 26, 1993
Tajikistan	Tajik ruble	May 10, 1995	May 15, 1995
Turkmenistan	Manat	November 1, 1993	November 1, 1993
Ukraine[a]	Karbovanets	November 12, 1992	November 16, 1992
	Hryvnia	September 2, 1996	September 2, 1996
Uzbekistan	Sum-coupon	November 15, 1993	January 1, 1994
	Sum	July 1, 1994	October 15, 1994

Source: Tonny Lybek, "Central Bank Autonomy, and Inflation and Output Performance in the Baltic States, Russia, and Other Countries of the Former Soviet Union, 1995–97," *Working Paper of the International Monetary Fund*, January 1999.
[a]Single-use coupons had already been issued in 1991 and multi-use coupons were introduced in January 1992.

eignty to Russia. Rather than submitting to the will of the CBR, these states responded by hastening the introduction of their own currencies. Distressed, Gerashchenko pushed for the creation of a "ruble zone of a new type"—over the protests of the Russian Ministry of Finance. Russia, Armenia, Belarus, Kazakhstan, Tajikistan, and Uzbekistan signed a tentative agreement to create this new zone in September 1993. The CBR's centralizing tendencies doomed this effort as well, though, as talks broke down in November over currency conversion issues, access to Russian ruble notes, and the CBR's demand that the other states give up their gold reserves.[67] By late 1993 most former Soviet republics had already issued their own currencies (see Table 3.5).

67. Ivan Zhagel, "There Is No Longer a Ruble Space, There Is a Ruble Zone," *Izvestiia*, January 25, 1993, trans. *Current Digest of the Post-Soviet Press* 45, no. 4 (1993): 28.

This solved the technical problem of CBR control over cash and credit emission, but in a messy way that pleased no one. Not only did the CBR's refusal to consider the creation of a higher, coordinating authority preclude the establishment of a federal-reserve-style system in the former Soviet Union, but from 1992 until the currency reform in mid-1993, Russia lost a great deal of money due to the CBR's backhanded attempts to keep the ruble zone together. Moreover, this second major unwanted display of the CBR's clout convinced Yeltsin and his economic team that the uncooperative bank had to be brought to heel.

The Balance of Power

Two related phenomena in 1993 and 1994 partially resolved this standoff between the politically autonomous, monetarily profligate CBR and the fiscally conservative, authoritarian executive. First, Yeltsin's dissolution of the Supreme Soviet and its aftermath changed the balance of power between the executive and parliament, weakening the CBR's ability to play the two sides off against each other. Yeltsin's bid to increase his influence began with a referendum on April 25, 1993, which asked voters whether or not they trusted the president's economic course. Yeltsin's victory in the referendum gave him additional leverage in his battle with the parliament and the CBR, and helped prompt his fateful decision to abolish the entire network of popularly elected soviets throughout Russia in September 1993. The Supreme Soviet itself refused to go without a fight, and the resulting bloody confrontation between partisans of the president and the parliament left the Russian "White House" bathed in inky black soot. Although Gerashchenko had supported the Supreme Soviet in the fight, despite widespread expectations to the contrary Yeltsin decided to "reappoint" him as CBR director. Yeltsin passed a decree subordinating the CBR to the executive until elections for a new lower house of parliament (the State Duma) could be held in December. The president believed that this would sufficiently stamp out the CBR's troublesome independence.

The December 1993 elections further complicated the political picture. Yeltsin expected these elections to reinforce his power, yet the results were mixed. On the one hand, the State Duma elections held a nasty surprise for Yeltsin. Yeltsin's unpopular, ineffective economic policies took their political toll, as nationalist and communist parties triumphed at the polls. This recreated the previous ideological division between president and parliament. On the other hand, the election simultaneously ratified Russia's first post-communist constitution by referendum. This constitution, which Yeltsin's team had drafted, reserved so much power for the president that the new parliament found it difficult to oppose him effectively. Rancor remained, but the power balance had shifted. By December, Gerashchenko's CBR had regained some political freedom from the executive, both because of the sharp rebuke Yeltsin had received from the electorate and because Gerashchenko by this point had gained supporters in Yeltsin's own cabinet (in particular, the support of another high-level Soviet-era apparatchik, Prime Minister Viktor Chernomyrdin). The CBR's ability to preserve its autonomy by playing the president and parliament off against each other, though, waned significantly after the constitutional defanging of the parliament.

The second major factor mitigating the standoff between the Central Bank and the executive was the greater influence that the IMF (and other international financial organizations) began to assume over Russian monetary policy in the wake of the 1992 financial catastrophe. This served to reduce the CBR's autonomy, since in order to receive IMF aid it had to at least appear to cooperate with the Fund's policy demands. Moreover, the 1992 events had taught the CBR harsh lessons about the dangers of credit expansion and misuse, souring Gerashchenko in particular on using uncontrollable commercial banks to disburse and monitor state loans. If the banks refused to use these loans to promote production, and if the CBR was not organizationally capable of forcing them to do so, then the CBR could no longer achieve its aims through bank-directed credit. Training programs run by the international financial institutions also began to socialize the central bank's staff into accepting more monetarist viewpoints. As a result, the CBR's policy preferences began to converge more closely with the IMF's and the executive's.

This overall decline in the CBR's autonomy ironically led it to adopt more conservative monetary policies and encouraged greater policy coordination between the CBR and the executive. A less "independent" CBR proved to be a more watchful guardian of the currency. Moreover, while IMF influence restricted the CBR's autonomy, it also served to increase its technical capacity. With the aid of international financial institutions, over the next few years the CBR introduced credit auctions, developed the treasury bill market, improved the payments system, enforced more stringent reserve requirements on commercial banks, achieved positive real interest rates, and introduced a "ruble corridor" to attempt to stabilize the exchange rate.

In spring 1993, the IMF offered Russia a $3 billion loan under the new Systemic Transformation Facility, with the condition that the CBR adopt more restrictive monetary policies. Three significant changes immediately followed. First, under pressure from both the IMF and the Ministry of Finance, in May 1993 the CBR agreed to participate in a credit policy commission run jointly by the Ministry of Finance and the CBR. This led to the introduction of credit ceilings for the CBR in May and the elimination of subsidized credits to enterprises in September.[68] Second, the CBR committed to achieving positive real interest rates. As a first step, in May 1993 the CBR and the government signed agreements limiting the CBR rate to no less that 7 percent below the interbank rate. In a further agreement, after April 1994 the CBR and IMF agreed to limit the discrepancy to 5 percent. In practice, though, by April 1994 the CBR's rate had already become consistently higher than the interbank rate. In a rapid turnaround, by 1995 the real interest rate on CBR credits became one of the most positive in the world. Combined with falling inflation and higher reserve requirements, this caused a serious credit crunch for commercial banks in late 1995. Finally, Russia developed a treasury bill market. As early as 1992, the CBR and the IMF had urged the Ministry of Finance to start raising money through the securities markets rather than drawing it directly from the Central Bank.[69] This came to pass with the first GKO sales in May 1993.

The CBR remained in the eye of the storm through Russia's rocky macroeconomic stabilization in 1994–95. Yeltsin fired Gerashchenko as CBR director in November 1994 after the ruble's value fell almost 30 percent against the dollar on "Black Tuesday" (October 11), in part due to Gerashchenko's defiant loosening of monetary policy. Although according to Russian law the president and parliament held joint responsibility for firing a CBR director, Yeltsin successfully dismissed Gerashchenko without even asking the parliament for its acquiescence. The subsequent appointment of Gerashchenko's long-time deputy Tat'iana Paramonova, who remained only an acting director throughout her year-long tenure, further eroded the CBR's autonomy.

The next Central Bank director, Sergei Dubinin, also found the CBR's autonomy challenged regularly by the executive. The parliament overwhelmingly confirmed Dubinin as the new director in November 1995, in part in the hopes that his noted economic conservatism would prevent him from aiding Boris Yeltsin financially in the upcoming presidential campaign.[70] However, immediately before the June 1996 presidential

68. This commission had been created by a Yeltsin decree of October 7, 1992, but it did not become active until Finance Minister Boris Fedorov took it over. The credit ceilings were subsequently exceeded in the fall of 1993, when, as usual, the agricultural lobbies pressed for credits for the harvest and the northern regions asked for credits to prepare for the winter.

69. The Ministry of Finance announced its official intent to create GKOs in its statement "Osnovnye usloviia vypuska gosudarstvennykh kratkosrochnykh beskuponnykh obligatsii" of December 1992.

70. Yegor Gaidar, remarks, Southern Economics Association Conference, November 25, 1996.

elections, Yeltsin forced the CBR to transfer $1 billion to the government to cover his campaign promises. Under severe protest, but preferring to aid Yeltsin rather than contribute to a potential Communist election victory, the CBR relented.[71] Ironically, when I had asked Dubinin just two months earlier whether or not he considered the CBR to be independent, he replied:

> We are a very, very strong ruling and supervising facility. We operate in the political context of my country, but by the law we have two main items as the basis of our independence . . . nobody [alone] can fire the chief of the central bank . . . and no one can ask me or anyone at the central bank to give credit to the government.[72]

While the CBR began to implement tighter monetary and regulatory policies overall, it remained a politicized, troubled, and secretive institution.

The Complexity of Change

As the short, tortured history of the Central Bank of Russia demonstrates, the creation of a politically autonomous central bank does not necessarily lead to restrictive monetary policies. While the CBR is an extreme case, other post-communist central banks have come under similar fire. For example, economist Domenico Nuti noted that the Polish central bank "is deemed to have a wider degree of responsibility than even the Bundesbank . . . These arrangements ought to allow for stricter control of inflation, preventing the government from promoting employment via inflationary monetary expansion and currency devaluations. Polish actual experience of 1994–96 is quite the opposite."[73] This should lead us to rethink our theories on central bank independence—both how we

---

71. Deputy CBR director Aleksandr Khandruev called the decision "politically understandable but economically wrong," while Dubinin appealed to the Supreme Court to try to stop the transfer, saying "This is not only our right but our duty." As the IMF noted, "It . . . calls into question the independence of the central bank." See CBR, "Bespretsedentnyi 'zaem'," *Ekonomika i zhizn'* 24 (June 1996): 4–5; John Thornhill, "Central bank attacks Yeltsin 'violation'," *Financial Times*, June 11, 1996, 2; Reuters, "Yeltsin Move on Central Bank Prompts Concern at IMF," June 7, 1996; Reuters, "Russia Tightens Credit After Pre-Election Binge," June 10, 1996; and Reuters, "Russian Central Bank Faces First-Ever Loss," July 25, 1996. Allegedly, though, the CBR did use FIMACO to prop up the GKO market before the election, and may actually have funneled money directly through FIMACO to Yeltsin's campaign (Powell and Albats, "Follow the Money").

72. Sergei Dubinin, interview with author, April 23, 1996, Washington, D.C.

73. Domenico Nuti, "Exchange Rate and Monetary Policy in Poland, 1994–96; or, The Case for Privatizing the National Bank of Poland," paper presented at the Fifth US-Polish Economic Roundtable on "Directions of Financial Reform in Poland: Domestic Challenges and Foreign Participation," Warsaw, October 23–25, 1996.

define independence and what we can and cannot expect of an "independent" central bank. Given the CBR's continuity of personnel, historical objectives, and technical capabilities, even a politically autonomous CBR cannot have been expected to internalize and implement new policy goals overnight.

In fact, conservative monetary policy in post-communist democracies has depended much more on the influence of international financial institutions, on societal consensus, and on the government's revenue needs. Estonia and Lithuania, two states eager to join the West, established currency boards to ensure monetary restraint; Bulgaria did the same, but only after a devastating financial crisis and change of government. Hungary, Poland, and the Czech Republic, states in the forefront of the movement to break free of the command economy and Soviet political yoke, initially created three of the most independent central banks in the region in order to send a positive message about their intentions to the IMF and the European Union. States like Romania and Ukraine, less sure of their paths, created legally independent central banks but in practice kept monetary policy under government sway. In short, central bank autonomy cannot substitute for a lack of political consensus on economic policy or for the technical ability to implement reforms. Yet unaccountable central banks themselves can perform an end-run around democratic procedures. Their very secretiveness provides a breeding ground for corruption, while making coordinated monetary policy difficult to carry out.

Furthermore, as the Russian case demonstrates, restrictive monetary policy alone is not enough to remold a state's economic institutions. Even when the CBR's political autonomy declined and it began to implement tighter monetary policies, the Russian economy refused to respond. Although inflation had fallen below 3 percent per month for six months running by the end of 1996, Russia enjoyed no comparable reversal of the dismal economic performance that had begun in Soviet times. Real GDP fell by 3.5 percent in 1996, domestic investment plummeted by 17 percent, and wage and pension arrears hit a new high of 40.2 trillion rubles ($7.4 billion).[74] Tax collection continually lagged well behind expected efforts, while interenterprise debts ballooned again to reach 400 trillion rubles ($75 billion) in June 1996.[75] Capital flight continued at high levels throughout the decade, and the Russian government replaced fleeing

74. Penny Morvant, "Yeltsin Orders Further Action on Wage, Pension Arrears," *OMRI Daily Digest*, October 20, 1996.

75. Penny Morvant, "Military Protests Lack of Funding," *OMRI Daily Digest*, September 20, 1996; and Natalia Gurushina, "Company Arrears Increase in the First Half of 1996," *OMRI Daily Digest*, September 10, 1996.

money with ever-increasing levels of foreign and domestic debt. Instead of responding to the restrictive monetary environment by restructuring or cutting back spending, enterprises and local governments increased their use of monetary surrogates such as veksels (defined kindly as "commercial paper"; less kindly as "IOUs"), barter, and accumulation of inter-enterprise debt. The federal government tried to meet its own budget targets on the expenditure side by not paying wages and pensions and on the revenue side by emitting an ever-increasing number of high-yielding GKOs. Rather than encouraging energetic economic restructuring, the CBR's restrictive monetary policies had simply highlighted the many other unresolved structural problems in the Russian economy. These poor policy choices clashing with perverse institutional legacies laid the groundwork for the CBR's unhappy role in the 1998 crisis. As we shall see in the following chapters, this same combination paved a path of fool's gold for Russia's commercial banks as well.

CHAPTER FOUR

Shock Therapy Meets Soviet Bankers

In an article entitled *A Bank for Real Men*:
"What's good for the bank is good for Russia."

—Sergei Evseev, Volgo-Don Bank, 1994

ussia's commercial banks prospered in the first few years after the breakup of the USSR, building political and financial powerhouses on beds of quicksand. The impact of the shock therapy attempt on the hybrid financial infrastructure that had evolved under Gorbachev made this possible. Although the government immediately undertook major price liberalization and privatization in 1992, political battles and institutional legacies prevented the corresponding macroeconomic stabilization from beginning until mid-1993. Rather than bringing widespread economic prosperity to Russia, the policies introduced in 1992 accelerated the decline in production, enriched the commercial banks, significantly de-monetized much of the Russian economy, and touched off a political firestorm. In 1992 alone, industrial output fell by 18 percent and agricultural output by 9 percent, while inflation reached 2,506 percent. As even the IMF later admitted, "the magnitude of decline has exceeded the depth of any depression in Russia during the previous seventy years and may have been on the same order as . . . in the United States between 1929 and 1933."[1]

---

1. Biswajit Banerjee et al., *Road Maps of the Transition* (Washington, D.C.: IMF, 1995), 55.

Moreover, the privatization program failed to provide investment capital to enterprises that desperately needed restructuring, and failed to create a new, broader-based, and more profit-oriented ownership structure for former state enterprises. The effort to privatize quickly left most enterprises under the control of their former managers, thereby legitimizing the results of earlier *nomenklatura* privatization.

During this poisonous era of liberalization without stabilization, the Russian banking system thrived and expanded. Despite the dramatic fall in GDP for the Russian economy as a whole, the GDP created in the financial industry from 1991 through 1994 grew by 57 percent.[2] Tellingly, by 1993 only 6 percent of banks deemed their financial condition "bad," while 63 percent of enterprises did so.[3] The banks' profitable manipulation of the inflationary environment, counterposed with the suffering of domestic enterprises, the limited foreign investment, and the restrictions on foreign banks in Russia, allowed the commercial banks to assume an increasingly significant role in Russia's political and economic system. Their financial activities, in turn, often exploited the banks' incestuous ties to political figures, government ministries, the CBR, and state enterprises, all of which further cemented the institutional links between the big banks and the Russian state.

Yet the bankers' expanding power masked significant underlying problems within the emerging Russian financial system. Institutional legacies from the Soviet period, combined with the cumulative effects of bank liberalization and the ill-fated shock therapy attempt, created a banking sector well-suited to exploiting short-term money-making opportunities but unable to perform the most basic tasks expected of banks in market economies. This chapter examines the intertwined growth of the banks' political and economic influence during these years of profit and expansion, exploring how Russia's commercial banks managed to enjoy an unprecedented boom period from 1992 until 1995 while simultaneously becoming estranged from both domestic enterprises and households.

Banks and Enterprises: The Creeping Divorce

In developed market economies, many banks make money primarily through deposit and loan operations with corporate customers. As Russia avowedly undertook a rapid transition towards a market economy,

2. Vladimir Popov, "The Financial System in Russia Compared to Other Transition Economies: The Anglo-American versus the German-Japanese Model," *Comparative Economic Studies* 41, no. 1 (Spring 1999): 1–42.

3. Elena Belyanova, "Banks and Policy," *Russian Economic Barometer* 3, no. 2 (Spring 1994): 20–21. These results average six surveys of banks and twelve surveys of enterprises in 1993. Each survey included 160–200 industrial enterprises, 75–100 agricultural enterprises, and 50–60 banks throughout Russia.

then, we might have expected over time to see a commensurate increase in both the extent and profitability of these activities for commercial banks. Instead, exactly the opposite occurred. Bank credit to enterprises dropped from 33.6 percent of GDP in 1992 to 12 percent in 1995, while enterprise and government deposits combined fell from 21.1 percent to 4.2 percent of GDP.[4] During this period, long-term loans to enterprises dropped below 5 percent of all loans.[5] In fact, an examination of bank balance sheets revealed that in 1994 far more Russian bank activity concentrated on processing payments than on dealing in deposits and loans.[6] Small businesses suffered the most; whereas 28.8 percent of entrepreneurs reported that they had access to bank credit in 1992 (already a tiny proportion), by 1997 the rate had fallen to 18.8 percent.[7] The creeping divorce of banks and enterprises became such a serious problem that in 1994 the European Bank for Reconstruction and Development (EBRD) initiated a special program to extend loans through Russian banks to investment-starved small businesses.[8] Nevertheless, banks seemingly prospered despite their estrangement from enterprises. Why did banks and enterprises choose to move away from one another?

At first, of course, they did not. Banks continued to credit enterprises as in the past, and the nominal value of commercial bank loans increased tenfold in 1992. The unstable, highly inflationary macroeconomic conditions of 1992 and early 1993 proved extremely profitable for the banks, as the CBR's real monthly refinancing rate fell to negative 12.2 percent, and inflation reduced the value of nonperforming Soviet-era loans to infinitesimal amounts.[9] Banks in any inflationary economy can profit by short-term, speculative financial activities such as currency exchange and trade transactions, interbank credit operations, and manipulating the float (the period of time during which banks process customer transactions). After all, merely holding hard currency or delaying payments

4. Organization for Economic Cooperation and Development, *OECD Economic Surveys: Russian Federation, 1997* (Paris: OECD, 1997); and Michael Bernstam and Alvin Rabushka, *Fixing Russia's Banks: A Proposal for Growth* (Stanford, Calif.: Hoover Institution Press, 1998), 35.

5. Central Bank of Russia, *Bulletin of Banking Statistics* 1, no. 20, 1995.

6. Popov, "The Financial System in Russia Compared to Other Transition Economies."

7. Gennady Polonsky, "Small Business in the Russian Provinces: Case Study Evidence from Volgograd," *Communist Economies and Economic Transformation* 10, no. 4 (1998): 519–37.

8. Yu. I. Shimanskii, "Soderzhanie, metody, i formy gosudartsvennoi podderzhki malovo predprinimatel'stva," in *Biznes i banki v sovremennoi Rossii,* ed. A. I. Arkhipov (Moscow: Institut ekonomiki Rossiiskoi akademii nauk, 1996), 103; and Catherine Belton, "EBRD Seeks to Calm Jitters Over New Lending Bank," *Moscow Times,* June 18, 1999.

9. European Bank for Reconstruction and Development, *Transition Report 1998* (London: EBRD, 1998).

transfers earned bankers a profit as the value of the ruble fell. While most banks could do well under these conditions (or at least keep their heads above water), those banks with good political connections prospered the most because they had easier access to hard currency licenses and foreign trade organizations.

But banks also made a great deal of money through loans in the inflationary environment, even though, given the negative real interest rates that even the commercial banks charged at the time, this result seems counterintuitive. How did they manage this feat? First, banks maintained large spreads between commercial deposit and lending rates throughout this period, which enabled them to capture revenue from the "inflation tax." Russian economist Mikhail Dmitriev gives three reasons for this: (1) insufficient competition meant that banks could provide low interest rates on deposits; (2) unlike other high-inflation countries, Russian banks did not index their deposits; and (3) early on, banking laws failed to limit the spread between interest rates on commercial deposits and loans. The study estimated that during this period, "inflationary redistribution" through Russian commercial banks measured 6–9 percent of GDP, with most of the money remaining in the banks themselves.[10]

Second, banks easily exploited institutional legacies and lax CBR regulation to make disbursing centralized credit profitable. Directed credits composed over half of the 1992 loan expansion, accounting for 3.5 trillion rubles of bank credits that year (23 percent of GDP).[11] The CBR increased centralized credit allocation dramatically after July 1992, when it simultaneously began offsetting previously accrued interenterprise arrears and eliminated card-file number two (*kartoteka dva*) in order to remove its ability to carry out any such general offsets in the future. Card-file number two was the accounting channel that had allowed the CBR to keep track of all payments orders among enterprises (and thus of interenterprise debt growth). The decision to eliminate card-file number two, made by Matiukhin in May and put into effect on July 1, aimed to reduce interenterprise debt by removing this accounting channel. Since the CBR could no longer monitor interenterprise debt through the card-file number two accounts, it could no longer choose or be pressured to offset this debt. After all, it would have no idea who owed what to whom. As David Woodruff has observed, this decision changed the political calculus of industrial directors because "the plausibility of a general solution to the problems particular enterprises faced as a result of price liberalization

10. M. E. Dmitriev, ed., *Rossiiskie banki nakanune finansovoi stabilizatsii* (St. Petersburg: Norma, 1996).
11. Ruben Lamdany, ed., *Russia: The Banking System During the Transition* (Washington, D.C.: World Bank, 1993), 8.

and inflation waned."[12] At this point, the unity of the industrial lobby disappeared and individual enterprises began to lobby the banking system and the government for cheap directed credits. This one-time offset and accounting change thus increased the perceived need for directed credits to lubricate the economy.

Although the CBR formally limited the interest rate spread on directed credits to 3 percent (on its face, not an attractive rate for banks), its technical inability to monitor the use of these credits meant that banks could safely ignore this directive. During this period, officials of the Volgograd CBR administration named raising the interest rate above the allowed 3-percent margin as the most common violation of banking norms in the region.[13] Similarly, banks would regularly accept directed credits earmarked for one use and divert them to another. Bankers also developed more involved strategies to get around this constraint. For example, an enterprise might receive a loan from one bank at the low CBR rate and then pass the money over to an enterprise-affiliated commercial bank to relend at a much higher rate.[14] Bankers waved off these excesses as a manifestation of "primitive capitalist accumulation," putting their training in Marxist-Leninist economics to strange use.

This combination of bank profitability and disingenuousness led to a "third wave" of bank creation. On the one hand, the money-making potential of the banking sector relative to other economic sectors encouraged the founding of additional zero banks. On the other, the proclivity of the banks to divert funds led yet more enterprises to create their own pocket banks, on the theory that an enterprise-controlled bank would not delay the enterprise's payments transfers and would lend centralized credits to it at the prescribed 3 percent margin. If the CBR could not control the banks, then enterprises would do it themselves. At the height of the banking boom, Russia had over 2,500 licensed commercial banks (see Table 1.1).

But beginning in late spring 1993, banks and enterprises mutually became less interested in interacting with one another. Enterprises pulled away from commercial banks because of the increasing and unwanted pressure to repay loans, because the CBR began to scale back on directed credits, because of their relative poverty and lack of acceptable collateral, because they believed (sometimes rightly) that corrupt banks would give criminals access to their account information, and, perhaps most impor-

12. David Woodruff, *Money Unmade: Barter and the Fate of Russian Capitalism* (Ithaca, N.Y.: Cornell University Press, 1999), 97.

13. Elena Dorofeeva, CBR Volgograd, "Khochesh' poluchit' kredit? Privatizirui predpriiatie," *Delovoe povolzh'e* 12 (June 1993): 7.

14. Svetlana P. Glinkina, "Privatizatsiya and Kriminalizatsiya: How Organized Crime Is Hijacking Privatization," *Demokratizatsiya* 4, no. 1 (Winter 1996).

tantly, because of the *kartoteka* system. Card-file number two (*kartoteka dva*) had been just one piece of this extensive accounting system. The *kartoteka* system—a Soviet-era legacy—allowed taxes, certain service bills, and court judgements to be collected directly from an enterprise's bank account. If an enterprise accumulated tax arrears, any money that appeared in its bank account became liable for confiscation. The electric power industry, railroads, and oil and gas suppliers could send an enterprise's bill directly to its bank, and if the account held money, they could be paid.[15] Moreover, if a private firm won a court judgement again an enterprise for nonpayment, money in the bank account had to be used to pay off these creditors according to a priority list. Not surprisingly, enterprises with tax arrears, with overdue bills, or with judgements pending emptied their bank accounts. The *kartoteka* system thus contributed substantially to the de-monetization of the economy, as enterprises simply dropped out of the financial system when they hit hard times. As an analysis by Kathryn Hendley, Barry Ickes, Peter Murrell, and Randi Ryterman observes, "The use of banks to facilitate tax collection, which might be efficient under normal circumstances, apparently leads to dysfunctional barter activity when this arrangement is combined with an enterprise system that has heavy tax arrears."[16] When combined with the *kartoteka* system, the impoverishment of Russian enterprises after the failed shock therapy attempt ironically decreased both state tax revenues and the state's ability to affect economic development through monetary policy.

From mid-1993 to 1995, banks drew away from enterprises as well for three primary reasons. First, directed credits became unprofitable for banks and by 1995 had dried up almost entirely. In March 1993, the *Russian Economic Barometer* indicated that 92 percent of surveyed banks disbursed directed credits, and over two-thirds believed that the success of their banks depended upon this activity. But by March 1994, when asked "Is it profitable for your bank to allocate directed credits?" 100 percent of respondents answered "No."[17] Why did this occur? In May 1993, the government passed a resolution making banks, not enterprises, financially responsible for the return of directed credits. The Central Bank of Russia, fed up with commercial banks misdirecting its money, rigorously en-

15. Woodruff, *Money Unmade*, 118.

16. Kathryn Hendley, Barry Ickes, Peter Murrell, and Randi Ryterman, "Observations on the Use of Law by Russian Enterprises," *Post-Soviet Affairs* 13, no. 1 (1997): 36.

17. "Commercial Banks: Recent Trends," *Russian Economic Barometer* 2, no. 3 (Summer 1993): 21; and Elena Belyanova, "Banking Sector in Transition," *Russian Economic Barometer* 3, no. 3 (Summer 1994): 35. On average, in early 1993 centralized loans represented 40 percent of these banks' borrowed resources. Sample size for these surveys conducted by the Russian Economic Barometer averaged between 40 and 60 banks, most of which were medium-sized. Approximately half were former specialized banks, and half new banks.

forced this rule. Combined with the slowing inflation and rising CBR interest rates in 1993, this suddenly made disbursing directed credits quite unattractive. In fact, the government and CBR began to experience the opposite problem; they could not find enough banks willing to disburse the centralized loans that they allocated. Banks would only accept this task if the enterprise customer seemed reliable, or if the bank itself was a former spetsbank or a pocket bank inclined to disburse risky credits.

Second, commercial banks did not participate significantly in Russia's initial privatization program. Interestingly, in late 1992 and early 1993 Russian bankers had anticipated that they would play a much larger role in enterprise privatization, with the majority planning to buy company shares or invest privatization vouchers.[18] But other activities proved to be safer and more profitable for the banks. The privatization program in Russia made it easy for managers to gain control of their own enterprises, and even a bank that ran its own voucher privatization fund initially could not acquire any more than 10 percent of an enterprise, a limit that was only raised to 25 percent for the 1994 privatization program. One study found that of 148 voucher funds interviewed, only 32 reported a bank as one of its founders.[19] As a result, few banks bought vouchers: in one survey, 53 percent of bankers said that their banks had reservations about acquiring vouchers because "it is difficult to invest vouchers profitably."[20] Without the opportunity to acquire meaningful stakes in privatizing enterprises, banks had little interest in participating in the process. Therefore most of them missed this opportunity to expand their connections to new enterprises.

Finally, banks began to make fewer loans on their own initiative as they learned that most enterprises were poor credit risks. In the Soviet era, state enterprises safely assumed that "loans" meant "grants," operated without consideration for profit, often made so-called "value-destroying"

18. See the survey reports in *Russian Economic Barometer* 2, no. 2 (1993): 23, and no. 4 (1993): 24. Like a number of post-communist states, Russia privatized its state-owned enterprises partially through vouchers. In voucher privatization plans, each citizen of a country is eligible to freely receive or cheaply purchase "privatization vouchers." They can then either invest the voucher(s) directly in a privatizing enterprise, sell the voucher(s), or place the voucher(s) in investment funds that gather numerous vouchers and bid them in blocks. Czechoslovakia pioneered this method in the post-communist world, arguing that voucher privatization represented the fairest, most equitable way to redistribute state-owned property.

19. Roman Frydman, Katharina Pistor, and Andrzej Rapaczynski, "Investing in Insider-Dominated Firms: A Study of Russian Voucher Privatization Funds," in *Corporate Governance in Central Europe and Russia,* ed. Frydman et al. (Budapest: Central European University Press, 1996).

20. "Commercial Banks in the Voucher Market," *Russian Economic Barometer* 2, no. 2 (Spring 1993): 21–23. The survey was taken from October 1992–March 1993.

goods, and had nontransparent accounting systems. As a banker in Riazan' observed, "Of course, we can't analyze the situation of our debtors over a period of five years, like your professors suggest. And they all try to hide their balances . . . in general, there is nothing concrete to tell you who is trying to rip you off."[21] Similarly, Russian commercial bankers had little experience with tasks such as evaluating loan applicants, which take years even for would-be Western bankers to learn.[22] In a December 1994 survey, in response to the question, "Is it necessary to strengthen the level of preparation of personnel in the banking sphere?" every single banker answered "Yes."[23] Agreeing, Oleg Matveev, an economist in the Riazan' office of the CBR, stated that "the main problem we run into with the opening of commercial banks is the quality of the staff."[24] Although commercial bankers took a number of steps to remedy this deficiency (opening over 50 financial training centers by 1995), expertise could not accumulate quickly enough to improve loan management before major mistakes were made. For example, Astrobank (the favored bank of St. Petersburg's intellectuals) gave a one billion ruble loan to Petersburgskii Tekstil, although Menatep had just sued the company for not returning another large loan.[25] In a second case, in early 1995 a scandal broke out when the supposedly reputable firm Erlan defaulted on numerous loans from some of the biggest banks in Russia. It turned out that although Erlan had been successful at first, it soon went into the red and began a string of borrowing from one commercial bank to pay off loans from another. Not surprisingly, many banks suddenly became much choosier about their borrowers. A small pocket bank rebellion even began in 1993, as some suffering pocket banks managed to wrest control from their founders by continually issuing new shares that their affiliated enterprises could not afford to buy.[26]

Perversely, this creeping divorce increased the proportion of bad loans in the commercial banking system. According to the CBR, by November 1994 banks held 13.7 trillion rubles in overdue loans (23 percent of all

21. Liudmila Komarova, Director of the Analysis Department, Mesherabank, interview with author, March 14, 1995, Riazan'.

22. For an excellent summary of this dilemma and its consequences, see O. M. Bogdanova, "Problemy formirovaniia i upravleniia bankovskimi kadrami," in Biznes i banki v sovremennoi Rossii, ed. Arkhipov, 63–73.

23. Surveys by Cassandra research service, reported in the CBR publication Monitoring bankovskoi politiki 1 (1995): 33.

24. Oleg Matveev, lead economist, Department of Licensing, CBR Riazan', interview with author, September 2, 1994, Riazan'.

25. Peter Rutland, "Bankruptcies Loom in St. Petersburg," OMRI Daily Digest, November 14, 1995.

26. Woodruff, Money Unmade, 105–6.

loans), while in some banks the ratio reached 90 percent.[27] On the demand side, as we have seen, many enterprises became wary of interacting with the banking system unless they had no other options. A survey of enterprises at three points in 1993 confirmed that enterprises which considered themselves to be in a "bad" financial position were much more likely than other enterprises to have received loans from two or more banks.[28] On the supply side, as banks with options ceased making all but the safest loans, the major lenders became former spetsbanks, pocket banks, and zero banks lending to affiliated organizations. In these situations, customer quality took a back seat in lending decisions. The former spetsbanks in particular often stuck their heads in the sand and continued to give unwisely large amounts of credit. They often granted these loans at subsidized (and occasionally at zero) interest rates without the bank conducting any sort of acceptable credit review process. For instance, Zapsibkombank in Tiumen' oblast' stated in its annual report that "the credit policy of the bank gives shareholders the right to receive immediate credit on preferential terms. In 1993 the bank granted loans totaling 78 million rubles to its shareholders (or 47 percent of the total). This sum included 16 million rubles in privileged credits which allow shareholders to save an average of 2 million rubles a year."[29] The case for lending cutbacks should not be overstated; banks did continue to grant credits to enterprises. The amounts in real terms simply became smaller, and the circles of connection tighter.

The bank-enterprise divide and the perpetual environment of uncertainty in Russia increasingly split the economy into two halves. On one side, a small money-based economy developed, inhabited by banks, a few profitable enterprises, and individuals. Cash rubles, precious metals, and—most importantly—dollars circulated throughout this system. After rising steadily for several years, in October 1995 purchases of hard currency by Russian citizens hit a record level of $3.1 billion.[30] During 1993–94, banks concentrated their financial activity on the foreign currency markets and, increasingly, on the interbank lending market. On the other side, a nonmonetary economy appeared, inhabited by most enterprises and a growing group of local governments.[31] Interenterprise debt,

27. Tat'iana Paramonova, address to the Third International Congress on Banking in Russia, December 1994, printed in Association of Russian Banks (ARB), *Informatsionnyi biulleten' (Spetsial'nyi vypusk)*, 1995.
28. *Russian Economic Barometer* 3, no. 1 (1994): 9.
29. Zapsibkombank, "Annual Report, 1993."
30. V. P. Plakin, "Nekotorye aktual'nye problemy i tendentsii razvitiia bankovskoi sistemy Rossii," in *Biznes i banki v sovremennoi Rossii*, ed. Arkhipov, 30.
31. A book on money and banking necessarily cannot do justice to the fascinating intricacies of the nonmonetary economy in Russia. The best work on this subject includes

barter, veksels, and other surrogate monies became the currency of this alternative economy. After being wiped out by the CBR in summer 1992, interenterprise debt started expanding significantly again by October 1993, at the same time interest rates finally had reached market levels. Barter reared its head then as well. According to one survey of enterprise directors, the average percentage of barter in sales rose from 5 percent in 1992 to 40 percent by 1996.[32] Although creditors always preferred payment in cash, they would accept payment in kind if the alternative was receiving no payment at all. It made no sense for enterprises to cut off their cash-poor customers completely and bring the supply chain to a grinding halt. This put an economic cycle into motion that Woodruff has aptly called the "barter of the bankrupt." Enterprises increasingly devoted their time and resources not to production and restructuring, but to re-bartering and selling goods received from their customers.

Finally, veksels (from the German wechsel, or bill of exchange) began to appear throughout Russia by 1994 as enterprises, banks, and local governments sought to unravel the chain of arrears and substitute surrogate financial instruments for time-consuming barter.[33] In their simplest form, enterprises in a supply chain might pass veksels along to each other instead of paying in hard-to-come-by cash. Regional governments and banks found themselves drawn into the veksel net as well. Banks (most prominently Tver'universalbank) quickly learned to profit by emitting their own veksels that could be redeemed for cash after a certain date, or by making loans to enterprises in veksels instead of cash. Governments began to accept veksels for tax payments and used them to pay their own debts to enterprises; soon, they too began emitting their own. In Riazan', the oblast' administration joined forces with three commercial banks to introduce veksels, believing it would unravel the interenterprise debt chain in the oblast'. By 1994, almost two billion rubles-worth of veksels circulated in Riazan' oblast'.[34] Volgograd started using veksels even earlier, and by 1994 almost 100 billion rubles-worth had entered into circulation in the

Woodruff, *Money Unmade*; Clifford Gaddy and Barry Ickes, "Russia's Virtual Economy," *Foreign Affairs* 77, no. 5 (1998): 53–67; and Barry Ickes and Randi Ryterman, "The Interenterprise Arrears Crisis in Russia," *Post-Soviet Affairs* 8, no. 4 (1992): 331–61, and "Roadblock to Economic Reform: Inter-Enterprise Debt and the Transition to Markets," *Post-Soviet Affairs* 9, no. 3 (1993): 231–52.

32. Hendley et al., "Observations on the Use of Law by Russian Enterprises."

33. On the beginning of the veksel' trade, see especially Woodruff, *Money Unmade*, 149–61; *Veksel' i veksel'noe obrashchenye v Rossii* (Moscow: Banktsentr, 1994); and "Vsaimozadolzhennost' predpriatii i veksel'," *Biznes i banki* 6, no. 172 (February 1994): 1.

34. Nikolai Reunov, "Vekseli kak sredstvo ot udavki neplatezhei," *Priokskaia gazeta*, September 30, 1994, 1; and A. Shtrikov and A. Volkov, "Ispol'zovanye vekselei pozvoliaet budzhetu polychat' pribyl' i chastichno pogashat' vzaimnuiu zadolzhennost' predpriatii," *YeZh-Rus'* 8 (February 23–March 1, 1995): 7.

oblast'. Veksels, however, could not solve the nonpayments problem; despite veksels, by January 1995 nonpayments in Volgograd oblast' had risen to 2.3 trillion rubles.[35] Veksels merely represented unexpected local circumventions of the CBR's central austerity program.

Therefore, by mutual agreement, banks and enterprises became increasingly economically separated between 1993 and 1995. This split proved dangerously destabilizing for Russia's economic and political development. Bank loans did not provide the capital required to start up small businesses and foster a middle class. De-monetization reduced the power of the Russian federal government to control the economy, and contributed to political decentralization as local governments participated in surrogate monetary systems. Finally, the relative economic power of commercial banks in Russia gave them unprecedented leverage in the political system. Although any average, medium-sized bank in the United States would dwarf the largest commercial banks in Russia, in a cash-starved society the man with pocket change is king (see Table 4.1). This particularly benefited the well-established Moscow zero banks and the largest remnants of the spetsbank system.

Retail Banking: The Customer Comes Last

Given the separation between banks and enterprises, we might have expected commercial banks to turn towards retail banking as an alternative source of profit. After all, Russian households have no choice but to operate in the cash economy; they must pay for groceries and other consumer goods in currency. Here, though, commercial banks faced a different obstacle—Sberbank. Sberbank held significant initial advantages over other banks in this arena. It controlled over 90 percent of all household deposits in 1992; its branches spanned the length and breadth of Russia; households paid their bills directly through their local Sberbank branch; and the government explicitly insured deposits in Sberbank. Despite these advantages, Sberbank's share of the retail market had dropped to less than 60 percent by January 1995 (see Table 4.2). But it then shot back up, and as of September 1996 Sberbank held 72.5 percent of all household deposits.[36]

The fall and rise in Sberbank's popularity speaks volumes about institutional legacies and bank behavior in Russia. Sberbank initially squandered its monopoly position in the savings market because of its compla-

---

35. Ivan Shabunin, administrative head of Volgograd oblast', "Oblast' budet konkurirovat' s finansovymi kompaniiami," *Delovoe povolzh'e* 3 (January 1995): 1.

36. Praim-TASS, "Novosti," *Finansovye izvestiia*, October 3, 1996.

Table 4.1. The leading Russian banks (by assets) as of January 1996 (in millions of rubles)

Bank	City	Assets	Capital	Net profit
1. *Sberbank*[a] (1)[b]	Moscow	119,824,868	6,099,889	3,010,424
2. *Vneshtorgbank* (2)	Moscow	26,066,736	3,764,350	875,083
3. *Agroprombank* (3)	Moscow	18,622,009	275,509	na
4. ONEKSIMbank (7)	Moscow	17,717,302	1,370,596	260,727
5. Inkombank (4)	Moscow	14,686,940	1,052,618	806,354
6. *Mosbiznesbank* (6)	Moscow	13,110,620	640,478	482,539
7. Rossiiskii Kredit (5)	Moscow	11,982,206	557,032	400,351
8. International Financial Company (MFK) (10)	Moscow	11,265,122	1,120,847	207,889
9. Imperial (9)	Moscow	10,100,994	996,003	395,220
10. *Moscow Industrial* (8)	Moscow	10,017,547	527,385	609,219
11. Menatep (12)	Moscow	9,962,400	625,027	285,877
12. *Unikombank* (14)	Moscow	8,960,225	469,296	463,639
13. *Promstroibank* (15)	Moscow	8,173,556	487,892	435,813
14. *Bank St. Petersburg*	St. Petersburg	8,136,274	139,342	131,294
15. International Moscow Bank (13)[c]	Moscow	7,088,619	731,741	206,038
16. Stolichnii Bank (11)	Moscow	6,696,978	867,715	36,162
17. *Tver'universalbank*	Tver'	6,114,373	262,228	81,604
18. *Avtobank* (20)	Moscow	5,771,314	615,759	331,008
19. *Vozrozhdenie* (16)	Moscow	5,647,559	376,954	171,132
20. *Promstroibank St. Petersburg*	St. Petersburg	5,383,508	349,026	348,931

Source: Rating analytical center, "Krupneishie banki Rossii" <http://www.rating.ru>
$1 = 4,622 rubles (1/1/96)
[a] Italics designate state-owned or former specialized banks.
[b] Rank in January 1995 shown in parentheses.
[c] 40% of stock owned by former specialized banks.

cent, Soviet-style operations. In answer to an interview question, one Riazan' banker snidely observed, "Our Sberbank is so conservative, to find out what has changed the least in the banking system you should talk to them."[37] Sberbank offered low, unpredictable interest rates on deposits and absolutely terrible service. Most Sberbank depositors who had significant amounts of money in their accounts before 1991 saw those savings obliterated by hyperinflation. As the Professional Association of Workers of Local Industry and Communal Enterprises in Riazan' observed in an open letter to Yeltsin in 1994, "deposits that would have been enough to buy a car a few years ago, now . . . aren't enough to buy a child's bicycle."[38]

37. Riazan' banker, interview with author, September 1994, Riazan'.
38. Ol'ga Ignatova, "Piketami po gasfondu?" *Priokskaia gazeta*, February 18, 1994, 1.

Table 4.2. Year-end household ruble savings
(in billions of redenominated rubles)

	Total household ruble deposits	Total ruble deposits held in Sberbank[a]
1992	na	90%
1993	na	60
1994	28.3	58.6
1995	70.6	65.3
1996	118.4	76.2
1997	148.2	79.2
1998	149.5	85.3
1999	211.1	88.0

Sources: Russian Economic Trends, "Monthly Update" <http://www.hhs.se/site/ret/update>; CBR, *Bulletin of Banking Statistics* 2 (1994, 1995, and 1996); CBR, "Annual Report 1997" and "Annual Report 1998"; and Bank of Finland, "Russian and Baltic Economies: The Week in Review" <http://www.bof.fi/env/eng/it/weekly>.
[a] If we also included household foreign exchange deposits, Sberbank's share of the total household deposit market would be consistently lower (e.g., about 74 percent for both 1998 and 1999).

Sberbank's interest rates during the transition period were determined in cooperation with the CBR and the Ministry of Finance.[39] Negative real interest rates on deposits persisted until late 1995. From 1992–93 real interest rates averaged an astonishing negative 93 percent, while they rose to negative 40 percent in 1994 and early 1995.[40] To make matters worse, the government effectively confiscated a great deal of state-owned Sberbank's funds in 1992 and repaid the debt in the spring of 1993 at low interest rates, leaving its real value substantially reduced.

In addition, Sberbank sometimes took it upon itself to unilaterally lower interest rates on current deposits. As the director of Volgograd Sberbank charitably observed after customers complained, "If you don't read what you sign, then it's your problem. When we raised our rates four times no one took us to court."[41] Newspapers across the country regularly

39. Lamdany, ed., *Russia: The Banking System during the Transition,* 19. However, at least the Moscow Sberbank gave preferred interest rates on deposits and loans to shareholders. According to one staffer there, this explained why many commercial banks bought shares in Sberbank. Nikolai Kil'diushev, head of the hard currency credit department, Sberbank Moscow, interview with author, July 7, 1995, Moscow.

40. Bernstam and Rabushka, *Fixing Russia's Banks,* 39.

41. Yurii Voinov, "Nashi liudi privykli k sberknizhkam," *Delovoe povolzh'e* 10 (March 1995): 10.

ran stories decrying the egregious, Soviet-style attitude that Sberbank adopted towards its customers. A typical article from Volgograd observed that "Every day our eyes and ears are beaten with ads attracting deposits of the population . . . Only at our hometown Sberbank, like many other monopolistic state structures, does the opposite often occur—clients are chased away like obtrusive flies."[42] A 1993 survey carried out by Moscow's Sberbank found that although customers appreciated Sberbank's convenience and stability, its interest rates and range of services were not competitive. Pensioners, in fact, provided its most loyal customer base. Like the Russian Communist Party's supporters, it seemed as if Sberbank's main constituency would literally die out over time if it did not change its ways.[43]

Where were Sberbank's customers going? Surprisingly, most did not turn to one of the hundreds of new commercial banks. In fact, most commercial banks initially did not bother to compete in the retail market. Commercial bankers surveyed stated that this was due to their lack of facilities for servicing individual depositors, the high costs of doing so, and the unwillingness of households to deposit their money in other banks.[44] Commercial bankers greatly preferred attracting enterprise clients and working on the short-term credit and currency markets. As Viktor Tsybko, vice-president of a respected Volgograd zero bank, stated, "It is more profitable to work with strong clients than with the masses, which each have three rubles in their pocket. We are not a charity organization."[45] Naturally, the poor interest rates and service at Sberbank, the dearth of competition from other banks, the reality of high inflation wiping out people's savings, and the economic naivete of much of the Russian population provided a perfect breeding ground for pyramid schemes, pawnshops, and loan sharks. As a result, fly-by-night scammers captured much of the market that Sberbank lost in 1993.

42. P. Lipchenko, "Kakoi bankir otkazhetsia ot deneg?" *Volgogradskaia pravda*, November 14, 1992, 1. See also V. Konovalov, "Zazvuchit li v Gosbanke roial'?" *Volgogradskaia pravda*, December 24, 1991, 5. Konovalov discussed the poor service at Sberbank and the difficulty clients experienced withdrawing money there. He stated, for example, that one Saturday "it turns out that there isn't any money at Sberbank and none is expected. In addition, communal services payments aren't being accepted, inasmuch as the cash register isn't working."

43. Moscow Savings Bank, "Moscow Savings Bank Customer Survey Analysis," March 24, 1993; "Bank location, fast service, bank stability, historical relationships with the bank, and communal payment services were most frequently mentioned as important reasons for banking at MSB. Attractive interest rates, a broad range of services, and payroll remittance services were generally not considered compelling reasons for banking at MSB. . . . Pensioners use more MSB services, are less likely to use competing banks . . . and weigh their historical relationship with the bank more heavily than do young and middle aged customers."

44. *Russian Economic Barometer* 3, no. 3 (Summer 1994): 37.

45. Viktor Tsybko, Russkii Yuzhnii Bank, quoted in Viacheslav Dudenko, "Novye Russkie na Russkom yuge," *Delovoe povolzh'e* 40 (October 1994): 5.

Pyramid schemes in particular represented a major financial scourge for Russia's citizens. Infamous companies such as MMM, *Russkii Dom Selenga* ("Russian House of Selling"), and *Russkaia Nedvishimost'* ("Russian Real Estate") began to appear in 1992 during the beginning of the voucher privatization process, masquerading as legitimate voucher investment funds. These companies sold investors shares in their own funds (accepting either money or vouchers) and often promised impossible returns of well over 1,000 percent a year. Their slick advertising campaigns and the financial windfalls for the first investors allowed these schemes to spread like wildfire, with the crippled and divided government unable to stop them. MMM, one of the largest funds, crashed in early 1994, taking many people's life savings with it. Others soon followed.

Sberbank's share of household deposits began to edge up again after the first funds crashed. According to the director of Sberbank Volgograd, every time a fund went under they gained new clients.[46] One family in Volgograd provided an instructive example of consumer behavior during this period. They put their privatization vouchers in a pyramid scheme, and received no dividends. They deposited their money in a small local bank and for a time made a profit from its high rates, but then the bank burned down and stopped paying its depositors. So they decided to return their money to Sberbank, despite its comparatively low interest rates, because the state guaranteed their deposits there.[47] The president of Bank St. Petersburg observed that "The best lesson for the country as a whole seems to have been the MMM fiasco. . . . The scandal actually taught the Russian people the lessons of capitalism, perhaps for the first time."[48] This statement seemed somewhat optimistic, however, considering that bilked depositors tended to blame the government rather than the pyramid schemes for the loss of their savings. Sergei Mavrodi, the director of MMM, even managed to get himself elected to the Duma after the fund's collapse by promising to use his position to find a way to refund investors. In reality, he wanted the immunity from prosecution that Duma deputies enjoyed, and did not bother to attend sessions of the Duma after his election.

Sberbank's advantage in security persisted through this period because, despite several attempts, Russia did not develop a deposit insurance sys-

46. Yurii Voinov, "Nashi liudi privykli k sberknizhkam."
47. Interview in Volgograd, April 18, 1995. Confirming this view, in an October 1994 survey 53.8 percent of Russians said that Sberbank was reliable, while only 14.9 percent said the same about commercial banks. Survey of 1500 people in 12 regions of Russia, conducted by the Center of Social Prognosis and Marketing. CBR, *Monitoring bankovskoi politiki* 1, no. 5 (1995): 38.
48. Yurii Lvov, advertisement for Bank Saint Petersburg, *Euromoney*, September 1994, 137.

tem for commercial banks. The reason was simple—the Central Bank wanted commercial banks to design and fund it, while the bankers felt that the CBR should do so. Both wanted the security, but neither wanted to pay for it. Moreover, the sheer number and diversity of banks, combined with the uncertainty in the economy, made it difficult to estimate how well-financed the plan would need to be and how often depositors might need to draw upon it. Tekhnobank president Garegin Tosunian spoke for the commercial bankers when he stated, "the means for creating this fund and originally financing its activities may be granted by the state in the form of subsidized credit with a lengthy term of repayment."[49] The CBR, on the other hand, preferred that the commercial banks set up and police their own voluntary fund. The CBR and the commercial banks completely ignored Yeltsin's two decrees on the matter (from 1993 and 1994) because of this fundamental difference in opinion. The Duma passed its own legislation to create a special, separate deposit insurance fund in November 1995, but Yeltsin vetoed it.[50]

Belatedly reacting to the crash of many pyramid schemes and small commercial banks, the CBR further helped Sberbank by tightening regulations on the ability of commercial banks to accept deposits from the public. The CBR first declared that the amount of bank deposits from individuals could not exceed a bank's capital. Commenting on this regulation, one Volgograd banker said, "Of course it's ridiculous. These measures can only lead to the population beginning to store money in their stockings."[51] Then, as of January 1, 1995, the CBR began enforcing regulations that allowed banks to attract deposits from the public only if they had: 1) been operating for over one year; 2) published an audited annual report; 3) followed the CBR's regulations; 4) kept a 10 percent reserve fund for deposits; and 5) maintained reserves to cover loan losses.[52] This kept all but the largest commercial banks out of the retail market.

Yet the enduring legacy of this period harmed Sberbank, commercial banks, and the government alike. Many Russians lost trust in banks altogether and invested in hard currency or in goods.[53] According to *Fi-*

---

49. Garegin Tosunian, *Bankovskoe delo i bankovskoe zakonadatel'stvo v Rossii* (Moscow: Akademiia narodnogo khoziaistva pri pravitel'stve RF, 1995), 162.

50. Pavel Medvedev, "Bankovskoe zakonadatel'stvo ne uspevaet za razvitiem bankovskoi sistemy," *Finansovye izvestiia*, February 1, 1996; and Peter Rutland, "Protection for Depositors and Investors," *OMRI Daily Digest*, March 22, 1996.

51. Arkadii Makarov, general director, Volgoprombank, quoted in Ol'ga Kosonozhko, "Volgoprombank: chem bol'she bank, tem men'shche protsenty," *Delovoe povolzh'e* 11 (March 1995): 11.

52. Main Department of the CBR for Riazan' Oblast', "Komu doverit' svoi sberezheniia?" *Priokskaia gazeta*, February 2, 1995, 2.

53. Nor did they deposit their hard currency. According to EBRD estimates, as of 1995 only $10 billion of the $43 billion possessed by Russian citizens and enterprises was held in

nansovye izvestiia, by 1994 only about 8 percent of individuals kept any savings in a bank.[54] As Bank of Finland economist Pekka Sutela notes, this rate is far lower than the 18 percent average in East European states, while other developing countries boast rates even higher.[55] This meant that little household money circulated in the financial system to be invested in the Russian economy. For the commercial banks, this restricted yet another standard, nonstate, potentially lucrative source of finance. For the government (Sberbank's majority owner), Sberbank's failure to capture the "mattress" savings of the population robbed it of significant financial resources that it might have directed towards additional state expenditures.[56] Sberbank's nickname, after all, is the "Ministry of Cash." For Sberbank itself, this institutionalized tie to the state prevented it from diversifying its activities and operating as a for-profit institution. Of course, none of this dented Sberbank's position as the largest bank in Russia, with the widest branch network and the dominant position in the retail banking market. Sberbank persevered because of the legacies bestowed on it by its unique position in the Soviet economic system. Russian households paid the price.

Political Power, Economic Interests

Commercial banks, relatively wealthy yet without reliably profitable inroads into enterprise and retail markets, reinforced their tenuous prosperity by solidifying and redefining their relationships with politicians. As economic decentralization and political democratization became the order of the day, bankers coalesced into an identifiable, influential interest group. Bankers formed numerous representative organizations during this era, including the Association of Russian Banks (ARB), several regional banking groups, and groups uniting the former

---

domestic bank accounts. Peter Rutland, "Russians Hold $43 Billion," *OMRI Economic Digest*, November 17, 1995. A survey of 4,000 Russians in 1995 found that 53 percent preferred not to keep their savings in banks. Richard W. Stevenson, "In New Economy, Russians Cannot Rely on Their Banks," *New York Times*, September 12, 1995, 1.

54. See A. V. Molchanov, *Kommercheskii bank v sovremennoi Rossii: Teoriia i praktika* (Moscow: Finansy i statistika, 1996), 37.

55. Pekka Sutela, "The Role of Banks in Financing Russian Economic Growth," *Post-Soviet Geography and Economics* 39, no. 2 (February 1998): 96–124.

56. The April 1995 revised "Law on the Central Bank of Russia" required the CBR to divest itself of its stakes in Sberbank and Vneshtorgbank, but apparently no one thought about how this would be carried out or whether or not the CBR would be paid for its shares. After a long, public wrangling over its fate—and many commercial banks drooling over the chance to get in on the privatization—in June 1995 the Duma declared that the privatization could not go ahead without "special enabling legislation," which never appeared.

spetsbanks.[57] Foreshadowing an important later trend, public political pronouncements by high-profile bankers occasionally complemented the activities of these organizations. For example, during the rancor surrounding Gaidar's dismissal as prime minister in December 1992, leading Moscow bankers such as Most Bank's Gusinskii, Inkombank's Vinogradov, and Menatep's Khodorkovskii authored the statement "Entrepreneurial Political Initiative—92," which called upon the executive and the parliament to cooperate with one another in forming economic policy.

The Association of Russian Banks, formed in 1991 with 65 members, became the largest national organization uniting commercial bankers. It wisely chose a well-connected president, Sergei Yegorov. Not only had Yegorov held several high-level positions in Gosbank, but he was a CPSU member until 1991 and a top advisor to the Central Committee.[58] As of June 1995, the ARB united 1,058 banks and financial organizations (e.g., auditing firms), representing over 40 percent of all Russian banks and including the great majority of large commercial banks. Although the ARB carried out a multitude of functions, it primarily served as a legislative lobbying organ for commercial banks. According to Yegorov, during the seventeen meetings of the ARB council held between 1991 and 1993, fully 47 percent of the issues addressed dealt directly with "representation and protection of bank interests in bodies of executive and legislative power."[59] It is especially striking to compare the drafting process for the 1990 banking laws, written with only moderate input from commercial bankers, with the lengthy process for writing the revised versions of these laws. The ARB took a leading role in the drafting process, while numerous commercial banks, other banking associations, and the Financial Services Volunteer Corps (FSVC) provided substantial commentary. Moreover, commercial bankers who also held seats in the State Duma sat on all of the parliamentary committees responsible for the legislation.[60]

From 1992 through 1995, the ARB lobbied strongly for changes to the payments system, for providing state preferences for banks that invested in the economy, and for restructuring the 1990 Law on Banks and Bank-

57. Center for Analytical Information on the Political Situation of Russia, *Doklad #3: Obshchenatsional'nye obshchestvennye ob'edineniia predprinimatelei v sfere obrashcheniia (finansovyi i torgovo-posrednicheskii kapital)*, Moscow, June 1994.

58. Anvar Amirov, *Kto est' kto v bankovskoi sisteme Rossii* (Moscow: Panorama, 1996), 31–32.

59. Sergei Yegorov, "Otchetnyi doklad o rabote soveta ARB za 1991–1993 gg.," *Biznes i Banki* 21, no. 187 (May 1994): 5.

60. Viktor Ivanov and Mikhail Loginov, "Al'ians vlastei s bankami sokhranilsia," *Kommersant-Daily*, January 25, 1995; and Duma Deputy Pavel Medvedev, interview with author, Moscow, June 19, 1995.

ing Activity. More importantly, it fought particularly hard against the CBR. Not only did the ARB press (usually unsuccessfully) to lower the Central Bank's interest rates and its minimum reserve and capital requirements, it attempted to bleed power from the CBR by lobbying for the creation of a National Banking Council, for a separate governmental body to regulate banks, and for official recognition as the lead organization representing banking interests in Russia. The ARB also actively campaigned against the confirmation of Tat'iana Paramonova as CBR director in 1995 because of, among other things, the higher reserve requirements that she placed on commercial banks in early 1995 as the acting director. ARB pressure proved instrumental in the Duma's decision to reject her candidacy—despite strong support from Boris Yeltsin.

Regional banks and the former spetsbanks also founded several banking associations to defend their joint interests in relations with the government and the Moscow commercial banks. By mid-1995, eighteen banking associations had appeared in regions as varied as Bashkortostan, Murmansk, and Sakha. Associations created by the former spetsbanks included *Rus'*, an association of former Zhilsotsbanks; the *Association of Sberbanks*, for Sberbanks of the CIS; and *Rossiia*, an association of Promstroibanks. Thirty-four Promstroibank branches started *Rossiia* in late 1990 after the spetsbanks split up, and Promstroibank Russia director Yakov Dubnetskii led the group. By 1995 it had over 100 member banks. According to G.I. Denisov, the association's vice-president, one of its main goals was "to actively defend the legal interests of banks in all structures of state power . . . We try to actively take part in the working up of legal projects . . . [and] to introduce propositions on clarifying the laws . . .". *Rossiia* used its good connections with the government to get the government to help banks issue long-term credit profitably (through concessions, "cartel" agreements among enterprises and bankers mediated by the CBR, and so forth).[61] It also succeeded in getting tax breaks for association members.

Equally as important, beginning with the December 1993 Duma elections, bankers actively financed national political campaigns.[62] Bankers

61. Interview with G. I. Denisov, vice-president of the Association of Joint-Stock Commercial Industrial-Construction Banks "Rossiia," in *Bankovskii zhurnal* 1 (1995): 30–32.

62. ARB, "Obshcherossiiskie ekonomicheskie elity: skhematicheskii portret," *Informatsionnyi biulleten'* 10 (1995); Victor Yasmann, "Bankrolling Russia's Political Parties," *Jamestown Monitor* 1, no. 25, part 3, December 1, 1995; Ivan Rodin, "The LDPR Has So Far Received the Most Money," *Nezavisimaia gazeta*, December 5, 1995, 2; Leonid Bershidsky, "The Murky World of Campaign Cash," *Moscow Times*, September 24, 1995, 15; Elisabeth Rubinfien, "Russia's Businessmen Learn How to Use Political Financing to Wield Influence," *Wall Street Journal*, December 6, 1993, A11; Sander Thoenes, "Behind the Parties, Banks Loom Large," *Moscow Times*, December 3, 1993, 1; and "Russian Tycoons: Entrepreneurs Piling Up the Wealth," *Moscow Tribune*, May 30, 1995, 6.

felt that the old Supreme Soviet had not been amenable enough to their influence, and wanted to ensure their representation in the new legislative body. Many politicians quickly came to depend upon this support. With the exception of the Communist Party, Russian political parties suffered from youth, disorganization, and low levels of name recognition. In a country the size of Russia, it took a great deal of money to finance the kind of campaign necessary to familiarize voters with a party's political message and leading candidates. Moreover, as we have seen, few other economic interest groups had the financial clout with which to provide this support. This combination of circumstances gave the wealthiest bankers a decided advantage in dealing with Russia's new representative political institutions.

In the State Duma elections (the first nationwide, post-Soviet Russian elections), bankers supported a wide variety of parties and candidates. As the ARB itself wrote, "Banks took an active part in financing election campaigns to the Federal Assembly in December 1993. . . . They supported blocs and candidates of absolutely all political stripes, and several banks supported several blocs at the same time."[63] Russian electoral law made this a natural strategy, as half of the deputies were elected through party list voting (where a voter chooses a party rather than a particular candidate), and half through single-member districts. The bulk of the bankers' support went to "reformist" parties such as Russia's Choice (Yegor Gaidar's party, at the time identified with Yeltsin), Grigorii Yavlinskii's Yabloko Party, and the Party of Russian Unity and Accord. Oleg Boiko (president of Olbi and of Natsional'nyi Kredit bank) supported Russia's Choice and served as the party's executive director. Al'fa Bank also helped to fund Russia's Choice, and its president Petr Aven appeared at number 16 on the party list. Most Bank claimed to support Yabloko, Russia's Choice, and a third unnamed "democratic" party. The majority of its funds went to Yabloko, as Most Bank's director Vladimir Gusinskii had close personal ties with Yavlinskii. Menatep Bank also supported Yabloko in 1993. Moreover, according to Yavlinskii's finance director, both Most and Menatep had provided Yabloko with copying machines, fax machines, and office supplies. The ARB itself backed the Party of Russian Unity and Accord, as well as other undisclosed parties. The ARB's main strategy, though, was to support banker-candidates regardless of party. In one case it went even further—the former vice-president of Inkombank, Aleksandr Turbanov, revealed that the ARB "found" him a spot on the party list for the Party of Russian Unity and Accord.[64] Turbanov served in

63. ARB, "Obshcherossiiskie ekonomicheskie elity," 38.
64. Aleksandr Turbanov, Duma deputy and member of the Committee on the Budget, Taxes, Banking, and Finance, interview with author, June 29, 1995, Moscow.

the Duma from 1993–95, and afterwards became the deputy director of the Central Bank of Russia.

While no one knows the exact amounts spent on the 1993 elections, it is widely acknowledged that parties spent far more than they officially reported.[65] Although the 1993 election laws limited corporate donations to 150 million rubles for political blocs and 1.5 million for candidates, these regulations proved easy to avoid. A single bank, for example, could set up any number of shell companies that could each contribute to the cause.

Did this spending pay off for the bankers? In the broadest sense, probably not. No straightforward relationship between spending and votes emerged. Russia's Choice ended up with 15.6 percent of the total seats in the Duma, but Vladimir Zhirinovskii's Liberal-Democratic Party of Russia (LDPR) beat it out in the party list voting, earning 22.9 percent of the vote (and 14.2 percent of the seats) to Gaidar's 15.5 percent. Meanwhile, the Communists and the Agrarians gained 10.7 percent and 7.3 percent of the Duma's seats, respectively, while spending little. Yabloko garnered only 5.1 percent of the seats, while the Party of Russian Unity and Accord lagged still further behind with 4.0 percent.[66] Yet ARB president Yegorov correctly viewed the results in a more positive light. He observed that "In the new parliament the interests of banks are represented more competently than in the former Supreme Soviet . . . Eight former bankers are on the Committee on the Budget, Taxes, Banks, and Finances."[67] In short, bankers had gained substantial representation on the committee that most affected their interests. Moreover, they had established themselves as the primary source of campaign financing for business-minded parties and politicians.

This accumulation of political power resulted in several well-publicized showdowns and deals involving prominent bankers. The animosity between Yeltsin and Moscow mayor Yurii Luzhkov underlay many of the battles in the capital city. For example, the long-standing political alliance between Vladimir Gusinskii and Luzhkov so frightened Yeltsin and his entourage that on December 2, 1994, masked gunmen from Yeltsin's personal security service raided Most Bank's headquarters (located in the Mayor's building), roughed up some of the staff, and prompted Gusinskii

65. In total, the parties officially claimed to have spent 4.62 million rubles on the election, with Russia's Choice on top at 1.92 million rubles, followed by the Party of Russian Unity and Accord at 830 thousand rubles. For a breakdown of official Central Electoral Commission numbers and an analysis of lobbying efforts in the 1993 elections, see Andrei Neshchadin et al., "Political Lobbies In Russia: Copying the Worst or a Change for the Better?" *Business in Russia*, June 1995, 46–56.

66. Stephen White, Richard Rose, and Ian McAllister, *How Russia Votes* (Chatham, England: Chatham House, 1997), 123.

67. Yegorov, *Otchetnyi doklad*, 4.

to flee the country for a few months. Aleksandr Korzhakov, the head of Yeltsin's security service, referred to these efforts against Gusinskii as "Gus'" hunting (in English, "goose hunting").[68] According to the ARB, this had been only the most recent attempt to intimidate a certain group of Moscow banks, and the association sent an open letter to Yeltsin demanding that he guarantee the legal protection of these banks.[69] In another example, Oleg Boiko of Natsional'nyi Kredit claimed that he and other prominent bankers played a key role in the formation of the pro-Yeltsin Duma bloc *Stabil'nost'* (Stability) in early 1995. According to rumors that circulated widely around Moscow, financiers invited a number of unaffiliated Duma deputies to a dacha for the weekend and offered them monetary incentives to create this new bloc.

But more importantly, how did bankers use the political leverage they had gained in parliament, with the executive, and with the political allies who had helped found and support their banks? Overwhelmingly, bankers wielded their power as an interest group and as political patrons to attempt to protect themselves from competition and to strengthen their status as agent banks. In other words, instead of pressing for the creation of a transparent market environment and greater freedom to conduct their activities, banks asked the state to provide them preferential conditions and closer state ties. In this way, they expanded their money-making abilities without having to further engage enterprises or households. Three developments demonstrate this perverse dynamic: the restrictions on foreign banks, the growth in "authorized" banks, and the character of the GKO market.

The Anti-Foreigner Campaign

The big Russian banks successfully pushed through legislation limiting the number and scope of foreign banks in Russia while they built up their own financial empires and client bases. The campaign against foreign banks began in 1992, even though few foreign banks had then expressed interest in entering the Russian market. Credit Lyonnais, the first foreign bank licensed in Russia, gained permission to open a branch in 1991 but only began operations in late 1993. Despite the seemingly small threat, Russian bankers made foreign banks a key political issue. Importantly, politically influential Moscow banks most strongly opposed foreign

68. Interfax, "Intsident u zdaniia merii," *Delovoi mir*, December 6, 1994; *Kommersant-Daily*, "Ataka na predmostnye ukrepleniia," December 6, 1994.
69. Mikhail Koslov, "Sobytiia bankovskoi zhizni," *Denezhnyi rynok*, December 1994, 8; and Petr Brangov, "Vladimir Gusinskii zhdet, shto shto-to sluchitsia," *Kommersant-Daily*, December 7, 1994.

competition. According to a poll of bankers in 32 regions, 55 percent opposed allowing foreign banks to operate under the same conditions as domestic ones in Russia, while only 35 percent were in favor and 10 percent were neutral.[70]

Accordingly, in 1992 the ARB prepared draft legislation to restrict the establishment of foreign bank branches. CBR director Gerashchenko, belying his public image as an anti-Western reactionary, opposed the ARB on this issue and worked consistently to bring foreign banks into the country. Gerashchenko, for example, quashed a draft parliamentary bill in October 1992 that would have revoked the license of Credit Lyonnais and strongly limited foreign bank access to Russian customers.[71] While the Supreme Soviet existed, the banks and the CBR remained in a legislative stalemate, as foreign banks remained restricted in some respects but not prohibited outright.

The downfall of the Supreme Soviet and the bankers' strong influence in the December 1993 Duma elections turned the tide against the CBR. This began a pattern of pre-election capitulation by Yeltsin and his allies to the Moscow bankers. That November, Yegor Gaidar, who had previously favored allowing foreign banks access to Russian markets, met with a group of influential bankers and then announced that the bankers had persuaded him of the need to restrict foreign banks. According to Sergei Zverev of Most Bank, "Probably Gaidar's comments are the result of the fact that there is an election underway."[72] Just days later, on November 17, Yeltsin issued a decree freezing the entry of new foreign banks until January 1996 and prohibiting existing foreign banks from working with Russian customers (unless they had already done so, which grandfathered Credit Lyonnais and BNP-Dresdner Bank). This decree restricted foreign banks far more than envisioned in previous draft legislation under consideration in the Supreme Soviet, and took many by surprise. As Gerashchenko observed bluntly, "This decree is very weird."[73] The government fully repealed the decree only in April 1995, and retained many other restrictions on foreign bank activities. Such decisions provided Russian banks with the "breathing space" they so wanted, yet sharply con-

70. "Are Foreign Banks Welcome to the Russian Market?" *Russian Economic Barometer* 2 no. 1 (Winter 1993): 26–28.

71. Yelena Makovskaia, "Foreign Banks in Russia: I Would Choose Credit Lyonnais Because Lenin Banked There," *Kommersant* 26 (July 5, 1993): 14, trans. *FBIS Central Eurasia*, August 9, 1993, 64.

72. Quoted in Elisabeth Rubinfien, "Russia's Businessmen Learn How to Use Political Financing," A11.

73. Quoted in Reuters, "Gerashchenko: Economy Is a 'Whorehouse'," November 24, 1993. Gerashchenko went on to say that Yeltsin imposed the decree because of pressure from banks during the electoral campaign.

trasted with the state's avowedly liberal economic policies in other spheres.

Authorized Banks

The designation of "authorized" (*upolnomochennye*) banks to handle the finances of the federal, regional, and local governments represented an egregious post-Soviet display of political favoritism. Authorized banks appeared in late 1992 and 1993, when commercial bankers persuaded the central government to allow banks other than Sberbank, Promstroibank, and Agroprombank to manage its funds. In the absence of reliable enterprise clients, the state held more potential as a customer for commercial banks. Authorization naturally benefited the largest and best-connected banks, and banks vied especially hard to capture the lucrative business of federal government agencies and foreign trade organizations. When a bank acquired the accounts of a major government organization such as the customs agency, it instantly shot up to the top level of bank rating lists. These empowered banks tended to be first-wave zero banks, former spetsbanks, or banks that were "born authorized . . . created under the aegis of governmental structures" such as ONEKSIMbank.[74]

Indeed, many banks were founded precisely in order to capture government revenue. ONEKSIMbank (the United Export-Import Bank) and MFK Bank (the International Financial Company) exemplified the phenomenon of "instant" zero banks created after 1992. Vladimir Potanin, founder of ONEKSIMbank, worked in the USSR Ministry of Foreign Trade for seven years before striking out on his own. He founded the Interros foreign trading company in March 1990, making money through his ministry connections. In February 1992, Potanin and Mikhail Prokhorov of the International Bank for Economic Cooperation (IBEC, a key foreign trade bank for the Eastern bloc) created MFK Bank in cooperation with Sberbank, Vneshekonombank, Interros, and IBEC. They not only used IBEC assets as deposits and charter capital, but acquired many of IBEC's powerful foreign trade clients.[75] Potanin founded ONEKSIMbank itself in 1993 with the support of these same foreign trading associations, and MFK became the *de facto* junior partner of ONEKSIMbank. By January 1996, ONEKSIMbank had become the fourth and MFK the

74. Ol'ga Kryshtanovskaia, RAN Sociological Institute, "Banki, oblechennye doveriem vlastei," *Izvestiia*, February 8, 1995.

75. Jonas Bernstein, "Nickel for your thoughts?" *Russia Review*, February 26, 1996, 22–24. It is also likely that a great deal of Communist Party and KGB money was "liberated" through the International Bank for Economic Cooperation before 1992, which would explain where the bank got the $300–400 million in start-up capital that it transferred to the International Financial Company.

eighth largest Russian banks by assets (see Table 4.1). ONEKSIMbank set up its main office in the old IBEC building, and the biggest export enterprises in Russia—including key representatives of the oil, diamond, metals, and weapons industries—became its shareholders and clients. From the beginning, ONEKSIMbank served as an official agent of the Russian government for servicing Russia's foreign trade operations. Authorized banks such as ONEKSIMbank and MFK relied on government bureaucracies for their revenues, but politicians became equally as dependent on the banks for support.

Local government resources were also highly sought after, as the case of Moscow demonstrates.[76] In one of the first cracks in the spetsbank domination of budget funds, the Moscow city government authorized Most Bank and Menatep Bank to manage a portion of its budget in February 1993. The two banks split 7.5 billion rubles earmarked for local enterprises.[77] By July 1994, the Moscow city government had designated fourteen authorized banks. Of the group, Most, Menatep, and Tekhnobank held by far the largest number of accounts, with Most Bank controlling the primary current account of the city's Finance Department. In exchange for placing city budget funds in these banks, giving city guarantees for the banks' loans, and "creating favorable conditions for the functioning of these banks and their branches on Moscow territory," the City of Moscow charged the banks with investing its money, funding municipal projects, developing a municipal bond market, carrying out the basic financial needs of municipal agencies, acting as sponsors and donors for the "social and cultural acts of the city administration," and in general serving as financial advisors to the government. In January 1994, these authorized banks formally created a six-member council in order to coordinate their activities and attempt to protect their status.

Authorized banks quickly became the wealthiest in Russia.[78] By 1995 the biggest banks held the accounts of the federal tax authorities, customs authorities, and Finance Ministry, among others. The Finance Ministry served as an especially profitable "client," because it would take out loans from its authorized banks (loans guaranteed by the government) to cover temporary budgetary shortfalls, and then pay the loans back with interest. The state Audit Chamber estimated that banks earned about $1.32 billion

76. See Mezhbankovskii Finansovyi Dom, *Upolnomochennye banki pravitel'stva Moskvy: Kontseptsiia i tekhnologii raboty* (Moscow: Delo Ltd., 1994).

77. Irina Demchenko, "Moscow Government Authorizes Commercial Banks to Distribute State Credits," *Izvestiia*, February 9, 1993, 4, trans. *Current Digest of the Post-Soviet Press* 45, no. 6 (1993): 23.

78. See Association of Russian Banks, "50 Vedushchikh predprinimatelei v Rossii," *Informatsionii biulleten'* 7 (1995): 37.

in this way in 1995–96.[79] Authorized banks controlled vast resources and made good profits without risk or long-term investment, all because of their connections to the state.

The GKO Windfall

When commercial banks entered the treasury bill market, they successfully lobbied to restrict foreign entry in the market's early stages of development, and persuaded the state to designate authorized banks as primary dealers of GKOs. The government, looking for cash to finance its budget deficit after it had sworn off direct CBR financing, introduced GKOs in March 1993 and soon made them extremely attractive to the commercial banks. GKOs yielded consistently high annual returns (an average of 136.8 percent in 1994) and the state made GKO profits tax-free. The Ministry of Finance chose twenty-six favored banks as primary GKO distributors and kept foreigners out of the first treasury bill auctions. Afterwards, the state limited the percentage of GKOs offered to foreigners and the yields that foreigners could earn, protecting the high yields for domestic buyers. Importantly, though, the government did not introduce GKOs in order to "buy off" the commercial bankers and to persuade them not to lobby for continued monetary and credit emissions, as Daniel Treisman has argued.[80] Rather, the IMF pressured Russia to develop a treasury bill instrument for noninflationary financing of the budget deficit, the government eagerly embraced a way in which to raise money that did not depend on the dysfunctional tax system, and the CBR actively sought the introduction of GKOs both as the first necessary step in devel-

79. According to the auditor, ONEKSIMbank, Menatep, MFK, Moscow National Bank, Vozrozhdenie, and Sberbank were the leading players. Mark Whitehouse, "Auditor Claims State Lined Banks' Pockets," *Moscow Times*, June 6, 1997.

80. Daniel Treisman, "Fighting Inflation in a Transitional Regime: Russia's Anomalous Stabilization," *World Politics* 50 (January 1998), 235–65. Treisman argued that the persistent drop in inflation after January 1995 occurred because the government's introduction of GKOs persuaded politically powerful bankers that conditions of low inflation were preferable to those of high inflation. Inflation had yielded significant profits for the bankers in 1992, as we have seen. However, by late 1993 leading Moscow bankers had easy access to the GKO market, found distributing centralized credits unprofitable, and were operating with positive real interest rates, making an inflationary environment less attractive. If Treisman's theory were correct, inflation would have continued the downward spiral it began in mid-1993 rather than spiking from July 1994 through January 1995. Instead, inflation receded from January 1995 through 1998 because by that time the government could reliably finance its persistent budget deficit through noninflationary means such as the GKO market (soon opened to foreign participation), foreign loans, and revenue from the loans-for-shares program. Moreover, it could then hold the exchange rate steady by means of the ruble corridor introduced in July 1995. Unfortunately, lagging tax collection and high GKO yields made this strategy successful only temporarily.

oping its open market operations and as a means by which to reduce the pressure to finance the budget deficit using CBR funds.

Banks, as the only Russian commercial entities with access to large amounts of investable cash, were the natural customers for this new market. Once the CBR's real interest rates became consistently positive and the CBR began holding banks (rather than enterprises) responsible for overdue directed credits in 1993, banks could no longer exploit these credits for survival. Moreover, by mid-1993 inflation had begun to slow and the early signs of monetary stabilization ate into bank profits. As a result, GKOs became an increasingly lucrative and attractive source of revenue for the commercial banks. Banks with access to the market rationally channeled available resources in this direction. In fact, the banks funneled "unavailable" resources earmarked for other uses into the market as well: banks were often accused of delaying payments transfers to play the market, or of putting money they held as "authorized" banks towards GKO purchases (in effect, lending the government its own money). Vneshekonombank director Anatolii Nosko, for example, was dismissed in February 1996 for "speculating in Russian treasury bills with funds earmarked for repaying foreign debts."[81] According to the State Tax Service, banks invested an average of 60 percent of their credit resources in GKOs.[82] Therefore, the regular primary government sales of GKOs pulled in a great deal of money from the banking system, and extensive secondary GKO markets developed in the major cities. By mid-1995, total trading on the secondary market had reached the equivalent of $136 million per day.[83] In the first six months of 1995, the government issued enough treasury bills to cover 46 percent of the budget deficit, and the total outstanding GKO debt reached 35.7 trillion rubles ($7.9 billion).[84] In total, the government financed 70 percent of its 1995 deficit through GKOs.

The government freely admitted, however, that it used revenues from the sale of current GKOs to pay off GKOs coming due from earlier releases. CBR official Andrei Kozlov, asked in 1995 if treasury bills were just a government pyramid scheme, did not lay anyone's worries to rest when he responded that GKOs were "not a pyramid, but a column."[85] The government came to depend upon falling yields and increasing sales volumes

81. Natalia Gurushina, "Head of Vneshekonombank Dismissed," *OMRI Daily Digest*, February 9, 1996.

82. Artyom Shadrin, "From Inflation to Investment Banking," *Business In Russia* 76 (April 1997): 55.

83. Thomas Sigel, "Russian Treasury Bills: An Overview," *OMRI Economic Digest*, October 1995.

84. Natalia Gurushina and Thomas Sigel, "Circulation of Treasury Bills Fuels Inflation," *OMRI Economic Digest*, November 17, 1995.

85. Andrei Kozlov, remarks, Russian-American Bankers' Forum, July 30, 1995.

to sustain the ever-expanding GKO market, inasmuch as it continued to run a vast budget deficit and was unable to collect enough revenue through the tax system. Therefore, the GKO market, while temporarily lucrative for the banks, was little more than a shell game as long as government tax revenue and GDP continued to stagnate. Ultimately, this made the burgeoning GKO market a ticking time bomb for the government, the Central Bank of Russia, and the commercial banks alike.

In sum, bankers' exertion of their political power against foreign banks, in favor of "authorized" banks, and to gain preferential access to the GKO market represented bank exploitation of the state, as the bankers used their influence to heighten their status as agent banks. Furthermore, the executive branch was far more complicit than the parliament in this process. Despite the Yeltsin government's reformist reputation, the executive regularly went out of its way to accommodate favored banks in exchange for political support. Yeltsin's penchant for ruling by decree made this kind of policy particularly easy to carry out. Finally, authorization and GKO access began to divide the banks into haves and have-nots, with connected Moscow banks benefiting most from these developments. While enterprises spun off into the nonmonetary economy with the state unable to stop them, well-connected banks used their predominant position in the cash economy to extract the state's own cash resources. Accordingly, power itself continued to bleed away from the state.

Law and Lawlessness

The Russian state's impotence began to be reflected in an increasingly frightening environment of lawlessness. The existing legal and regulatory regime itself was part of the problem, especially in the early 1990s. Not surprisingly, because the USSR's original banking laws and regulations referred to a state-controlled monobank system, legal reformers had difficulty adjusting them to suit the changing banking sector. As Duma member Pavel Medvedev put it, "The Central Bank has run into unsolved problems—as if it entered into conditions of a regulatory vacuum."[86] Nature abhors a vacuum, and in the Soviet tradition all possible bodies rushed in to try to regulate commercial banking. Since 1988, Russian governing bodies have subjected commercial banks to: 1) "laws" and "resolutions" of the USSR Supreme Soviet; 2) "laws" and "resolutions" of the two Russian parliaments; 3) "decrees" of the president; 4) "letters," "telegrams," and "instructions" of Gosbank and the CBR (simultaneously

86. Pavel Medvedev, "Bankovskie zakonoproekti: trudnie puti prodvizheniia," *Biznes i banki*, May 1994: 1.

during 1990–91); and 5) instructions from the Ministry of Finance, the Tax Inspectorate, and the Securities Commission. As Riazan' banker Boris Khitrov stated, "about 80 percent of the decrees (*ukazy*) of the president are simply not fulfilled. To fulfill all of the norms that exist today is practically impossible."[87] Several bankers whom I interviewed in early 1995 had not read or even heard of the new draft laws on the central bank and on commercial banking. In addition, as bankers at the May 1995 ARB conference loudly complained, local governments often passed laws contradicting national laws and CBR instructions.

Yet many laws did get passed and rationalized, capped by the new Civil Code in 1995 and the revised laws on central and commercial banking in 1995 and early 1996. Western nongovernmental organizations like the Financial Services Volunteer Corps commented on the draft banking laws, and the IMF and World Bank often made loans conditional on the adoption of Western-style economic legislation. The introduction of this legal framework revealed a second, more insidious problem: the state's inability to effectively enforce existing laws. As Kathryn Hendley points out, "institutional changes have not prompted Russian economic actors to shift from a reliance on networks of personal relationships to a reliance on law."[88] The top-down legal reforms, combined with the decentralization engendered by liberalization and privatization, did not appreciably change Russian bankers' attitudes towards the rule of law. In short, there was little demand for these laws from below. Instead, the banks used the laws for their own purposes when it seemed to benefit them immediately (for example, by filing harassing lawsuits against each other), and otherwise put their efforts towards subverting and bypassing them.

The combination of the confused and inefficient legal system, the persistent disregard for the rule of law fostered in Soviet times, and the short-term outlook of the bankers often led them to do whatever they wanted to do, whether or not the law forbade it. As Menatep's Mikhail Khodorkovskii observed, "I have never broken the law in a direct sense. But if a law gets in my way—it's not important if it's good or bad, I seek out a crack in it, I think of a way to get around it. Loopholes can be found in any law, and I use them without thinking about it for a second."[89] In *Comrade Criminal,* Stephen Handelman quotes another young banker as say-

87. Boris Khitrov, interview with author. For other examples from the regions, see A. Grishin, "Reshitsia li problema neplatezhei, esli etim po-prezhnemu budet zanimat'sia tol'ko Tsentrobank," *YeZh-Rus'* 15 (December 22–28, 1994): 1; and Valerii Surganov, "Tol'ko s razresheniia Goskomimushchestva," *Delovoe povolzh'e* 17 (July 1993): 5.

88. Kathryn Hendley, "Legal Development in Post-Soviet Russia," *Post-Soviet Affairs* 13, no. 3 (1997): 229.

89. Mikhail Khodorkovskii, in *Biznesmeny Rossii: 40 istorii uspekha* (Moscow: OKO, 1994): 172.

ing: "Older people have an ethics problem. By that I mean they *have* ethics. To survive I can break a law if I need to, and the risks aren't too large."[90] An official in the licensing department of the Riazan' CBR confirmed this attitude. "If we tell a commercial bank to do something, they say to us, 'Show me where that is written' and I cannot do it. Now they are more clever than before. They see all of the holes in the laws and they use them!"[91] In many cases, this situation forced politicians to justify bank activities in law *ex post facto* or change certain laws forbidding bank activities that had become widespread. Similarly, bankers felt that they could not rely on the law or the courts to protect their rights. For example, the unpopular bankers found little support from the police or the judicial system in cracking down on recalcitrant clients. In fact, banks sometimes "need[ed] to turn to organized criminal groups for help in retrieving loaned money," because it was not always possible to get it back in a "civilized way."[92] Therefore, although the bankers actively lobbied to affect legislative outcomes (especially on easily enforced standards regarding foreign banks, licensing requirements, and so forth), the post-Soviet banking system did not significantly change its day-to-day practices in response to legal reforms from above.

This boded ill for the inculcation of democratic norms based on the rule of law, as crime and corruption increasingly posed a serious threat to the healthy development of both the Russian banking system and the Russian state.[93] As one banker candidly admitted to me in 1994:

> [Organized crime] is one of the most important problems for us. . . . Their strength is growing very rapidly because they are penetrating into administrative and government bodies. They are succeeding in penetrating into the management of the enterprises that are our customers. . . . Now they are growing wiser, more experienced . . . and they need banking institutions to perform their own financial operations. . . . They are trying to impose controls on all of us.

Soviet-era legacies combined with the freewheeling, anything-goes atmosphere after 1987 allowed this proliferation of criminal activity. The in-

---

90. Stephen Handelman, *Comrade Criminal: Russia's New Mafiya* (New Haven: Yale University Press, 1995), 345.

91. Oleg Matveev, lead economist, Department of Licensing, CBR Riazan', interview with author, September 2, 1994, Riazan'.

92. CBR Volgograd press release, "Shto govorili na soveshchanii," *Delovoe povolzh'e* 28 (July 1994): 6.

93. For an excellent overview of early criminal penetration into the Russian banking sector, see Garegin Tosunian, ed., *Bankovskii biznes v Rossii: Kriminologicheskie i ugolovno-pravovye problemy* (Moscow: Delo Ltd., 1994).

terpenetration of crime, finance, and politics had its roots in Soviet times when bribes and other types of lawbreaking "greased the wheels" of the system. The command economy bred illegality and corruption, especially during the 1970s and 1980s. Numerous groups that operated on the Soviet black market were well-organized, with long-standing networks ready to take advantage of the changing environment. Soviet citizens and leaders alike had little respect for the law, and this attitude persisted in the "new" Russia. Moreover, institutional legacies left Russians with little ability to cope with financial crimes. The Soviet-era legal system made it difficult to identify and prosecute white-collar capitalist criminal activities. At the same time, opportunists could take advantage of the primitive Russian payments system, the lax auditing and accounting standards, and the dual monetary circuit to, in effect, create money out of thin air. The de-monetization of the Russian economy contributed to this dynamic, as did the punitive but irregularly enforced taxation system.

As the economy became more decentralized, the problems of these legacies became evident. Crime became endemic: according to the Interior Ministry, 7,600 "economic crimes" occurred in the banking sector in 1994, most of which were incidences of theft or embezzlement.[94] However, it is important to realize that Russians used the words "mafia" and "organized crime" quite loosely. The Interior Ministry called groups of more than two people committing crimes "organized." Statistics on organized crime activity, therefore, were highly unreliable. Moreover, the public believed that wealthy businesspeople must have come by their money unethically. Although this was often true, it fed into the perception that the "mafia" controlled every aspect of the Russian economy.

In fact, the bankers' relationship to crime and corruption was one of both participation and victimization. The banks could not be described as innocent victims of the criminal world. They continually broke the law by falsifying their books, underpaying their taxes, and using enforcers to help them collect loans, to give only a few examples. Moreover, bankers often facilitated criminal transactions such as money laundering, turning Russia into a dollar sinkhole.[95] For example, about $20 billion in cash was shipped to Russia in 1994, accounting for 10 percent of the U.S. cash held overseas at the time.[96] Russian banks established numerous offshore

94. F. I. Shamkhalov, "Ekonomicheskaia prestypnost' v Rossii: Dinamika, tendentsii, i faktory rosta," in *Biznes i banki v sovremennoi Rossii*, ed. Arkhipov, 123–24.

95. Yevgenii Vasil'chuk, "Rossii pora izbavliat'sia ot reputatsii mezhdunarodnogo tsentra griaznykh deneg," *Finansovye izvestiia*, June 6, 1995, 3.

96. Knut Royce, "Dollars Pouring into Russian Stew," *Long Island Newsday*, March 24, 1995. The article also cites Jack Blum, a Washington lawyer who has investigated money laundering for the U.S. Senate, who stated that "Russia has become possibly the best single place to launder the proceeds of a crime. What you do is ship the cash to Russia, use the cash

branches (particularly in Cyprus and the Caribbean) that simplified money laundering.[97] Russia soon acquired the dubious reputation as one of the easiest places in the world to launder currency, a reputation further enhanced by the Bank of New York scandal in 1999 that led to U.S. congressional hearings into alleged Russian money laundering through U.S. financial institutions.

Russian banks facilitated much garden-variety capital flight as well. In fact, according to published balance-of-payments information, impoverished Russia became a net exporter of capital as early as 1994.[98] While estimates vary widely, the most reliable statistics demonstrate that Russia lost at least $100 billion in capital flight during the 1990s, an amount far exceeding the $22.4 billion the IMF loaned to Russia during this same period and about two-thirds the amount of Russia's total external debt (see Table 1.2). Russians most commonly used false import contracts to expatriate this capital. In this scheme, a bank or enterprise makes an import contract, buys hard currency to pay for the imports under the aegis of that contract, and pays the hard currency to the foreign company. The foreign company, though, never sends the import goods to Russia. More simply, a Russian organization might agree to pay an artificially inflated price for the imported goods. The foreign seller then transfers the extra money to a foreign bank account held (often indirectly) by the Russian organization. In another popular method, a Russian enterprise or bank contracts to export goods abroad at an agreed world price. Upon receipt, the foreign customer complains about the quality of the goods, so the Russian partner "lowers" the price. The full value of the goods remain abroad, and the Russian and foreign counterparts split the expatriated proceeds from their sale. These "foreign" companies, of course, were often Russian-controlled. Numerous Russian intermediary organizations also arose that would facilitate this process for a price. The rush to avoid Russian regulation and taxes even spawned a journal for the would-be rich named *Offshorny*.

Yet the bankers were victims of crime as well as willing participants. At first, organized criminal groups primarily demanded protection money from banks or refused to repay their loans.[99] According to some estimates,

---

to buy a real commodity like oil or aluminum or whatever . . . then you sell the commodity for a price in the European market, and all of a sudden your money is all legitimate."

97. See Douglas Farah, "Russian Crime Finds Home in Caribbean: Colombian Drug Ties Suspected As Secretive Banks Proliferate," *Washington Post*, October 7, 1996, A15; Pamela Constable, "From Russia with Chutzpah," *Washington Post*, August 18, 1996, F1; and Chris Hedges, "Cyprus Shores Wash Dirty Money," *New York Times*, June 15, 1995, A10.

98. See G. K. Beliaeva, ed., *Ekonomicheskaia bezopastnost': Finansy, banki* (Moscow: Institut Ekonomiki RAN, 1996).

99. Aleksandr Zhilin, "The Financial Crime of the Century," *Prism*, Jamestown Foundation 1, no. 25, part 2, December 1, 1995.

criminals extorted money from 70–80 percent of privatized enterprises and commercial banks.[100] Rapidly, the demands of the criminals grew and became more sophisticated. They sought information on the amount of money held in enterprise accounts or perpetuated various scams on banks—including the infamous "Chechen affair"-style ripoffs (which Tosunian of Tekhnobank estimates to have cost the banking system as a whole a minimum of 3.5 trillion rubles).[101] Gaining loans under false pretenses proved popular as well. In June 1993, for example, a criminal group used three shell companies to get 1.5 billion rubles-worth of loans from eight leading banks (including Kredo Bank and Finist Bank) on the strength of forged import contracts. The group immediately converted part of the money into hard currency and sent it to Mexico.[102]

Organized criminals used a number of methods to encourage banks to cooperate with them. The simplest—bribing bank officials—was probably the most widespread. More ambitious groups managed to infiltrate banks, getting their own people hired (known as "rats") and then using them to embezzle money and find the bank's weaknesses.[103] Most dramatically, though, criminals carried out an ongoing terrorism campaign against bankers. The campaign reached its peak in 1993, when criminal groups carried out 23 armed attacks on bankers and their families.[104] Many Russian banks closed on December 7, 1993, to protest the lack of police protection for endangered bankers after the murder of Rossel'khozbank (Agroprombank) director Nikolai Likhachev.[105] The carnage continued in the following years, but the murders became more selective. Sixteen bankers were killed in 1994, while in July 1995 the high-profile president of Yugorskii Bank, Oleg Kantor, was fatally stabbed in the neck at his dacha. Two months earlier, Kantor's deputy, Vadim Yafiasov, had been gunned down in his BMW. As ARB spokesman Aleksandr Zagriadskii observed, "[Kantor's] was not an unmotivated murder. It is linked to big money. . . . The economic situation is such that the criminal world keeps trying to win control of the banking sphere."[106] In August 1995, Ivan Kive-

100. *Izvestiia*, "The Russian Mafia Assembles Dossiers on Important Officials and Politicians," January 26, 1994, 1–2, trans. *Current Digest of the Post-Soviet Press* 46, no. 4 (1994): 14–15.

101. Tosunian, ed., *Bankovskii biznes v Rossii*, 39. For more on the Chechen affair and similar operations, see chapter 3.

102. Ibid., 36.

103. Georgii Shvyrkov and Boris Klin, "Agent mafii," *Kommersant* 20 (May 30, 1995): 44–48.

104. Garegin Tosunian, ed., *Bankovskii biznes v Rossii*, 32; and F. I. Shamkhalov, "Ekonomicheskaia prestypnost' v Rossii," in *Biznes i banki v sovremennoi Rossii*, ed. Arkhipov, 132.

105. Steve Liesman, "Banking: Dangerous Business," *Moscow Times*, December 22, 1993.

106. Simon Saradzhian and Christian Lowe, "Top Banker Slain; Businessmen Call for Protection," *Moscow Tribune* 136, no. 683 (July 21, 1995): 1.

lidi, the head of the Russian Business Roundtable, was killed; in total, nine of the Roundtable's thirty leaders were murdered that year.[107] Not surprisingly, in a survey of bankers in December 1994, 52 percent rated the safety level of their employees as "poor."[108]

The authorities did little to interfere. In 1993, a journalist exclaimed, "Not one of the numerous murders of bankers has been solved. . . . As a result of the authorities' inaction, to put it mildly, key places in the banking system will be won by gangsters."[109] Of the 560 contract killings committed in 1995, police solved only 60.[110] Police officers, underpaid and overworked, were not averse to bribe-taking.[111] Yet at root, law enforcement officials plainly did not care about dead bankers. As Moscow police colonel Anatolii Davydov bluntly pointed out, "Money leads to crime—evil is where money is."[112]

As a result, bankers had to protect themselves. Moscow bankers quietly circulated a list of "corrupt" banks or those under the control of criminal gangs. The ARB published information on various schemes perpetrated on banks and how to avoid them. Bankers regularly staged protests and pushed for greater protection from the police. For example, on November 17, 1994, bankers and entrepreneurs in Riazan' wrote an open letter to the oblast' administration, the mayor, and their Duma representative asking them to do something about the "dangerous atmosphere of banditry" in Riazan' and threatening not to pay their taxes if their wishes were not heeded. The next day, the head of the oblast' administration announced the creation of a special task force to battle crime and corruption.[113]

But bankers did not rely merely on pressure and persuasion—they took their safety into their own hands. Most big-city banks hired private security guards to counter the threat from organized crime. A third of a bank's staff could be security guards, and large banks invested a great deal of money in high-tech security systems.[114] Even in provincial Riazan', em-

107. Shamkhalov, "Ekonomicheskaia prestypnost' v Rossii," 132.

108. Surveys by Cassandra research service, reported in the CBR publication *Monitoring bankovskoi politiki* 1 (1995): 29.

109. Mikhail Leontiev, "Gangsters Are Counting On Power," *Segodnia,* December 8, 1993, trans. *Current Digest of the Post-Soviet Press* 45, no. 49 (1993): 11.

110. UPI, "Russia Boosts Efforts to Combat Murder," May 29, 1996, Clari-net news service, e-mail distribution. The article goes on to say that "reports of bankers shot down in the stairwells of their apartments, picked off by marksmen while leaving their cars, or blown up by bombs while opening doors have become regular filler items in the Moscow press."

111. For example, see excerpts from the speeches of Deputy General Prosecutor Yuri Chaika and General Prosecutor Yuri Skuratov in *Moscow News* 28 (July 18–24, 1996).

112. Associated Press, "Report: Russia's Crime Rising," November 15, 1994, Clari-net news service, e-mail distribution.

113. "My ne khotim byt' ubitymi zavtra," *Priokskaia gazeta,* November 17, 1994, 1.

114. A study done by the European Union estimated that "the security arm of most

ployees of the municipal bank often carried guns.[115] The biggest banks created their own commercial security organizations, well-armed and trained, that resembled nothing so much as private armies. By December 1993, 21 percent of Moscow banks had formed their own security services.[116] Roughly 50 percent of security service executives formerly worked for the KGB, 25 percent were former Interior Ministry employees, and 25 percent had been in the Chief Intelligence Administration or armed forces.[117] The ARB itself formed a special arm called Amulet that dealt solely with bank security. It, along with nearly a dozen major banks, sponsored the "Kriminal Show '94" competition pitting these private bank security services in contests of skill against each other, with weapons as prizes.[118] This represented both another kind of tie between banks and the state, as well as an implicit challenge to the state's monopoly on the legitimate use of violence.

It is difficult to estimate how much outright control organized criminal groups actually have gained over banks. Russian sociologist Ol'ga Kryshtanovskaia (citing figures from the Interior Ministry) has argued that criminal organizations in Moscow oblast' have invested heavily in banking and financial structures, and that in 1995 organized crime controlled approximately 400 banks (about 16 percent of all banks at that time).[119] As a famous 1995 article in *Long Island Newsday* noted:

> A secret report on Russian banks last year by the CIA listed 10 of the largest 25 banks as reportedly 'linked to organized crime.' Several of these banks, including Menatep, Inkombank, Unikombank, and Stolichnii bank, received hundreds of millions of dollars in U.S. cash last year, according to knowledgeable sources. The crime links range from influence over certain officers of the bank to outright control, sources said. Menatep, for example, is 'controlled by one of the most powerful crime clans in Moscow,' according to the CIA report. Representatives of the four banks denied that they had any links to criminal organizations.[120]

medium-sized banks formed about 25 per cent of their total staff." John Thornhill, "On the Edge of Instability," *Financial Times*, April 11, 1996, 6.

115. Aleksei Kireev, Director, Zhivago Bank, interview with author, September 1, 1994, Riazan'.

116. Garegin Tosunian, ed., *Bankovskii biznes v Rossii*, 32.

117. Ol'ga Kryshtanovskaia, "Mafia's Growing Power Detailed by Sociologist," *Izvestiia*, September 21, 1995, 5, trans. *Current Digest of the Post-Soviet Press* 47, no. 38 (October 18, 1995): 1.

118. Michael Specter, "Lyubertsy Journal; Guns for Hire: Policing Goes Private in Moscow," *New York Times*, August 9, 1994, A4.

119. Kryshtanovskaia, "Mafia's Growing Power Detailed by Sociologist," 3.

120. Royce, "Dollars Pouring into Russian Stew."

However, these claims are impossible to verify, and probably overstate the case. In general, smaller banks proved more susceptible to criminal takeovers than larger ones. As Amulet's Aleksandr Krylov pointed out:

> The most widespread method [criminals use to take over a bank] is to place a bank in a difficult position and force it to cooperate with criminal groups by employing the artificial non-repayment of loans. The criminals suggest some profitable conditions under which to return the money to the bank. The banker agrees. The bandits return the money, having received the opportunity to take part in the management of the bank, and then take the bank completely under their control.[121]

This method is much less effective against a large bank with an extensive security service of its own. The exact percentages, types, and levels of organized crime control over Russian banking will probably never be known. Clearly, though, crime and corruption have touched the majority of Russian banks in one way or another.

Most immediately damaging, the actual and perceived criminalization has contributed to anti-banker (easily transferable to anti-capitalist) sentiment in Russia. People do not trust bankers, and many feel that banks have accumulated money and property dishonestly. This has been in part a vestige of Soviet attitudes, which viewed those who made money without producing goods as parasites. Bankers have fed into this perception, though, with their conspicuous consumption, their ties to organized crime, and their high-profile wheeling and dealing. Average Russians delight in poking malicious fun at the materialistic "New Russians" who became rich during these years. As one joke went:

> After a terrible crash, a banker stumbled from his car, one arm completely ripped away. He turned, looked at his car, and wailed, "Oh, no, my Mercedes!" An onlooker shouted, "Forget your car, what about your arm?" The banker stared down at his bleeding stump and began another plaintive wail—"Oh, no, my Rolex!"

This public sentiment has had political resonance. In the wake of a significant scandal in 1995, even one of Yeltsin's own advisors suggested nationalizing some of the banks, while hardliners like Working Russia Party leader Viktor Anpilov proclaimed, "Let the current bankers work for the Central Bank. Whoever does not like it—there's enough room at the

---

121. Shvrykov and Klin, "Agent mafii," 45.

lathe."[122] Bankers' bad reputations have discouraged Russians from keeping their money in banks, have undermined the popularity of "the market," and have left the bankers open to challenges from nationalist and communist demagogues.

The CBR's Crackdown

Two trends put an end to the "golden age" of Russian banking.[123] First, macroeconomic stabilization took hold as the state reduced monthly inflation to single digits and the CBR's refinance rate skyrocketed. This occurred both because of IMF pressure and because the CBR no longer felt that subsidizing banks improved the condition of enterprises. Inflation began falling in mid-1993, and from late 1993 through the fall of 1994, CBR credit policy (and interest and exchange rates) fluctuated rapidly. Inflation-based profits ended entirely for the commercial banks after "Black Tuesday"—October 11, 1994—when the ruble's value dropped almost 30 percent, in part as a response to the CBR's typically heavy autumn credit emissions to support the agricultural sector and Northern regions. As a result, CBR director Viktor Gerashchenko, acting Finance Minister Sergei Dubinin, and head of the Federal Currency and Export Control Service Viktor Krunia all lost their jobs. By 1995, the CBR had begun to rely almost entirely on credit auctions for refinancing commercial banks. Moreover, in July 1995 the CBR introduced the "ruble corridor," announcing its intention to defend the ruble-dollar exchange rate within a prescribed band. As a result of these developments, 587 banks finished 1994 with losses on their books, and in 1995, the number rose to over 800.[124]

Second, the CBR began to crack down on problem banks. It actively began to withdraw licenses after a long period of refusing to do so under Gerashchenko. The first bank failure in Russia did not occur until October 1993, and in that particularly egregious case, "the bank's founders . . . borrowed 4 billion rubles from the central bank, converted it into $4 million, sent it to 'an exotic offshore location,' and then disappeared."[125] Yet by the end of 1995, the CBR had stripped licenses from over 300 banks.[126]

---

122. Quoted in Michael R. Gordon, "Yeltsin's Communist Rival Tries to Moderate His Message," *New York Times*, May 21, 1996, A10.

123. This is Dmitriev's term for the high-profit years from 1992 through 1994.

124. Molchanov, *Kommercheskii bank v sovremennoi Rossii*, 42. These are particularly notable figures because of the lax accounting standards of the CBR—if Russian commercial banks did their books according to Western standards, the number of loss-making banks would likely be much higher.

125. Leyla Boulton, "Moscow Review May Force Bank Closures," *Financial Times*, October 22, 1993, 16.

126. Molchanov, *Kommercheskii bank v sovremennoi Rossii*, 42.

The Central Bank also tightened the screws by continually raising the reserve and capital requirements for commercial banks. Not only did the reserve requirements for banks more than double between January and August 1995, but the CBR announced that as of January 1999 the minimum level would be set at the ruble equivalent of five million ECU (a number that only a handful of banks had surpassed at that point).[127] The control-oriented CBR had become determined to consolidate the Russian banking sector into a smaller, more manageable form.

The August 1995 collapse of the interbank credit market represented the final break with the golden age. Banks had grown reliant on their ability to make and take overnight credits on the interbank market, considering this to be a completely safe endeavor. Banks' balance sheets increasingly felt the squeeze, however, as interenterprise debt kept mounting, the CBR increased reserve requirements and interest rates, and the exchange rate stayed stable. In mid-August, overnight interbank rates soared as some large banks faced serious liquidity and repayment problems. As a result, Mosbiznesbank's failure to make a 400 billion ruble ($90 million) interbank payment on August 24—caused by a malfunctioning computer modem—brought down the entire interbank house of cards, with over 150 banks subsequently missing overnight payments.[128] Although the CBR stepped in with emergency refinancing credits to leading banks, the crisis sent several banks into temporary or permanent bankruptcy (including Natsional'nyi Kredit, Lefortovskii Bank, and Chazprombank) and destroyed much of the national interbank credit market.

By 1995, then, banks found themselves in a difficult situation. Their inflation-driven income sources had been cut off, and they began to face hard budget constraints for the first time. But they could not yet emulate Western banks, which typically gather their resources through loans and individual deposits. True long-term enterprise loans could not serve as a reliable means of profit for Russian banks, and Sberbank's near-monopoly on the retail banking market made that strategic option difficult to pursue for all but the largest banks.

So what were banks to do, if they could not operate like banks? Russia's commercial banks—with the active participation of the state—devised two major and opposing kinds of "solutions" to this problem. First, they could invest more heavily in the treasury bill and stock markets. Eventually fu-

127. By May 1996, only 5 percent of commercial banks had equity capital of over 20 billion rubles (about $4 million at the current exchange rate). Natalia Gurushina, "Bank Statistics," *OMRI Daily Digest*, May 9, 1996. On reserves, see Joel Hellman, "Russia Adjusts to Stability," *Transition (OMRI)*, May 17, 1996, 6–10.
128. See *The Economist*, "And Then There Were 2,500," September 2, 1995, 69.

elled in part by Western loans and investment, this development led to another apparent boom in Russian banking, even though the real economy itself had not recovered. The growth of these two quasi-closed, Moscow-based financial markets made it increasingly difficult for regional banks and smaller banks to reap the windfalls, and exacerbated the polarization between the strongest, best-connected banks and the rest. These developments also damaged the power of umbrella banking interest groups like the ARB, as both large and small banks began to complain that the ARB no longer represented their interests.[129] Second, banks could reforge their ties to enterprises by joining financial-industrial groups (FIGs), which were industry-led for the weaker, regional banks and bank-led for the powerful, Moscow-based banks. (See the following 2 chapters.) In a manifestation of the irony of autonomy, these "solutions" contributed to the increasing concentration of capital in Russia without encouraging real investment in enterprises, stifling both political and economic competition.

By 1995, the biggest Moscow-based commercial banks controlled comparatively significant assets while the government, industry, and agriculture desperately needed money. The Russian government thus became ever-more dependent on the bankers' financial resources both to fill the holes in its budget and to fund political campaigns. The power of the banks carried a price for Russia, as bankers used this clout primarily to promote a patronage-based economic system that further reinforced their formal and informal ties to the state.

Moreover, the bankers supported the cause of political democracy in Russia only insofar as they could manipulate democratic institutions to maintain their preferential economic positions. The interaction of Soviet-era legacies with the uncertainty and decentralization of the immediate post-Soviet era, in short, created a parasitic and short-sighted stratum of banks in Russia whose apparent success rested on decidedly unstable foundations.

129. Aleksandr Pol'ianskii, "Assotsiatsiia volkov i ovets," *Delovye liudi* 79 (July 1997): 58–61.

C H A P T E R   F I V E

For a Few Rubles More: Banking in Russia's Regions

It all starts at the top and hits us down here.

—Riazan' banker, 1995.

Although banks blossomed in Russia's regions during Gorbachev's liberalization and the shock therapy attempt, after the subsequent financial stabilization and the CBR's crackdown on weak banks, bank failures, rapid consolidation, and the incursion of strong Moscow banks tore apart Russia's regional banking community. Financial power flowed strongly towards the center as Moscow banks swept into previously protected regional markets.[1] In January 1995, eleven of the twelve broad regions of Russia had more local banks and branches than branches of banks headquartered outside the

---

1. Interregional branching expanded everywhere except the Far East, and in all but three regions, more interregional branches than within-region branches appeared. William Pyle, "Inter-regional Credit Markets in Russia," *Post-Soviet Geography and Economics* 38, no. 8 (1997): 478–98. Although the CBR did not directly identify the regions from which these interregional bank branches came, evidence indicates that the vast majority were branches of Moscow banks. Only the largest banks can support branch networks, and 62 of the top 100 banks in 1997 were Moscow banks. Additionally, my fieldwork in Riazan' and Volgograd revealed that Moscow banks controlled most of the out-of-region branches opened in both cities. Moscow banks expanded outside of Moscow, but banks in the regions, when they expanded, tended to stay within the region (excepting perhaps opening one branch in Moscow). Among the over 30 banks Klimanov and Lavrov identify as having an "all-Russian regional strategy," Moscow banks overwhelmingly predominate. See V. V. Klimanov and A. M. Lavrov, "Regional'naia strategiia kommercheskikh bankov Rossii," *Region: ekonomika i sotsiologiia* 4 (1998): 106–21.

Table 5.1. Regional distribution of banks and branches

Region	Regional banks		Branches of regional banks		Branches of nonregional banks	
	January 1996	January 1999	January 1996	January 1999	January 1996	January 1999
City of Moscow	993	667	227	142	249	65
Northern	70	30	137	38	120	152
Northwest	79	53	93	46	167	151
Central (without Moscow)	167	103	301	85	438	594
Volgo-Viatskii	80	41	120	65	163	196
Central Black Earth	35	17	100	32	181	184
Volga (Povol'zhkii)	193	100	403	139	234	320
North Caucasus	334	153	414	221	292	352
Urals	182	106	442	230	268	351
Western Siberia	200	99	271	184	298	276
Eastern Siberia	83	42	175	104	189	208
Far East	133	51	250	87	161	199
Baltic (Kaliningrad)	29	14	28	7	26	25

Source: Central Bank of Russia, *Bulletin of Banking Statistics* 2 (1996 and 1999).

region, and only 27 percent of banks made their headquarters in Moscow. Yet by January 1997, regional banks comprised only 38 of the top 100 Russian banks (by assets) and Moscow banks represented 41 percent of *all* commercial banks in Russia. By January 1999, Moscow banks held 87 percent of the total assets of the Russian banking system, and local banks outnumbered branches of out-of-region banks (overwhelmingly Moscow-based) in only two areas, excepting Moscow itself—the North Caucasus and Western Siberia (see Table 5.1).[2] While Moscow overflowed with banks, regions lost more and more control over their own financial resources. What accounts for this boom and bust, this rapid decentralization and reconsolidation of Russia's regional banking system?

After 1993, institutional legacies and policy choices combined to put Russia's regional banks in much weaker financial positions than their Moscow counterparts. Regional banks, most of which were either pocket banks or descendants of the spetsbanks, relied on local enterprises for loan and deposit activity. Since these enterprises had become caught up in the spiral of nonpayments and barter plaguing Russia, they dragged their affiliated banks down with them. But Moscow banks, because they

---

2. CBR, *Bulletin of Banking Statistics* 2 (1999): 98. The January 1999 figures represent a high-water mark for Moscow-based branching, since the effects of the August 1998 crisis had not yet resulted in formal branch closings.

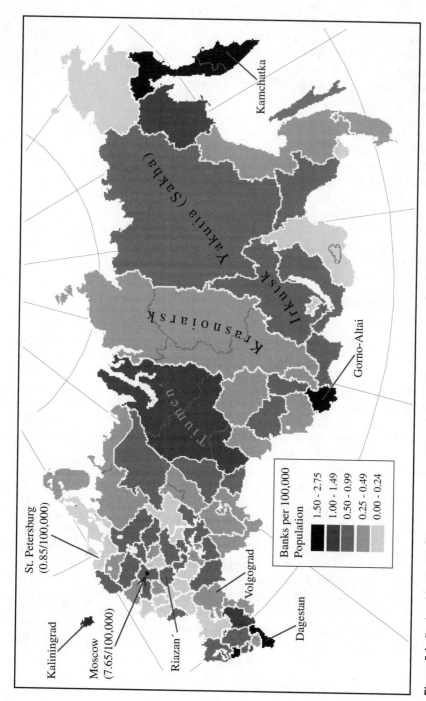

Figure 5.1. Regional banks (1999) per 100,000 population (1995), not including branch banks

could take advantage of the GKO market, their status as authorized banks, the currency market, and other nonlending avenues of profit, avoided this debt trap far more easily than their regional competitors. Ironically, this gave the biggest Moscow-based banks an opportunity to expand into the regions (over the strong protests of regional bankers) precisely because they had not been weakened by granting loans to cash-starved Russian enterprises. This phenomenon rapidly concentrated financial capital in Moscow, in sharp opposition to the political decentralization and industrial de-monetization occurring at the same time.

Soon, the only regions with more than one strong local bank were those that had both independent, powerful regional authorities and economies supported by raw-materials industries and foreign trade. Instead of unifying the Russian economy as Yeltsin and Gaidar had hoped, the period of relative macroeconomic stability between 1994 and 1998 exacerbated the split between the cash and noncash economies, and placed ever-more power in the hands of Moscow's financiers.

Squeezing the Regions

The largest regional descendants of the spetsbanks seemed to stand the best chance of holding back the Moscow onslaught. These banks prospered until 1994 by exploiting their initial institutional advantages. Indeed, in a 1993 survey, 75 percent of former spetsbank staff and 72 percent of new commercial bank staff agreed that former spetsbanks operated under better conditions than did the new commercial banks. While employees of the former spetsbanks identified their long-standing links with clients, more reliable clientele, and more skilled personnel as the cause, the new commercial bankers cited the ability of the former spetsbanks to obtain centralized loans, their preferential CBR requirements for capital and reserves, their probable state support in case of bankruptcy, and their better offices and facilities as pivotal.[3]

Not surprisingly, the jealous new commercial bankers were right. In fact, the old state banks' insolvent clients, dangerous level of specialization, and poorly trained staffs turned out to be their biggest weaknesses in the changing economic environment. Fortunately for the unwitting spetsbankers, these disadvantages were, at least at the beginning, often more than offset by the boons provided by their unique, historical position in the Soviet economic structure.

The largest former spetsbanks began their private lives with wide branch networks throughout Russia, which enabled them to reach far

---

3. *Russian Economic Barometer* 2, no. 3 (1993): 26.

more clients and markets than could the new commercial banks. The importance of this factor cannot be underestimated—two of the most common obstacles for new commercial banks were acquiring decent buildings in which to operate and expanding their branch networks. In June 1993, former spetsbanks represented 14 of the 15 banks with the most branches in Russia; as late as 1998, former spetsbanks still occupied 10 of the top 15 spots.[4] These branch networks allowed former spetsbanks to control banking in the regions by keeping intact their monopoly structures, political connections, and industry ties. Old branch networks of Promstroibank often dominated regional banking. In Riazan', as of September 1994, PRIO-Vneshtorgbank (created in part from Promstroibank and Agroprombank branches) had 23 branches, Agroprombank itself had 13, and Mesherabank (a former branch of Zhilsotsbank) had 1, while only two other banks had even a single branch office.[5] In Volgograd, as of mid-1995 Agroprombank had 34 branches, Sotsbank (created from Zhilsotsbank) had 18, and Volgoprombank (created from Promstroibank) had 9, while no other regional commercial bank had over 5.[6] Gosbank's descendants often continued to expand their branch networks through mergers and construction, frequently without regard for the financial consequences. Sberbank's new nine-story regional headquarters building in Volgograd, under construction in 1995, was to include a "Sberbank Academy," restaurant, sporting facilities, and a hotel.[7]

Their range, connections, and long history also allowed the former state banks to receive vital CBR authorization to carry out various lucrative activities (such as dealing in hard currency) earlier than most other banks. The difference between the haves and have-nots became particularly stark outside of Moscow. For example, of the 27 commercial banks in Volgograd in 1995, only Agroprombank and Volgoprombank had "general" licenses for dealing in hard currency, and Sotsbank was the only one with a "special" (more limited) hard currency license. Considering the profitability of hard currency operations in Russia's unstable transitional economy, this represented a significant advantage for the former spetsbanks.

Finally, one cannot dismiss the power of name recognition and established market presence. These well-known banks needed to spend far less

---

4. In 1998, all fifteen of these banks had forty or more branches. Klimanov and Lavrov, "Regional'naia strategiia kommercheskikh bankov Rossii."

5. "Perechen' bankovskikh uchrezhdenii Riazanskoi oblasti," *Bankirskii dom* 7 (September 1994): 2.

6. "Bankovskaia set' Volgogradskoi oblasti po sostoianiiu na 1.1.95 g.," *Delovoe povolzh'e*, no. 3 (January 1995): 5.

7. V. Zhuravlev, "Na podriade u russkikh—nemetskie firmy," *Delovoe povolzh'e* 37 (September 1994): 1.

on advertising than other banks. On the list of banks that spent the most money on advertising in 1995, the first former spetsbank to appear was Tver'universalbank, at number seven.[8] The spetsbanks at one point serviced every enterprise and individual in Russia. Therefore, these clients were theirs to lose—new banks had to lure accounts away from the former spetsbanks in order to build up their clientele. Moreover, in this period of turmoil, many people tended to turn back to the familiar and the safe. The former spetsbanks and state banks tried to capitalize on this tendency in their advertising—as Sberbank Volgograd's slogan put it "One old friend is better than two new ones." These particular Soviet-era legacies, then, gave them a leg up on their competition.

Yet Gosbank's regional descendents soon began to suffer for the same reasons that they had once prospered. Their political connections in the regions, their tight ties to their industrial and agricultural shareholders, and their distance from the rough competition in Moscow became severe liabilities in the changing national economic environment. The August 1995 crash of the interbank credit market and the CBR's more restrictive regulatory, reserve, and interest rate policies put increasing strain on the regional banking system. By 1996, Moscow banks increased their annual profits by 75 percent while regional banks saw a 27 percent fall in profits.[9] Three trends in particular solidified this dynamic.

First, the regional banks had a difficult time taking advantage of the new GKO market in Moscow. Their distance from the center made it hard to process transactions in the under-computerized environment, while the government chose Moscow banks to serve as its authorized primary GKO dealers. With GKO yields heavily outstripping the rate of inflation until after the 1996 presidential elections, this significantly disadvantaged the regional banks. Equally as troubling, the national payments system remained extremely slow, with monetary transfers between the center and the regions often taking two weeks or more. This effectively cut the regional banks out of the Moscow-based interbank credit market. These developments left the regional banks more reliant than ever on their local enterprise customers and regional administrations, just at the time when these actors faced severe cash crunches of their own.

Moreover, the regional banks had relatively little money to invest in profitable speculative activities. In particular, they enjoyed far less access to government resources than did the Moscow banks. Authorized Moscow

8. Sberbank was number 18, Promstroibank was number 32, Vneshtorgbank was number 43, and Agroprombank did not appear in the top 50. Sergei Veselov, "Banki ustanavlivaiut rekordy v reklame," *Finansovye izvestiia*, March 1, 1996, 3.

9. Lana Simkina, "Banking in Russia's Regions," May 28, 1997, BISNIS Report, U.S. Department of Commerce.

banks held an astonishing 94 percent of all federal budget funds circulating in the banking system (these funds amounted to over three times more than all regional and local government funds in banks combined).[10] Fourteen regions held no federal budget funds at all in their banks, while Sverdlovsk, the second-ranking region behind Moscow, held only 1.2 percent. In an economic environment where the federal government remained by far the most desirable client for banks, the political decision to place state monies in favored Moscow banks strongly and immediately affected the balance of power within the banking system.

Meanwhile, many regional and local governments began to concentrate their funds in a smaller number of banks, and made greater demands on the banks they did use. As a Volgograd banker put it, "Commercial banks are ready for cooperation with local government, but the government still isn't ready. The only thing that they want from us is money at a very subsidized interest rate."[11] A smaller number of banks thus became ever-more closely tied to regional administrations. Most disturbing for the provincial bankers, several regions and cities decided to create their own municipal banks (banks owned in part or in full by city and regional governments) as a way of ensuring greater control over budgetary funds. As Aleksei Kireev, the head of Riazan's municipal bank Zhivago, explained, "it became clear that [as a city] we need to concentrate our resources, to create a bank . . . that would serve the interests of the city. . . . The bank is an authorized agent of the city government and has complete control of the city finances."[12] Not only did Zhivago increase in influence over the course of the decade, but the municipal authorities continually increased their stake in the bank, and the bank took over a smaller, private competitor, Pereiaslavl' Bank.

In another example, Novosibirsk oblast' created its municipal bank in part because of the administration's unfortunate experience with an authorized bank. It had put oblast' monies into Sibirskii Torgovii Bank, once a rising regional star that had worked to facilitate interregional payments transfers. After the bank collapsed, the oblast' found it quite difficult to retrieve its money and hesitated to put its finances into yet another bank it could not control.[13]

Therefore, although the 1990 Law on Banks and Banking Activity ex-

10. CBR, *Bulletin of Banking Statistics* 2 (1999): 115.

11. Sergei Kostrov, Head of Planning and Financial Analysis, Russkii Yuzhnii Bank, quoted in Anna Stepanova, "Russkii Yuzhnii Bank prizyvaet sopernikov otkryt' zabralo," *Delovoe povolzh'e*, no. 12 (April 1994): 5.

12. Aleksei Kireev, director, Zhivago Bank, interview with author, September 1, 1994, Riazan'.

13. Irina Yasina, "Munitsipal'nye banki namereny dokazyvat' svoiu neobkhodimost'," *Finansovye izvestiia*, March 1, 1996.

plicitly prohibited the creation of municipal banks, they slowly began to appear. A Supreme Soviet resolution of July 22, 1993, permitted municipal bank formation on a limited, experimental basis, but municipal banks quickly outstripped the bounds of this resolution. Admitting defeat, lawmakers included a provision permitting municipal banks in the 1996 revised Law on Banks and Banking Activity. As Duma banking subcommittee member Pavel Medvedev observed, even though he was against the idea of municipal banks in principle, he came to realize that since many of them already existed in defiance of previous laws, it was more productive to regulate them than to outlaw them.[14] By 1996 municipal banks existed in Riazan', Novosibirsk, Voronezh, Tver', Petrozavodsk, and Moscow itself. Moreover, several regions had formed *de facto* municipal banks, where the oblast' or city government chose to work closely with only one main commercial bank and often took a financial interest in it (e.g., Briansk, Ivanovo, Kostroma, Lipetsk, Perm, and others).[15]

Municipal banks represented a reasonable yet dangerous solution to problems of local financial control in Russia. On the one hand, they allowed regional governments to handle their own funds, thereby retaining profits for themselves, directing investment to chosen projects, and avoiding the potential misuse of government monies by commercial bankers. Municipal banks, regional banks, and other types of sub-national, state-controlled banks exist throughout the developed and developing world. On the other hand, it created a serious problem of moral hazard for the cash-strapped regional governments. For example, Volgograd tried to create a municipal bank in 1993–94, but the attempt failed as local bankers charged that the municipal bank would operate under preferential conditions.[16] As international experience has often demonstrated, municipal banks can easily become regional pocket banks, further stifling competition and market development. In Brazil, for example, the federal government was forced to take over the regional banks in São Paulo and Rio de Janeiro in January 1995 after they had built up irrecoverable burdens of bad loans to their own state governments.[17] Either way, though, municipal banks spelled trouble for the regional banks.

Finally, the regional banks held a far higher proportion of both total loans and nonperforming loans than did the Moscow banks. In January

14. Pavel Medvedev, Duma deputy and member of the subcommittee on banking, interview with author, June 19, 1995, Moscow.
15. E. N. Chekmareva et al., "Opyt i problemy sozdaniia munitsipal'nykh bankov," *Den'gi i kredit* 11–12 (1994): 83–87.
16. For example, see Evgeniia Mikhailik, "Za stomillionnym kreditom," *Delovoe povolzh'e*, no. 18 (August 1993): 5.
17. Robert Taylor, "Feet on Fire," *The Banker*, April 1996, 80–82.

1995, even though Moscow banks represented 37 percent of all banks (and the vast majority of large ones), they accounted for only 13.3 percent of the credits granted to nonfinancial institutions and held only 4.7 percent of nonperforming loans in Russia.[18] The concentration of pocket banks and former spetsbanks in the regions explained much of this differential, because they engaged in extensive "connected lending" to their own shareholders and traditional customers. This went without saying for the pocket banks—after all, they had been created exactly for this reason. But for the former spetsbank branches, the ramifications of their close ties with specific sectors became much more obvious. While hyperinflation had virtually erased the former spetsbanks' burden of bad loans from Soviet times (unlike in Eastern Europe), these banks continued to make loans less on the basis of potential profitability than on political and economic connections. Each remnant of the former system started its new life with a narrowly focused bloc of clients—state-owned heavy industry for the Promstroibanks; agriculture for the Agroprombanks; and small business, housing, and trade for the Zhilsotsbanks. Former spetsbanks, therefore, tended to be no better off than the traditional customers that they carried with them from Soviet times. Because these banks had extremely concentrated loan portfolios, when a certain sector of the economy fell on hard times, the associated former spetsbanks naturally found themselves in jeopardy. Agroprombank and Promstroibank in particular found themselves saddled with—yet bound to support—some of the basket cases of the Russian economy. To make matters worse, former spetsbanks were also losing or having to share some of their more successful traditional customers.[19]

As a result of these three parallel developments, many of the former spetsbank branches and pocket banks in the regions began to experience grave financial difficulties. By mid-1994, for example, over half of Volgograd's banks had experienced such serious problems that the CBR prohibited them from accepting deposits from individuals.[20] When I visited one of these banks in the spring of 1995, I had the surreal experience of

18. Association of Russian Banks, "Sravnitel'nye pokazateli kommercheskikh bankov Rossii i Moskvy," *ARB Bulletin* 12 (1995): 48.

19. While only 58 percent of entrepreneurs said it was better to work with several banks in 1994, this number had risen to 78 percent by winter 1995. Survey of 3500 bank clients by Cassandra research service, published in Victor Lashchinskii and Yurii Okun'kov, "Bankiri ozhidaiut usileniia shtormovikh vetrov, sposobnikh potriasti finansovyi rynok," *Finansovye izvestiia,* January 26, 1996, 3.

20. A. I. Shirokii (nachal'nik Glavnogo upravleniia TsB RF po Volgogradskoi oblast), "O sostoianii bankovskoi sistemy i osnovnykh itogakh ee deiatel'nosti za 1994 god," press release, April 17, 1994.

interviewing the nervous director in his comfortable office while a woman outside screamed "Where is my money! What have you done with my money?!"

The fate of the two Volgograd banks that emerged from the Promstroibank break-up provide typical examples. The smaller, Traktorobank, decided to separate completely from the regional network in 1990 and associate itself with the massive Volgograd Tractor Factory. In effect, it became a pocket bank. When the factory began to have problems, so did the bank, and as a result a wealthy and notorious pyramid scheme (*Russkaia Nedvishimost'*, or "Russian Real Estate") bought it and four other small Volgograd banks. The larger, Volgoprombank, had a comparatively wide branch network and preserved its state privileges, but its poor service caused many of its better clients to flee.

In Riazan', the two banks that emerged from Promstroibank USSR suffered similar fates. The smaller one had no branches, and had kept its old management and clients. When I visited the bank in its out-of-the-way location, I met for two hours in the middle of the day with the bank's director and vice-director. During these two hours, no clients came into the bank and no one seemed to be working. Neither were computers in evidence; the director had an abacus and a calculator on her desk. In 1995, an outside group forcibly assumed control over this bank, and it was subsequently sold to an industry-led financial-industrial group. The larger Riazan' bank ran into problems granting loans to unscrupulous clients, and only survived by merging its finances and leadership structure with a more stable bank.

Agricultural Banks: Poverty in the Provinces

Agricultural banks—whether new banks, Agroprombank spin-offs, or Agroprombank itself—faced the most severe problems of any sectoral banks. About 25 percent of Russia's population lived in the countryside, with over 26,000 state farms controlling 90 percent of Russia's farmland (283,000 tiny private farms and private plots made up the rest).[21] Government attempts at land reform had hopelessly stalled, and the Russian agriculture sector, twisted by years of collectivization and centrally directed mechanization, remained unprofitable and unproductive. The chain of interenterprise debt often began with agricultural enterprises, and farmers traditionally considered loans from Agroprombank to be gifts from the state. Considering that the state was one of the biggest agricultural goods procurers, that the state itself often did not pay farmers

21. Sander Thoenes, "Privately Better Off," *Financial Times*, April 11, 1996.

for their products, and that the government continually wrote off farm debts, this outlook seems quite reasonable.[22] The institutional framework of post-Soviet Russia made it all but impossible for banks to make money by working with farmers. The tales of three agricultural banks, Respekt-bank in Riazan', Volgogradskii Kommercheskii Agroprombank (VKAB), and Agroprombank itself, demonstrate this unfortunate dynamic.

Commercial banks founded anew in order to finance private agriculture folded quickly after the state stopped guaranteeing loans to private farmers. Ignoring the pleas of farmers picketing outside the Central Bank's Riazan' office, the CBR closed Respekt-bank, a zero bank, in 1994. This bank first encountered serious problems beginning in 1993 because the government did not pay the bank its subsidies on centralized agricultural credits, although it had promised to do so. According to the bank's calculations, this cost it 300 billion rubles. The president of the bank complained that it was impossible to run an agricultural bank ". . . if the government won't support the agrarian sector as is done in civilized and even in uncivilized countries."[23] Until 1993, private farmers had received loans from banks like Respekt through guarantees from the Association of Peasant Farms and Agricultural Cooperatives of Russia (AKKOR).[24] After the state cut these loans off, according to Dale Van Atta:

> the new individual farmers are finding their interests increasingly aligned with the old large farms, rather than with the macroeconomic reformers who advocate tight state credit. Without any alternative source of capital, private owners can only demand state subsidies and protectionist policies just as their former bitter enemies, the farm chairmen, have been doing.[25]

Respekt-bank, like other new agricultural banks, did not stand a chance without state support.

VKAB, a large independent spinoff of Agroprombank USSR in Volgograd, met a similar fate. The agricultural sector in Volgograd oblast' lay in shambles. As early as 1992, only 15 percent of farmers finished the year with profits. As of May 1, 1993, agricultural enterprises in Volgograd had received a total of 12.5 billion rubles in loans (9.8 percent of all credit investment in the oblast'), and of this, 78 percent (9.8 billion) was

22. Natalia Gurushina, "Yeltsin Issues Decree to Support Agro-Complex," *OMRI Daily Digest,* April 17, 1996.

23. Tat'iana Dmitrieva, director of Respekt-bank, "Starye trudnosti pozadi. Novye—vperedi," *Bankirskii dom* 15 (December 1993): 2.

24. Thoenes, "Privately Better Off."

25. Dale Van Atta, "Agrarian Reform in Post-Soviet Russia," *Post-Soviet Affairs* 10, no. 2 (April–June 1994): 162.

centralized credit. VKAB had disbursed 78.4 percent of these credits, while Rossel'khozbank (Agroprombank) disbursed only 2.4 percent, and other still-independent branches of the former state agricultural bank were responsible for all but 5.8 percent of the rest.[26] As in other areas, the federal government slowed its subsidy payments on these credits in 1993. Farmers were supposed to pay only 28 percent in interest, but because the state had regularly been late in reimbursing VKAB for the difference, the bank charged the farmers the regular CBR rate (over 100 percent). It did not matter to the farmers—they could not pay the bank back in any event. But just for the month of April 1993, according to VKAB, the federal budget owed—and did not pay—VKAB 1.68 billion rubles to cover this subsidy.[27]

Moreover, despite being one of the largest, most privileged, and most politically connected banks in the region, the bank remained mired in corruption and inefficiency. In January 1994, an auditor accused three Volgograd banks, most notably VKAB, of "transferring 336.5 million rubles of subsidized credits directed to the oblast' [for agricultural needs] from the federal budget into the hands of entrepreneurs." In particular, the auditors claimed that the director of VKAB's financial department personally disbursed these credits in an unlawful manner, and that VKAB had diverted "tens of millions" in credits to a small company registered in Belgorod.[28] It had also spent far too much money building itself a gleaming new headquarters in the center of Volgograd. When I visited in 1995, the bank was clearly in deep trouble. The top official with whom I met lacked a computer, and in two separate phone calls during our meeting told his caller that "we have no money." When I tried to change dollars there after my interview, a guard stopped me, saying "No rubles today." I asked, "No rubles? Isn't this a bank?" and he laughed, replying "It's a Russian bank." These expensive indiscretions and nonperforming loans led the bank to take desperate measures to bring in money. In 1995, it raised interest rates to 220 percent and began to call in its loans.[29] By the end of 1995, VKAB's assets had been frozen, the bank had gone bankrupt, and, according to one source, "five million dollars had disappeared without a trace."[30] Lacking state support, solvent clients, and regulatory

26. CBR Volgograd, "Fermery zhivy kreditom," *Delovoe povolzh'e* 12 (June 1993): 8. For details on the evolution of Agroprombank into Rossel'khozbank, see chapter 2.

27. Interview with Elena Dorofeeva, vice-director of CBR Volgograd, in "Khochesh' poluchit' kredit? Privatizirui predpriiatie," *Delovoe povolzh'e* 12 (June 1993): 7.

28. "Volgogradskie milliony poshli v Belgorod," *Delovoe povolzh'e* 1 (January 1994): 1.

29. Gennady Polonsky, "Small Business in the Russian Provinces: Case Study Evidence from Volgograd," *Communist Economies and Economic Transformation* 10, no. 4 (1998): 519–37.

30. Ibid., 531.

oversight, the bank had no chance to develop into a transparent, stable financial institution.

Agroprombank itself became the single biggest basket case in the Russian financial system. Although the Agroprombank network fell apart in 1990–91, like a bungee cord many of the hundreds of briefly independent agricultural banks quickly snapped back into their original, integrated positions due to the devastating unprofitability of the Russian agricultural sector. By January 1994, one-quarter of all bank branches (excluding Sberbank) were branches of Agroprombank.[31]

Before 1995, Agroprombank emerged as a classically bizarre example of how a Russian bank could make money without a significant deposit base or solvent clients by relying on the appropriation and misappropriation of state largesse. In 1993, the Ministry of Finance funded 75 percent of Agroprombank's loans through subsidized, directed credit programs.[32] As Van Atta observed:

> Impersonal bank account funds can be converted into cash-in-hand and withdrawn by providing a sympathetic bank official with a small percentage of the transaction's value. The low, state-subsidized interest rates on agricultural credits made them attractive for other purposes and, as hyperinflation has made turning a quick profit in trade the only reasonable investment, more and more of the concessionary credits certainly have been diverted to other purposes.[33]

Agroprombank's financial operations, like the CBR's, remained shrouded in secrecy; in its final balance sheets for 1992 and 1993, the largest liability (and the second-largest asset) was "Other."[34] Yet Agroprombank officials interviewed in Riazan', for example, did not express concern about their bank's financial future. In fact, they took great pleasure in showing me the extensive, three-dimensional plans for their new downtown headquarters building.

By 1995, centralized credits to agriculture represented about 90 percent of Agroprombank's loans, and almost none were being paid back. At first the state decided to deal with the mounting insolvency by transform-

31. Central Bank of Russia, *Vestnik banka Rossii* 1 (February 16, 1994): 4.
32. As the World Bank observed, "The management . . . still operates under old procedures, and the bank is not profit-oriented. Its objectives are defined in terms of 'the need to protect farmers' and 'the interests of the country'." Ruben Lamdany, ed., *Russia: The Banking System during the Transition* (Washington, D.C.: The World Bank, 1993), 20. I confirmed the persistence of these attitudes in interviews with Agroprombank officials in Riazan' and Volgograd in 1995.
33. Van Atta, "Agrarian Reform," 172.
34. Agroprombank, "Annual Report, 1993."

ing these bad debts into debts of the state, which the Ministry of Finance converted into unattractive 10–year veksels paying 10 percent annual interest.[35] But in late 1996, the government, out of solutions, handed the ailing Agroprombank over to Moscow-based Stolichnii Bank Sberezhnii in exchange for Stolichnii's promise to continue disbursing subsidized credits to agriculture.[36] The renamed "SBS-Agro" planned to use Agroprombank's branch network to assault Sberbank's monopoly on the retail market. By the end of 1997, its retail empire had over 1,500 components, including 11 territorial headquarters, 67 branches, 9 subsidiary (*dochernie*) banks, and 1,450 outlet offices.[37] SBS-Agro thus further tied itself to the state to gain a competitive edge and to make it politically difficult to close the bank. As an official in the Ministry of Agriculture rightly observed, "These subsidies will exist for a long time, no matter how many 'reformers' appear."[38]

Challenges from the Center

The progressive weakening of the regional banks created a power imbalance that the Moscow banks quickly exploited. By 1999, Moscow-based banks had spread widely throughout Russia, but particularly focused on the wealthier, more export-oriented regions (see Figure 5.2). Several factors help to explain why the Moscow banks had become interested in regional expansion, despite the poverty and nonmonetary exchange proliferating in the provinces. First, the competition in Moscow had grown fiercer. Moscow banks competed strongly with each other in a variety of service areas, and such competition had begun to take its toll on profit margins. Moscow banks thus looked to the regions that lacked adequate banking services for new sources of the high profits to which they had become accustomed. Second, they "rediscovered" the idea of retail banking. In Russia, population density poorly corresponded with the number of banks in a region, reflecting most banks' earlier lack of interest in providing retail services.[39] However, the huge sums of money that the infamous pyramid schemes managed to collect from an unwitting Russian population opened some bankers' eyes to the potential of this

35. "Agroprombank vybiraet gosudarstvo," *Kommersant-Daily*, April 6, 1996, 6.
36. Evgenii Vasil'chuk, "Pravitel'stvo i SBS-Agro obeshchaiut navesti poriadok v kreditovanii agrokompleksa," *Finansovye izvestiia*, March 25, 1997.
37. SBS-Agro, "Annual Report, 1997."
38. O. M. Falileev, deputy director of the financial department of the Ministry of Agriculture, "Agroprom priglashaet banki k vzaimovygodnomu sotrudnichestvu," *Biznes i banki* 51, no. 217 (December 1994): 1.
39. V. V. Klimanov, "Territorial'naia organizatsiia bankovskoi sistemy Rossii," (ms, Moscow State University, Geography Department, 1997), 9.

market. Moscow banks such as Rossiiskii Kredit, Inkombank, and Stolich-nii Bank Sberezhnii thus began branching into the retail market, hoping to put a dent in Sberbank's near-monopoly. Finally, when the biggest Moscow banks began to form their bank-led financial-industrial groups (discussed in chapter 6), they needed to form bank branches in those regions where they had acquired enterprises. For example, ONEKSIMbank moved into Irkutsk and Saratov when it invested in Sidanko oil, and Menatep went to Irkutsk when it bought part of the Ust'-Ilimsk paper and pulp complex.[40]

This invasion of the "foreign" banks upset provincial bankers tremendously. They accused Moscow banks of stealing their best clients and employees, of not investing in the regions in which they operated, and of siphoning resources collected in the regions to invest in the Moscow GKO and interbank credit markets. I vividly remember an incident in 1995 when a Volgograd banker shredded a napkin with his pen as he furiously diagrammed the way in which Moscow banks pulled resources away from the region. As an economist at the CBR office in Riazan' noted:

> A situation that I don't like—and not just me—is when Moscow banks open their branches here. . . . Moscow banks play their own games and don't pay attention to local problems. Your shirt is closest to your own skin. They just try to get profits for themselves. They have greater credit resources, there is more competition in Moscow, and services are more extensive and cheaper. So they'll take customers from our independent Riazan' banks.[41]

A Volgograd banker echoed this concern, stating simply, "No one opens a branch in order to develop foreign (*chuzhuiu*) territory."[42] Not only did Moscow banks pull customers from local banks, but they began taking over some of the local banks themselves as the locals ran into problems.

In addition, most provincial banks could no longer count on their regional administrations and Central Bank divisions to throw up roadblocks to out-of-region banks as they had in the past. Before the regional banks began to suffer economically, this had been a key protectionist weapon for them. In many cases the CBR divisions and the administrations had

---

40. See Otdel Finansov, "ONEKSIMbank i MFK dvinulis' v regiony," *Kommersant-Daily*, December 26, 1996; Alexander Polyansky, "Banks: Providing for the Provinces," *Business in Russia* 76 (April 1997): 74–75; and Alexander Chernikov, "Resource-Rich Regions—Irkutsk Oblast on the Road to the Market," *Communist Economies and Economic Transformation* 10, no. 3 (1998): 381.

41. Oleg Matveev, lead economist, Department of Licensing, Central Bank of Russia, Riazan' office, interview with author, September 2, 1994, Riazan'.

42. Anatolii Valov, director of Volgofondbank, quoted in Anna Stepanova and Vladimir Teplitskii, "Pri slaboi ekonomike ne budet sil'nykh bankov," *Delovoe povolzh'e* 1 (April 1994): 1.

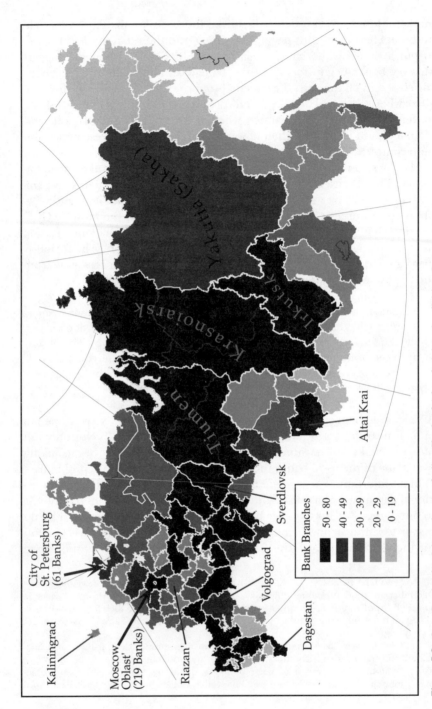

Figure 5.2. Out-of-region bank branches (excluding Sberbank) by administrative division, January 1999

been instrumental in setting up local banks in the first place, and did not want to see them get steamrolled by outsiders. Until February 1996, therefore, Russia's banking legislation required the requisite regional branch of the CBR to grant approval to any new out-of-region bank branch, approval that was often not forthcoming. Regional administrations, too, found it fairly easy to block the entry of Moscow banks by putting up legal and logistical barriers. For example, according to Avto-VAZbank officials, they would have set up a branch in Volgograd much earlier than 1996 "if there had not been a stubborn problem of a purely local character."[43]

This protectionist attitude had changed completely in most regions by 1996. Although regional CBR divisions remained wary of Moscow interlopers, they lost their power to block them. The ARB and the large Moscow banks pressed the Duma to include a statute in the February 1996 revised Law on Banks and Banking Activity that removed the right of the regional CBR offices to refuse entry to branch banks from other regions. At the same time, many regional administrations became less hostile toward the outsiders. This occurred both because the regional administrations needed more financing and services than local banks could provide, and because Moscow banks changed their expansion strategies to make themselves more attractive as regional partners.[44] Moscow banks promised to provide the regions with bank veksels (and to help set up local veksel programs), leasing operations, credit cards, faster payments transfers, and investment credits. In Krasnodar krai, for example, weak local banks and lack of investment concerned the administration so much that it actively began to court Moscow banks.[45] Administrators also found that the Moscow banks could do them personal favors. It was no coincidence, for example, that the 27–year-old daughter of oblast' administration head Ivan Shabunin became the director of the new bank branch in Volgograd of the Moscow-based Vozrozhdenie.

New strategies of the Moscow banks complemented this change of heart by regional administrators. Whereas earlier the banks had tried to bulldoze their way into regional markets and avoided working with many local customers, over time they developed more sophisticated methods. ONEKSIMbank, for example, would found subsidiary banks or buy out strong

43. Valerii Zhuravlev, "Bank, kotoryi natselen," *Delovoe povolzh'e* 25 (July 1994): 4.

44. Tat'iana Drygova, "Regional'nye vlasti i stolichnye banki pronikaiutsia vse bol'shei simpatiei drug k drugu," *Finansovye izvestiia*, August 22, 1996; Vladimir Kovalevskii, "Kolichestvo filialov sokrashchaetsia, no ne u stolichnykh bankov," *Finansovye izvestiia*, April 3, 1997; and Irina Yasina, "Otnoshenie mestnykh vlastei k moskovskim bankam zametno meniaetsia," *Finansovye izvestiia*, April 29, 1997.

45. Arbakhan Magomedov, "Krasnodar Krai: A 'Growth Pole' in the Transitional Economy of Russia?" *Communist Economies and Economic Transformation* 10, no. 3 (1998): 363–74.

local banks—like Primor'e Bank in the Far East—while retaining the original name and much of the staff. It opened its first subsidiary bank, BaltONEKSIMbank, in St. Petersburg in the fall of 1994. Moreover, when ONEKSIMbank moved into a region, it would first come to an arrangement with the local administration, "agreeing that the bank would become its agent for international settlements, and also provide expertise and carry out investment programs on that territory."[46] Moscow banks might commit to investing in the regions, or offer to help solve regional economic difficulties. Rossiiskii Kredit, for example, made a deal with Irkutsk oblast' to aid in solving their nonpayments problem, while Inkombank promised to participate in a regional investment program in Sverdlovsk oblast'.

Moreover, the federal government once again stood ready to help the largest Moscow banks in their endeavors. For example, in April 1996 the Yeltsin administration instructed the Ministry of Finance to guarantee loans that Stolichnii Bank Sberezhnii, Menatep, and ONEKSIMbank had granted to several regional authorities, including a $9 billion construction loan SBS made to the Republic of Adygei.[47]

In such ways, the Moscow banks continued their steady expansion into regional banking markets, a process which compounded the problems of the regional banks. By January 1995, Volgograd already had 15 branches of out-of-region banks, 11 of which were Moscow bank branches. Riazan' suffered a similar influx. For example, Mesherabank, a former Zhilsotsbank branch, did not prove large enough, connected enough, or progressive enough to remain a viable bank, especially after Riazan' created its own municipal bank and took much of Mesherabank's business away. As a result, in 1995 it became a branch office of Unikombank, a well-connected, larger, Moscow-based bank that had itself been formed from Moscow oblast' branches of Zhilsotsbank and Promstroibank. Most worrying for the regional banks, by 1995 even regions that maintained several authorized banks began to divide this status between local banks and the Moscow interlopers. Irkutsk had five authorized banks in the region, two regional and three Moscow-based.[48] An agreement signed in March 1995 in Volgograd authorized four banks to service the oblast' administration's off-budget funds, three Volgograd banks and one from Moscow (Vozrozhdenie).[49] Most Bank's branches in Vladimir and Saratov gained authoriza-

46. Klimanov and Lavrov, "Regional'naia strategiia kommercheskikh bankov Rossii," 119.

47. Natalia Gurushina, "Government Using Banks to Bail Out the Regions," *OMRI Daily Digest,* April 12, 1996.

48. Chernikov, "Resource-Rich Regions—Irkutsk Oblast on the Road to the Market," 381.

49. Administratsiia Volgogradskoi Oblasti, "O gosudarstvennykh i territorial'nykh vnebiudzhetnykh fondakh," *Postanovlenie* #153, March 30, 1995.

tion to service the local budget. As a result of this trend, by 1998 Moscow banks held 66 percent of all local budget funds.[50]

Yet this rapid expansion caused problems for the Moscow banks as well. They often had trouble managing their extended branch networks, particularly because none of the banks had computer systems linking all of their branches. Moscow banks knew the local markets poorly, and often had little control over their staff. For instance, one branch of a Moscow bank in Vladivostok lent money to friends of bank executives there. When the friends could not repay, the bank ended up with the almost worthless container of Chinese cigarettes that it had accepted as collateral.[51]

Similarly, because the Moscow banks needed to develop close relationships with regional politicians in order to branch successfully, they faced the danger of these relationships backfiring. ONEKSIMbank, for example, ran into trouble in both Vladivostok and St. Petersburg. In Vladivostok, its subsidiary, Primor'e, served as an authorized bank of the Primorskii krai administration—which was filled with political enemies of Vladivostok mayor Viktor Cherepkov. Therefore, when the city and ONEKSIMbank discussed a lucrative deal to grant veksel credits to the region in 1996, Cherepkov absolutely refused to allow Primor'e to be involved.[52] In St. Petersburg, Mayor Vladimir Yakovlev's attempt to transfer city treasury accounts to BaltONEKSIMbank set off a political firestorm as local banks banded together to protest and the powerful Communist Duma deputy Vladimir Semago vigorously objected to the plan.[53] This regional expansion, though initially lucrative for the Moscow banks, extended their reach and therefore their responsibilities and vulnerabilities.

Only a few regions managed to maintain strong local banks alongside those from Moscow during this period. These regions had two things in common: they had self-sustaining economic bases (because of natural resources and / or trade ties) and independent-minded regional governments. Without the strong economic bases, regional banks would not have had the strong clientele necessary to persist under the Moscow onslaught. Only 11 of 89 regions of the Russian Federation had more than one strong regional bank in 1998, and the majority of them boasted oil, metals, or other export and trade industries (see Table 5.2). Oil greased the regional economies of both Tatarstan and Tiumen'. Western Siberia,

50. CBR, *Bulletin of Banking Statistics* 2 (1999): 115.

51. Jeffrey Millikan, banking consultant, Barents Group, interview with author, June 26, 1995, Moscow.

52. Denis Demkin, "Meru Cherepkovu ne nravitsia bank Primor'e," *Kommersant-Daily,* October 29, 1996.

53. Yuliia Pelekhova and Igor' Ivanov, "Bankiry otbili biudzhetnye scheta Peterburga u BaltONEKSIMbanka," *Kommersant-Daily,* March 28, 1997; and Igor' Ivanov, "Peterburgskie banki izvlekli urok iz istorii s BaltONEKSIMbankom," *Kommersant-Daily,* April 18, 1997.

Table 5.2. Regions with
multiple strong local banks
(excluding Moscow)
(more than 40 million
rubles of authorized capital
as of September 1998)

Region	Banks
Tatarstan	7
Tiumen'	5
Sverdlovsk	4
St. Petersburg	3
Kemerevo	3
Bashkortostan	2
Nizhnii Novgorod	2
Samara	2
Rostov	2
Krasnoiarsk	2
Sakha (Yakutia)	2

Source: Central Bank of
Russia, *Bulletin of Banking Statistics* 12 (1998).

where Kemerevo and Tiumen' are located, enjoyed the highest GDP per capita of any Russian region, 14.38 million pre-1998 rubles (152 percent above Russia's average) and was second only to the Central (Moscow) region in aggregate GDP.[54] Seven of the 11 regions with strong local banks, in fact, proved wealthy and troublesome enough to make the elite list of "donor" regions (regions that were net financial donors to the federal government).[55] Others, such as Nizhnii Novgorod, had received extensive outside support from Moscow and from international financial and aid agencies.

Wealth could not ensure strong local banks, though, without the support of the regional administration. The Russian geographer Klimanov distinguishes the most "closed" areas of the country (Volga, Northern Caucasus, Urals, and the North and Far East) from more "open" territo-

54. *Regiony Rossii*, 1996. In what appeared at the time to be a victory for the Yeltsin administration, the ruble was redenomiated: 1,000 rubles became 1 ruble on January 1, 1998.

55. Seven regions of the eighty-nine were consistently "donor" regions from 1996–99: Moscow City, Lipetsk, Samara, Sverdlovsk, Bashkortostan, Krasnoiarsk, and Khanty-Mansi and Yamal-Nenets (both in the Tiumen' region). East-West Institute, "Who Are the Donor Regions?" *Russian Regional Report* 4, no. 20 (May 27, 1999); and Alexander Fyodorov, "The Regional Subsidy Cockfight," *Business in Russia* 93 (September–October 1998): 28–32. In 1999, other donor regions included St. Petersburg, Moscow oblast', Tatarstan, Perm, and Irkutsk.

ries (Moscow, St. Petersburg, Central Black-Earth, Northwest, Volgo-Vi-atskii, and Central).[56] In the "closed" regions, regional administrations did the most to support local banks and restrict the Moscow banks. Tatarstan, for example, avidly protected its local banks. Although it did allow a few Moscow branches to open when they promised to provide credit to local enterprises and budget funds, the administration never relaxed its suspicion that these banks drained money from Tatarstan and continued to favor local banks.[57] This did not come without a price for the local banks. Tatarstan used its legal status as a republic within the federation to mandate that each bank in the region be at least one-third owned by the Tatarstan administration.[58] Nizhnii Novgorod took measures to protect its local banks in 1996 by passing a law labeling any Moscow bank an illegal monopoly if it gained a 35 percent market share.[59] Bashkortostan, long a politically autonomous and secretive republic, refused to make any administrative arrangements at all with Moscow banks until 1997, when it allowed Mezhprombank to introduce nationally linked plastic ATM cards into the region in exchange for granting credits to the region's pension fund.[60] The combination of regional wealth and governmental support of local banks did not prevent Moscow banks from expanding into these regions, but it did ensure that Moscow banks could not dominate them.

Importantly, the large regional banks did not play the same kind of powerful political role in their regions as the Moscow banks did in national government. While these regional banks operated under comparatively preferential economic conditions, politically they survived on the sufferance of the regional authorities, who demanded much of the banks in return.

Regional Banks: Strategies for Survival

Regional banks reacted to this competition as best they could. Further consolidation was the first and most natural strategy for most regional banks. Relatively strong regional banks continued to absorb smaller ones, and sometimes joined with each other in order to fend off competition. This spate of bank takeovers effectively continued to reassemble the old state banking networks. By the end of 1997, the CBR

56. Klimanov, "Territorial'naia organizatsiia," 18.
57. See Guzel' Fazullina, "Tatarstan," *Ekspert* 11 (March 23, 1998).
58. Klimanov, "Territorial'naia organizatsiia," 17.
59. Natalia Gurushina, "Nizhnii Novgorod Against Financial Monopolies," *OMRI Daily Digest*, November 7, 1996.
60. Vladimir Kovalevskii, "Moskovskomu banku pozvoleno sozdat' plastikovuiu platezh-nuiu sistemu Bashkirii," *Finansovye izvestiia*, March 27, 1997.

had registered 320 banks as "liquidated owing to takeover."[61] In a different kind of tie, the former Rostov branches of Agroprombank, Promstroibank, and Zhilsotsbank signed an agreement of cooperation and exchanged packets of shares.[62] Because of their local knowledge and connections, often this was enough for such banks to maintain a solid position, and it led to a greater concentration of financial resources in a smaller number of banks. Banks also formed regional organizations to protect their interests. In 1995, Volgograd banks formed a coordinating council with eight members, including the four largest former regional spetsbanks and the favored bank of the local administration (Kor Bank). Riazan' bankers formed their own regional organization in 1995 as well, with the chairman of the largest bank, PRIO-Vneshtorgbank, appointed as its head. Novosibirsk did the same, creating a regional banking association in 1995 that excluded local branches of Moscow banks.[63] While such associations could help protect local banks to a certain extent, in no instance did they prove decisive in keeping Moscow banks out of a region.

Most importantly, regional banks tied themselves more formally to regional enterprises by participating in the creation of industry-led financial-industrial groups (FIGs). At this point, the connection between banks and enterprises, which had frayed after 1992, was reforged. Russia's FIGs can be broken down into two major groups: bank-led and industry-led. The bank-led FIGs emerged as Russia's biggest banks began to acquire shares of privatized or privatizing companies. These banks tended to focus their interest on lucrative export or consumer industries, and succeeded in gaining control over many of Russia's leading enterprises. Industry-led FIGs, on the other hand, were generally based on old industrial ties, concentrated in depressed industrial sectors (particularly defense), and located in the regions. By 1996, both regional banks and regional enterprises had become so desperate for survival that they once again bonded together in order to protect each other and pressure the state for succor.

The banks participating in these industry-led FIGs were usually either local banks or, occasionally, Moscow-based banks that provided little actual support to other FIG members. Industry-led FIGs started consolidating informally in early 1993, but their numbers initially remained small. We can trace the development of industry-led financial-industrial groups by looking at the number of FIGs entered in the government's official FIG registry. (For a variety of reasons, bank-led FIGs typically found it undesirable to register themselves.) Despite Yeltsin's 1993 decree promoting FIGs, only

61. CBR, *Bulletin of Banking Statistics* 2 (1999): 67.
62. "Mestnye banki ukrepliaiut pozitsii," *Delovoe povolzh'e* 7 (February 1995): 1.
63. Viktor Titov, "Novosibirsk," *Ekspert* 11 (March 23, 1998).

7 FIGs had registered by the beginning of 1995. This number had grown to 28 by January 1996, and to 46 by January 1997. By July 1997, there were a total of 70 registered FIGs and about 100 more in the process of formation—it took approximately one year from the initial group formation to official registration.[64] Although the number of financial-industrial groups appeared impressive, registered FIGs often existed primarily on paper. The Russian government did not provide statistics on FIG profits, interenterprise arrears, or tax indebtedness.[65] In addition, numerous unregistered industry-led FIGs emerged around the country. Although the government did not collect official statistics on unregistered FIGs, all evidence indicates that they functioned much like their registered compatriots.

These industry-led FIGs served two primary purposes for their members: they allowed enterprise owners (either its managers or the state) to maintain control over company activities, and they reduced the economic risks inherent in operating in Russia's uncertain transitional conditions. Russia's initial privatization program (carried out from June 1992 through June 1994) laid the groundwork for the eventual creation of industry-led FIGs. Most enterprises (73 percent) chose to privatize themselves through "Option 2," which gave 51 percent of an enterprise's shares to its workers and management at nominal cost. In addition, an average of 20 percent of the rest of the shares in enterprises was given away in exchange for vouchers, not cash. This rapid privatization process yielded insider-controlled, cash-poor, change-averse enterprises. In this situation, many of them naturally turned to their old trading and financial partners for support in the effort to survive without giving up control to outsiders, an effort actively encouraged by many regional governments. When the banks began to suffer as well, they gained an incentive to cooperate with these enterprises in FIG creation.

Moreover, the central government created financial-industrial groups from above by encouraging (and sometimes forcing) enterprises still under majority state ownership to form FIGs. Certain state actors saw this as a way to maintain central control over enterprise activity and investment and hoped, through these FIGs, to carry out an activist industrial policy.[66] The state played a leading role in creating groups such as Skorostnoi Flot, Magnitogorsk Steel, the Russian Aviation Consortium, Nosta-Truby-Gaz,

64. Maria Tarasova, Director of Information Department, Association of Financial-Industrial Groups, interview with author, Moscow, July 18, 1997.

65. As of mid-1996, only 15 registered FIGs were estimated to be active. These 15 "are primarily those whose participants include metallurgical and raw materials enterprises, and this success has been achieved as a result of increased export." Moisei Gelman, "Finansovo-promyshlennye gruppy," *Delovoi mir,* June 27, 1996.

66. European Bank for Reconstruction and Development (EBRD), Credit Department, "Russian Financial-Industrial Groups" (ms, February 1997).

Ruskhim, Sokol, Volzhskaia Kompaniia, Interkhimprom, and the Kamenskaia Agricultural-Financial Group, among others, in some cases establishing them by presidential decree.

These FIGs (particularly those created from below) were also designed to help industries and regions achieve stability in unstable conditions by creating vertically integrated and closed production cycles, centralizing contract enforcement, facilitating barter arrangements, and spreading risk over a number of enterprises.[67] Economic and legal uncertainties encouraged enterprises to work with only a limited number of trusted partners, in most cases reforging and reinforcing ties from the Soviet-era economy. In addition, as Barry Ickes, Peter Murrell, and Randi Ryterman aptly observe, participating in a FIG enabled enterprises to carry out "informal profit-seeking activities," especially tax avoidance.[68] Finally, this search for economic stability included the belief that unified FIGs had a better chance of attracting foreign investment and government subsidies than did lone enterprises. Industry-led FIGs thus tended to form readily around troubled industries, notably defense, and tended to include fairly large enterprises in economically strapped regions (see Table 5.3).

These poor banks and underfunded, insider-dominated enterprises regularly and actively lobbied the state for support. In fact, even Yeltsin's original December 1993 decree promising aid to financial-industrial groups clearly resulted from lobbying by enterprise directors.[69] Their political supporters included a number of Russian government agencies, political parties, and lobbying organizations, including the Ministry of Industry, the Ministry of Economics, Civic Union, the Communist Party, Aleksandr Lebed's Congress of Russian Communities, the Union of Industrialists and Entrepreneurs, the Union of Manufacturers, and the League of Defense Enterprises.

For this group of politicians and industry supporters, huge Soviet-style conglomerates, vilified by Yeltsin and Gaidar's government in 1992, became the purported answer to Russia's investment woes. They began encouraging the development of financial-industrial groups in the hopes that FIGs would help to reverse the continual fall in production and

67. Kathryn Hendley, Barry W. Ickes, Peter Murrell, and Randi Ryterman, "Observations on the Use of Law by Russian Enterprises," *Post-Soviet Affairs* 13, no. 1 (1997): 19–41; Barry W. Ickes, Peter Murrell, and Randi Ryterman, "End of the Tunnel? The Effects of Financial Stabilization in Russia," *Post-Soviet Affairs* 13, no. 2 (1997): 105–33; Jane Prokop, "Industrial Conglomerates, Risk Spreading, and the Transition in Russia," *Communist Economies and Economic Transformation* 7, no. 1 (1995): 35–50; Irina Starodubrovskaia, "Financial-industrial Groups: Illusions and Realities," *Communist Economies and Economic Transformation* 7, no. 1 (1995): 5–19.
68. Ickes et al., "End of the Tunnel?"
69. Vladimir Buyev, "A New Soviet Economy," *Moscow Times*, February 12, 1994.

Table 5.3. Enterprises in registered financial-industrial groups by sector, 1997

Defense	163	19.0%
Food Processing	80	9.3
Chemical	72	8.4
Construction	49	5.7
Metallurgy	41	4.8
Mining	36	4.2
Agriculture	33	3.9
Machine-Building	32	3.7
Textiles	28	3.3
Trade	24	2.8

Source: Association of Financial-Industrial Groups, "Svedeniia o finansovo-promyshlennykh gruppax, vnesennykh v reestr FPG Rossiiskoi Federatsii" (April 1997).

dearth of investment in Russian industry. Invoking the example of South Korean and Japanese conglomerates, some government officials saw FIGs as a potential way to direct state investments, promote foreign investments in Russian industry, achieve economies of scale, and gain competitiveness on the world market.[70] Oleg Soskovets, first deputy prime minister until his firing in June 1996, particularly advocated this view and headed the Interagency Commission on Assistance with the Organization of Industrial Joint-Stock Companies and FIGs. In January 1996, the supporters of industry-led FIGs created a lobbying association under Soskovets's leadership, the Association of Financial-Industrial Groups, which stated that its main objectives were to defend the legal rights and interests of its members, to participate in drafting new legislation on FIGs, to coordinate the economic activities of financial industrial groups, to help establish new FIGs, and to represent the association's interests to the government.[71] Over 40 FIGs, as well as numerous other economic organizations, became official members of the association in the hopes that it would advance their political and economic interests.

70. Reportedly, Russian government officials particularly began supporting the concept of FIGs after a high-level Russian delegation visited South Korea in late 1992. EBRD, "Russian Financial-Industrial Groups."
71. Association of Financial-Industrial Groups, "Zasedaniem Soveta Assotsiatsii FPG Rossii: Konseptsiia deiatel'nosti Assotsiatsii Finansovo-Promyshlenykh Grupp," October 17, 1996; Association of Financial-Industrial Groups, "Assotsiatsiia finansovo-promyshlennykh grupp," brochure, July 1997.

The state acted at all levels to pass legislation promoting financial-industrial groups. Numerous decrees, regulations, and laws spelled out in glowing terms what FIGs were, what they could do for the economy, and what benefits their members would receive. The state promised registered FIG participants tax breaks, the transfer of state shares in member companies to the FIG, government loan guarantees, lower reserve requirements for participating banks, privileged involvement in state investment projects, and other boons. Government officials, enterprises, and banks held endless meetings, conferences, and roundtables to discuss ways to foster FIG development, and several government agencies were involved in registering, regulating, and promoting FIGs. Even the Anti-Monopoly Committee, which might have been expected to hold a dim view of FIGs, presented few obstacles to their development.

In practice, though, the government did not support the registered FIGs. Until a January 1997 decree allowing FIGs to keep consolidated balance sheets, they received no systematic tax breaks.[72] The CBR refused to lower the reserve requirements for banks participating in FIGs, while the State Property Committee proved extremely reluctant to directly transfer state shares in FIG-affiliated companies to the FIGs as provided for in the legislation. Only two FIGs, Ruskhim and Nosta-Truby-Gaz, were able to pry shares in their enterprises from the State Property Committee after their registration.[73] The registered industry-led FIGs were not given the opportunity to participate in special state investment programs and received few state loan guarantees. The roots of this neglect lay in unsurprising places: the government's dearth of money for such handouts (especially under the IMF's watchful eye), a lack of cooperation among the government agencies that would need to carry out the legislation, and the declining political power of the leading supporters of industry-led FIGs.

Industry-led FIGs did not prove to be mighty engines of Russian economic growth and restructuring, to put it mildly. For example, government officials supporting FIGs regularly pointed to the Nizhnii Novgorod-based chemical-sector FIG, Ruskhim (one of the first FIGs), as an example of a dynamic, active FIG with great economic potential.[74] In 1994, the State

72. Although the 1995 law on FIGs technically allowed the groups to keep a consolidated balance sheet, Article 13.2 of the law demanded that the Russian government pass a decree elucidating how these consolidated balance sheets were to be constructed. When this decree finally appeared, it represented a major victory for FIGs, enabling those that were registered to pay fewer taxes. They had been requesting such a decree for several years on the pretext that it would allow FIGs to keep unprofitable members in their group. The government conceded in the hope that this tax privilege would encourage unregistered FIGs to register.

73. Konstantin Baskaev, "Finansovo-promyshlennye gruppy oboidutsia bez sredstv biudzheta," *Finansovye izvestiia*, May 29, 1997.

74. Andrei Bagrov, "Predpriiatiiam FPG razreshili platit' nalogi khorom," *Kommersant-Daily*, June 10, 1995.

Property Committee even agreed to transfer the state's shares of two of the strongest chemical companies in the oblast' to Ruskhim. But in 1997 the oblast' initiated proceedings to reacquire these shares, claiming that Ruskhim did nothing at all to restructure or invest in these enterprises and refused to pay workers their wages. According to Boris Nemtsov, the former governor of the oblast' who later became Yeltsin's first deputy prime minister, Ruskhim and the other FIGs were "the ugliest form of mafia privatization and unlawful theft of state property."[75]

In another example, when asked to name some successful FIGs, out of the entire range of 70 possibilities an official of the Association of Financial-Industrial Groups listed four—three in agriculture and one in defense—all of which were associated with weak banks and involved troubled industries.[76] She felt that one in particular, the Belovskaia FIG in Kemerevo oblast', merited special praise because it institutionalized a barter arrangement between the region's mining and agricultural sectors. The collective farm members grew food, the food processing members processed and packaged it, and then they traded it to the mining members for coal. Since barter represented at least 40 percent of all trade taking place in Russia by 1997 and tended to follow established chains of production, it does not seem surprising that industry-led FIGs served to expedite and legitimate it.[77] However, by no stretch of the imagination can one consider this to be a positive step towards market-oriented restructuring and investment. If these represented the good examples, what were the other FIGs doing?

The underlying conundrum for industry-led FIGs was that they needed investment capital in order to restructure. Yet the investment capital could not or would not come from their associated banks. This is confirmed by examining the kinds of banks that chose to affiliate themselves with registered financial-industrial groups—fewer than half of the FIGs registered as of April 1997 had as a member a bank rated in the top 200 by assets.[78] Given that these top 200 banks held 85 percent of the assets of the entire Russian banking system, FIGs without such a bank as a member could hope for little in the way of investment from their financial partners.[79] Indeed, a study conducted by the European Union's TACIS pro-

75. Mikhail Larin, "Ruskhim mozhet lishit'sia dvykh predpriiatii," *Kommersant-Daily*, February 14, 1997.

76. Tarasova, interview with author, 1997.

77. Hendley et al., "Observations on the Use of Law."

78. Association of Financial-Industrial Groups, "Svedeniia o finansovo-promyshlennykh gruppakh, vnesennykh v reestr FPG Rossiiskoi Federatsii," April 1997. Rating, "Krupneishie banki Rossii," rating of top 200 banks by assets as of January 1997, *Izvestiia*, February 13, 1997.

79. Aleksandr Turbanov, Deputy Director of the Central Bank of Russia, "Sostoianie bankovskoi sistemy strany i perspektivy ee razvitiia," *Biznes i banki* 28, no. 350 (July 1997).

gram confirmed that fully four-fifths of registered FIGs received no more than short-term financing from their affiliated banks, and 30 percent received no financing whatsoever.[80] Similarly, these FIG-affiliated banks could not depend on their impoverished enterprise-partners for support. FIGs did not make their members better, only collectively bigger. Without state resources and privileges, these FIGs typically represented desperate attempts by banks and enterprises to stay in business in the absence of restructuring or investment. FIGs, mergers, associations, and similar lines of defense could not protect the regional banks from their Moscow competitors, nor revitalize Russia's declining industrial and agricultural base.

Riazan's Uberspetsbank

To further clarify the confusing and conflicting patterns of Russia's regional banking development, we will now turn to an extended case study of a typical large regional bank, PRIO-Vneshtorgbank in Riazan'. This bank's development epitomizes the way in which big Russian regional banks grappled with the post-Soviet economy by relying on state support and Soviet-era legacies to arise and compete while also engaging the market in creative ways. The history of the bank demonstrates how combining the institutional advantages of former spetsbanks, the protection of an affiliated state bank, and the connections and energetic leadership of a new commercial bank allowed PRIO-Vneshtorgbank to dominate the Riazan' region until 1998. Importantly, though, it also shows why few regional banks could realistically have adopted such a strategy: because of the extensive, long-term political and economic ties it required, no more than one or two banks in most regions could follow this kind of path.

Riazan' oblast' is an average, economically depressed region of Russia. As of 1999 it had only 7 local banks (with 8 total branches), no lucrative natural resources, and numerous marginal collective farms. Many of its major enterprises were a part of the economically troubled military-industrial complex. Nevertheless, by exploiting its political connections with the local government and Central Bank of Russia, merging with three former state banks, and pursuing an active management strategy, the small commercial bank Prioskii became PRIO-Vneshtorgbank, the most powerful bank in the Riazan' region and the 138th largest bank by assets in Russia in 1998. PRIO-Vneshtorgbank managed to stifle competition in the local banking market, drop its unwanted agricultural clients, foster its political ties with local and national leaders, and make money on the short-term currency and loan markets—all without making risky, long-term financial investments in Riazan' oblast'.

80. Vera Krasnova, "Bez deneg i bez strategii," *Ekspert* 22 (June 15, 1998): 27–28.

Named for the river Oka that flows through the city of Riazan', city leaders founded tiny Priokskii bank in October 1989. It was the first new commercial bank in Riazan', officially registered on December 6, 1989, with an authorized capital of five million rubles. Its then 28–year-old president, Vladimir Mazaev, previously directed the finance division of a major industrial enterprise, while the head of its board of directors, Aleksandr Kalashnikov, directed the large enterprise Agropromsnab. Not coincidentally, Kalashnikov's father formerly headed the oblast' communist party. Eighteen local enterprises joined together to provide the bank's start-up capital. At first the bank had only three staff members, with small office facilities inside the Riazan' Gosbank headquarters building. One original staffer recalls that "Our first acquisition was an adding machine, and after several months a Xerox appeared."[81] But with the help of the state, Priokskii grew quickly—it had over 5,000 clients by September 1994.[82]

Local Riazan' political and economic elites created the bank for their own purposes, as a way to gain more control over local finances and draw resources from the central government. Priokskii began its life as a commercial bank with the support of the local Gosbank branch, communist party organs, and government in Riazan'—support without which it could not have arisen. One bank employee stated that "From the very first, the leadership of the oblast' department of Gosbank supported us. It must not be forgotten that its head, Tamara Aleksandrovna Pigilova, was among those who initiated the creation of the first commercial bank in Riazan'."[83] The City Executive Committee of the Communist Party in Riazan' also became one of its founders, transferring 1.5 million rubles of its money to Priokskii bank in March 1990, soon after the bank began operations.[84] According to a vice-president of the bank, Oleg Churbanov:

[the local government] helped us politically in creating new branches . . . they gave us the opportunity to develop. This was the time when they could stop everything by the movement of a finger. . . . We were not getting loans from the central bank at the time because . . . they distributed state finance only among state-owned banks, Agroprombank and Promstroibank.[85]

81. Valentina Ul'ianova, Head of the Auditing Department, PRIO-Vneshtorgbank "V nachale byl faktoring," *Bankirskii dom* 8 (November 1994): 2.

82. PRIO-Vneshtorgbank fifth anniversary advertisement in *Priokskaia gazeta*, December 6, 1994, 3. As an interesting aside, PRIO-Vneshtorgbank celebrated its fifth birthday by paying for one day's free travel on public transportation for the entire city.

83. Ul'ianova, "V nachale byl faktoring." Tamara Pigilova remained the head of CBR Riazan' through 1999.

84. V. Volodin, "Finansiruet gorispolkom," *Priokskaia pravda*, March 23, 1990, 1.

85. Oleg Churbanov, vice-president, PRIO-Vneshtorgbank, interview with author, March 14, 1995, Riazan'.

Then, thanks to its political connections and the impending commercialization of the spetsbanks, this small commercial bank got the opportunity to merge with some of the region's breakaway branches of Agroprombank USSR in October 1990. It acquired thirteen new branches in this manner, and changed its name to Agroprom-Priobank.[86] As Churbanov states, the banks merged in part because Agroprombank had its own building and Priokskii did not, but:

> the [other] reasons were mostly political, because there was heavy fighting between the Communist committees which at that time had a lot of power . . . and the local office of the central bank. The idea of the Communist Party was to create a huge agricultural bank that could involve all of the branches of the former state bank, and they chose this small commercial bank as the basis for the agricultural bank. . . . But the position of the Central Bank was vice-versa, because at that time they had an idea of creating a large amount of small local banks with capital of 2–3 million rubles. . . . This was the time when everybody was crazy about independence, and in every small province they tried to found banks, governments, treasuries, even banks for foreign trade. Mostly it didn't work. Life made everything reasonable. . . . After one year of this poor experience, they tried to restore the old system.[87]

Thus, the party patrons of Priokskii bank won out, and the bank grew. Over time the bank picked up more errant former branches of the old Agroprombank network that had tried to go it alone. In this way, the bank greatly expanded its branch network and gained access to Central Bank subsidized credits at a time when using such credits was profitable.

As a defensive measure against losing its independence and becoming a purely agricultural bank, Agroprom-Priobank then adopted Vneshtorgbank Russia as its patron, joined its loose regional network, and became PRIO-Vneshtorgbank on November 21, 1991. As Churbanov observed, "this was the time when Rossel'khozbank was founded . . . and at that time, due to political reasons, there was a strong danger that we would be taken over by Rossel'khozbank." Vneshtorgbank, although it owned 51 percent of PRIO's stock, played little role in management: Churbanov claimed that "Despite the fact that we are their daughter, we don't feel they are interested in us very much. . . . They don't take our risks at all. . . . They help us sometimes to receive additional resources, additional funds. . . . They are nice shareholders, because they are bankers and they

---

86. "PRIO-bank god raboty," *Priokskaia pravda*, May 8, 1991, 2.
87. Churbanov, interview with author, 1995.

understand our problems." PRIO-Vneshtorgbank completed its mergers with the biggest former spetsbanks in Riazan' on October 27, 1992, when it merged with Prombiznesbank (a former branch of Promstroibank USSR). This bank, like many of its Promstroibank compatriots, had accumulated numerous bad debts since 1990.[88] In particular, Prombiznesbank had given almost 10 million rubles to a shady cooperative enterprise called "Oktan" and tried to cover its mistakes by using other funds in a questionable manner. After the CBR published this information, the president of the bank was suspended at a special shareholder meeting and later fired. Prombiznesbank tried to sue Oktan, but Oktan representatives never showed up at the hearing. When the bank's shareholders asked the CBR for credits to bail them out, the Central Bank made it known that it preferred to reorganize the bank as a branch of another bank. PRIO-Vneshtorgbank saw the value in absorbing the clients, connections, and premises of a former spetsbank and used its regional political clout in order to do so.

PRIO-Vneshtorgbank, in an unusually overt move for a provincial bank, also got involved in local politics. Bank president Vladimir Mazaev himself ran in the March 1994 elections to the oblast' Duma, but came in second to a Communist. His telling political slogan was "Vote for the youngest candidate!" (In the opinion of one Riazan' banker who shall remain nameless, Mazaev lost because people "think bankers suck blood.") Mazaev observed that "to work in this economy, to be a businessman, a banker and be outside politics is impossible today."[89] PRIO-Vneshtorgbank financed the campaigns of several candidates for oblast' and city elections in 1994. It also distributed leaflets outlining the platforms of various candidates, including one who directed an enterprise that just happened to be a major shareholder in the bank. To keep people from throwing the leaflets away immediately, the bank had the weekly television schedule printed on the flip side.

Like all commercial banks in Russia in this period, PRIO-Vneshtorgbank found itself trapped between the state and the market, needing to have one foot in the past and one in the future in order to survive. The bank could not have emerged and prospered without the patronage of local political and economic elites, but in the changing environment this patronage could not in itself ensure success. PRIO-Vneshtorgbank's active

88. Main Department of the CBR for Riazan' oblast', "Ugroza bankrotstva," *Priokskaia gazeta*, February 6, 1992, 1; and Stanislav Yushkovskii, "Do bankrotstva delo poka ne doshlo, no . . . ," *Priokskaia gazeta*, February 26, 1992, 1.
89. Interview with president of PRIO-Vneshtorgbank Vladimir Mazaev, "My prishli v rynok nadolgo i khotim, shtoby nam doverili," *Priokskaia gazeta*, October 19, 1994, 1.

management thus continued to build on the bank's strengths—it explored new banking services, advertised widely, and loaned cautiously. For example, because of its connections, PRIO-Vneshtorgbank was the first bank in Riazan' to get a hard currency license (in December 1991), and it quickly turned this to its advantage by opening numerous exchange points and offering competitive rates. It bought and sold privatization vouchers and operated on the secondary GKO market. (Riazan' is only about 200 kilometers southeast of Moscow). PRIO-Vneshtorgbank also continually tried to attract new capital, even at times advertising in the newspaper for new shareholders. It controlled a local auditing company and an insurance company.

Like most regional banks, it held the majority of its assets (57 percent) in loans, representing over half of all of the loans granted by commercial banks in the oblast'.[90] Despite its spetsbank history, it began to restructure its portfolio away from directed credits in 1993 when this activity became unprofitable. As Mazaev stated, "It has become obvious that it is no longer possible to build credit policy on the basis of trust in the government" and "in the current situation giving credits to enterprises at preferential rates . . . is a road to nowhere."[91]

Perhaps most astonishingly, this agriculturally oriented bank managed to shed most of its agricultural clients in 1995 thanks to Agroprombank's return to the region. In 1991–92, the Russian agricultural bank Rossel'khozbank expanded into all regions of Russia, gathering old pieces of its ancestor, Agroprombank USSR, back into the fold. But when it could not get control of PRIO-Vneshtorgbank, it opened up a completely new branch network in Riazan' oblast', providing PRIO-Vneshtorgbank with a golden opportunity to hand off its bad clients. Churbanov described the process:

> Agriculture in this region is not profitable . . . our agricultural companies must receive straight donations from the government. Now these donations are given in the form of bank credit. This is not normal, because we as a commercial bank accept the credit risk and the risk is extremely high. . . . We managed to dispose of all the customers that were in the agricultural business [in three regions of the oblast']. We managed to pass them over to Agroprombank. . . . In other regions where we didn't manage to do this job, we totally stopped granting loans to the agricultural companies. This was a

90. Priokskii kommercheskii regional'nyi bank Vneshtorgbanka Rossii, "Annual Report, 1994."

91. Interview with Vladimir Mazaev, "Universal'nost'—garantiia stabil'nosti banka," *Bankirskii dom* 2 (March 1994): 1.

very difficult decision, but . . . the agriculture business is growing worse and worse. . . . They are not even able to pay back the interest [on their loans].[92]

Therefore, PRIO-Vneshtorgbank rid itself of the agricultural albatross and restricted its lending to more profitable sectors of the economy, an opportunity that most other former state agricultural banks had not enjoyed.

Nevertheless, PRIO-Vneshtorgbank continued to grapple with the serious problems stemming from Soviet-era institutional legacies that affected all Russian banks. Change had to be gradual, and had to take place within a larger institutional context where production levels continued to fall, organized crime continued to expand, and banking technology, laws, and staff abilities remained primitive. As the chairman of the board of PRIO-Vneshtorgbank (and former head of Prombiznesbank) Viktor Ganishin observed, "The problem for us today is how to turn the quantity of growth into quality . . . This is the work of a whole period, not less than five years."[93] PRIO-Vneshtorgbank needed to shed bad clients, train its staff, fend off criminal organizations, compete with branches of Moscow banks flooding into the provinces, deal with the tax authorities, give fewer credits to its shareholders, and cope with the disastrous financial situation of most enterprises in the oblast' (11.4 percent of PRIO's outstanding loans were overdue in 1995).[94] Mazaev complained that "we were always surprised at how differently the directors of [PRIO-Vneshtorgbank] branches thought about and understood our problems. Several work in the old ways, weakly orienting themselves to the market sphere and nonsensically making decisions that contradict the interests of the bank."[95]

Political ties, a large banking network, and early market presence were vital to PRIO's survival; but survival also depended on active leadership, diversified banking activities, and the willingness and opportunity to shed needy clients. As a result, it gained a prominent position in Riazan' and managed to crowd out much of the local competition. However, by late 1996 even PRIO-Vneshtorgbank felt the squeeze of competition from

92. Churbanov, interviews with author, September 1, 1994, and 1995. On the timetable worked out between the two banks for the customer transfer, also see Tamara Dudnik, "V Agroprombank—po grafiku," *Priokskaia gazeta*, August 17, 1994, 1.

93. Interview with Viktor Ganishin, Chair of the Board of PRIO-Vneshtorgbank, "Dorozhit' imenem banka, kak svoim sobstvennym," *Bankirskii dom* 9–10 (December 1994): 3.

94. Viktor Ganishin, "Uspekh dostigaetsia umnozheniem kapitala na tvorchestvo," *Bankirskii dom* 3 (March 1995): 3.

95. Vladimir Mazaev, "Zhizn' vnosit korrektivy v politiku banka," *Bankirskii dom* 3 (March 1995): 2.

Moscow banks, a poor regional economy, and Riazan's expanding municipal bank. In 1996, PRIO-Vneshtorgbank participated in the founding of a Riazan' financial-industrial group, ROSSA-PRiM (with ten local enterprises and an investment company), with the avowed aim of attempting to increase the level and security of investments in the region. Subsequently, it broke ties with Vneshtorgbank when Vneshtorgbank decided that it no longer wanted to support a subsidiary in Riazan'. Vneshtorgbank gave PRIO a choice between becoming a full-fledged Vneshtorgbank branch or buying out Vneshtorgbank's shares, and PRIO's managers decided to retain its independence.

After the August 1998 collapse of the financial system, PRIO survived but lost its predominant position in Riazan' to staid, but state-owned, Sberbank. Its president Vladimir Mazaev, looking for a more profitable niche, became the director of the affiliated Riazan' Machine-Tool Factory. Oleg Churbanov followed him there; when I talked to him again in the summer of 1999, this erstwhile banker was just about to leave for a three-week sales trip to the United States.

The Concentration of Power

Between 1994 and 1998, Russia's banking sector became far more concentrated both vertically and horizontally, as Moscow banks branched out and drew financial capital into the center, and regional banks merged or went under. Of course, this Moscow-based concentration in and of itself should not be surprising; in most states, financial power is concentrated in one or two city centers. Czech geographer Jiři Blažek notes three reasons for this trend: the need for a highly qualified pool of labor, access to top-notch support services and customers, and superior technological and infrastructural networks.[96] All of these resources will be most accessible in a state's core, and therefore finance will typically gravitate there. Where countries want to develop strong regional financial networks, the state must often step in to facilitate it. For example, the United States restricted interstate branching in order to support regional banks. On the other end of the ideological spectrum, China purposefully used its banking system to redistribute resources to poorer regions. State banks took in money from households and redirected a "substantial" amount of funds to support state-owned enterprises; between 1989 and

96. Jiři Blažek, "The Development of the Regional Structure of the Banking Sector in the Czech Republic and its Implications for Future Development," *Acta Universitatis Carolinae 1997 Geographica*, Supplementum, 265–83. Also see Paul Krugman, *Geography and Trade* (Cambridge, Mass.: MIT Press, 1991).

1994, it annually redistributed funds worth about 4 percent of GDP.[97] Even in Russia itself, the EBRD's Financial Institutions Development Project "twinning" program, aimed at developing the country's financial sector, took great care to focus as much attention on regional banks as on Moscow-based ones.

Why would a state want to step in and develop strong regional financial institutions if market forces tend to concentrate wealth and expertise in the center? Strong centralization, especially in large federal states, can cause undesirable results. It can lead, for example, to poor loan policy in the regions due to lack of local expertise, and to a concentration of loan resources in the center. Enterprises located on the periphery of countries with centralized financial systems typically enjoy less access to credit than those in countries with decentralized financial systems.[98] In fact, centralized financial systems encourage "regional drainage," in which banks collect money in the regions and lend it in the center.[99] This kind of development can be particularly problematic in a post-communist state like Russia, which needed heavy loan and investment activity in the regions in order to develop both a market-oriented economic infrastructure and the middle class necessary for stable democracy. The hyperconcentration of financial resources in Moscow during this period thus proved counterproductive to the dual political and economic transformation.

Yet the rapid concentration of financial power in Moscow cannot be attributed solely, or even primarily, to market forces. In such an expansive country, especially one that began its life with an extremely large and dispersed banking sector, concentration should have progressed far more slowly. Politics, not economics, caused this accelerated effect. When macroeconomic stabilization took hold, regional banks suffered far more than Moscow banks, enabling Moscow banks to expand. Decisions made by the Yeltsin government catalyzed the expansion of banks from the center by allowing Moscow banks to make significant profits on GKOs and as authorized banks, protecting them from foreign competition, and subsidizing their moves into the regions. The Moscow banks, in turn, gained these privileges from the central government as a result of their accumulation of political power after 1988. The Russian government did not believe that it was in its interest to encourage the development of regional

97. Nicholas Lardy, "The Role of the People's Bank of China in the Interregional Redistribution of Funds: Implications for Guangdong Province" (ms, July 1996).

98. R. W. Hutchinson and D. G. McKillop, "Regional Financial Sector Models: An Application to the Northern Ireland Financial Sector," *Regional Studies* 24, no. 5 (1990): 421–31; and D. J. Porteous, *The Geography of Finance* (Avebury, England: Aldershot, 1995).

99. Gunnar Myrdal, *Economic Theory and Underdeveloped Regions* (London: Gerald Duckwords, 1957).

banks, so instead it facilitated the concentration of resources in Moscow-based banks through a combination of trickle-down policies and political favoritism. Although this may have brought the Yeltsin government short-term political benefits, it threatened the long-term development of the Russian economy while placing ever-more power in the hands of a small clique of wealthy Moscow financiers.

CHAPTER SIX

Russia's Financial-Industrial "Oligarchy"

> Wherever there is big money, there is war. It should not be forgotten that transfer of ownership is taking place on an unprecedented scale in this country. Therefore, it should hardly be expected that all the norms of ethics and morals will be observed in this battle.
>
> **—Leonid Nevzlin, Rosprom, 1998**

Although Moscow banks used their political influence and relative economic power to expand their banking businesses into the regions, they adopted another development strategy based on these same strengths that proved even more fateful and controversial. Taking advantage of the Russian government's second-phase privatization program, several prominent Moscow banks formed extensive bank-led financial-industrial groups between 1995 and 1997. The appearance of these FIGs alternately caused elation, confusion, and consternation on the part of Western observers. Boris Berezovskii, head of the influential FIG LogoVAZ, boldly (though inaccurately) claimed that six of these conglomerates alone controlled as much as 50 percent of the Russian economy by 1996.[1] Could the bank-led FIGs

1. The so-called Group of Seven bankers consisted of Berezovskii; Vladimir Potanin, the head of ONEKSIMbank and its associated financial-industrial ventures; Vladimir Gusinskii, leader of the Most banking and media group; Mikhail Khodorkovskii, leader of the Menatep-centered financial-industrial empire; Petr Aven and Mikhail Fridman of Al'fa Bank and its associated ventures; and Aleksandr Smolenskii, head of SBS-Agro (formerly Stolichnii Bank Sberezhnii). This list left out the two other heads of influential bank-led FIGs: Vladimir Vinogradov of Inkombank and Vitalii Malkin of Rossiiskii Kredit bank. See Chrystia Freeland, John Thornhill, and Andrew Gower, "Russia: Wealthy Clique Emerges from Kremlin Gloom," *Financial Times*, October 31, 1996; and Chrystia Freeland, John Thornhill,

represent the first significant steps towards the revitalization of Russian industry, or did they represent merely another link in the long chain of speculative financial strategies that banks had begun forging in the Gorbachev era? The fate of Russia's entire market transformation seemed to hang on the answer to this question.

The major bank-led FIGs centered around Menatep Bank, ONEKSIMbank, Al'fa Bank, Most Bank, LogoVAZ, Rossiiskii Kredit Bank, Inkombank, and SBS-Agro. Several of these banks created holding companies for their enterprises with different names: Rosprom (Menatep), Interros (ONEKSIMbank with MFK bank), Al'fa Group (Al'fa Bank), and Most Group and Media Most (Most Bank).[2] They joined together the biggest private banks in Russia with many of Russia's largest industrial enterprises, reaching the height of their influence in 1997 (see Table 6.1). Although discovering the precise range of their holdings is difficult, they clearly had significant power. ONEKSIMbank's Interros group alone claimed to hold significant stakes in seven of Russia's twenty largest companies.[3] They included Noril'sk Nickel, Russia's sixth-largest company and biggest nonferrous metals producer; Sidanko, the fifth-largest oil company; and Novolipetsk Metallurgical Combine, the second-largest ferrous metals producer.[4] Other major bank-led FIG holdings in oil included Menatep (Yukos) and LogoVAZ (Sibneft'). Rossiiskii Kredit owned, among other enterprises, Russia's largest ferrous metals producer (Lebedinsk Ore Processing).

Soviet-era institutional legacies and the uncertain post-Soviet economic and political environment were primary factors in the emergence of bank-led FIGs. The traditionally close ties between enterprises and the state, the penchant for creating giant economic concerns, the insider-dominated transactions, the bureaucratized corruption, and the impor-

---

and Andrew Gowers, "Russia: Moscow's Group of Seven," *Financial Times*, November 1, 1996.

2. LogoVAZ is a special case, because although it is a financial rather than an industrial organization, the actual banks affiliated with the FIG are comparatively small [See Table 6.1]. Boris Berezovskii used his connections at AvtoVAZ to create LogoVAZ in 1989 as a company to distribute and sell Lada cars. Much of LogoVAZ's initial capital came from this sales relationship with AvtoVAZ and the resulting Russian Automobile Alliance (AVVA) scheme, as well as from special government deals and tax breaks. Over the years, Berezovskii became known for acquiring *de facto* control over companies in which he did not hold the majority of shares—companies such as ORT and Aeroflot—by putting people close to him in top management positions. See, for example, Dan Medovnikov and Aleksei Khazbiev, "Novaia operatsiia Kontserna AVVA," *Ekspert* 18 (May 19, 1997).

3. Craig Mellow, "Russia's Robber Barons," *Fortune*, February 3, 1997.

4. For a concise listing of Russia's top 100 companies by market capitalization at that time, see Joseph Blasi, Maya Kroumova, and Douglas Kruse, *Kremlin Capitalism* (Ithaca, N.Y.: ILR Press and Cornell University Press, 1996). This table does not, however, include details of company ownership.

Table 6.1. Selected business interests of the bank-led financial-industrial groups in 1997

Bank-led financial-industrial group	Financial affiliates, holding companies, and subsidiaries	Sectors of investment	Key stakeholdings and interests
Al'fa Group	Al'fa Bank; Al'fa Kapital; Al'fa Cement; Al'fa Art; Al'fa Estate; Al'fa-Eko; Al'fa-Om; New Holding; Volshkaia Kompaniia FIG	Cement (8 companies), oil, food processing, chemicals, trading More than 30 enterprises	Tiumen' oil; Liubiatov factory; Volzhkii, Nizhnii Tagil, and Spasskii cement plants; Tverkhimvolokono; Misha M; Smail; Mikromashina; Office-business center 'Arbat'; Dacha-building companies Rozhdestvono and Krilatskoe
Inkombank	Inkomkhim; Babaev Holding; Rusleskom; Ruskonditprom; Intermetall; Metallurgical Investment; Inkom-Kapital; Inkom-Trade; Dom-Inkom; Inkom-Fond; Inkom-Invest; Inkom-Start; Inkom-Gold; Inkom-Trast; Inkom-Ilim; Sochistroiservis; Inkom Mortgage; Nosta-Truby-Gaz FIG; Morskaia Tekhnika FIG	Confectionary (controlled 15% of the Russian market), metallurgy, aircraft, pipes More than 26 enterprises	Five candy factories (Babaevskoe, Rot-Front, Yuzuralkonditer, Sormovskaia, and Novosibirsk); SAMEKO (Samara Aluminum); Magnitogorsk Steel; Nosta; Sokol
LogoVAZ	AVVA; Ob"edenennyi Bank; AvtoVAZbank; Oil Financial Company; Financial Oil Company; Volga-Kama Group FIG	Oil, transportation, media	Sibneft'; Aeroflot; Andava (Swiss); ORT; *Nezavisimaia gazeta*; *Ogonek*; Novaia kompaniia; TV-6
Most Group	Most Bank; Media Most; Most Investment; Most Construction; Movis	Real estate, media 42 "operating companies" and 10 "property firms"	NTV; *Segodnia*; Itogi; Eko Moskvy; Sem' Dnei

Table 6.1. Selected business interests of the bank-led financial-industrial groups in 1997 (*continued*)

Bank-led financial-industrial group	Financial affiliates, holding companies, and subsidiaries	Sectors of investment	Key stakeholdings and interests
Menatep / Rosprom	Alliance-Menatep; Menatep International Financial Group; Menatepstroi-Komplekt; Menatep Invest; SKB-Samara; Menatep-Finance SA (Swiss); Novocherkassk Bank; Menatep Bank St. Petersburg; Laguna; Monblan; Menatep trading; IMPEX trading; Russian Trust and Trade JV; Progress Insurance; Russian Textile Consortium FIG; Eksokhim FIG	Oil, petrochemicals, food processing, textiles, metallurgy, construction, fertilizers, paper More than 40 affiliated enterprises	Yukos oil; Koloss; Apetit; Nitron; Ammophos; Avisma; Ust'-Ilimsk LPK; Murmansk Shipping; Orenburg Plant; Irkutsk Plant; Galeria Manezh; Volgotanker; Robot; Mibel; Pokrovka; Mosalsk; Independent Media Group; *Literaturnaia gazeta*
ONEKSIMbank/ Interros	MFK Bank (International Financial Company); Renaissance Capital; Banque Unexim Swiss; BaltONEKSIMbank; KabbONEKSIMbank; Primor'e Bank; ONEKSIM-Volga Bank; MFK-Moscow Partners; Garant Invest; ICFI; Interros-Oil; Interros-Dostoinstvo; Interros-Soglasie; Interros-Leasing; Interros-Impex; Interros-Estate; Rosinspekt; Rosekspertiza; Temp Eksim; Rimbak; KM-Invest; Mustcom Ltd; Svift; Volshkaia Kompaniia FIG	Oil, petrochemicals, shipping, metallurgy, railways, export trade, real estate, media Over 30 enterprises	Noril'sk Nickel; Sidanko; Sviaz'invest; East-West Shipping; Surgutneftegaz; UCS; Ulba; Novolipetsk Metallurgical Combine; Novokuznetsk Aluminum; Kuznetsk Metallurgical; Nitrogen; Irgiz; Phosphorit; Mikrodin Group; Energiia Group; Perm Motors; Oktiabr'skaia Railway; Lomo; Kovrov machine-building; Sorbent; Khimvolokno; *Izvestiia*; *Ekspert*; *Komsomolskaia pravda*

Rossiiskii Kredit	Rossiiskii Kredit holding; AO Kont; Roskreditinvest; RK-Garant; Ruskhim FIG; Sviatogor FIG; Tochnost' FIG	Metallurgy/mining (85% of bank's investments); chemicals, timber, hotels Over 40 enterprises	Lebedinskii Mining; Mikhailovskii Mining; Stoilenskii Mining; Urals Gold; Krasnoiarsk Aluminum; Orel Steel; Bezhetsk Steel; Novosibirsk Tin Plant; Berdsk Radio; Diffusion; Sapfir; RUMO; Vega
SBS-Agro	Stolichnii Bank Sberezhnii; Agroprombank; Zoloto-Platina Bank; Unified Depositary Company; Alikon Securities; Niva Chernozem'ia FIG	Agriculture, construction, retail trade, credit cards, media	STB (credit cards); *Kommersant Daily*; *Novaia gazeta*, ORT

Selected Sources: Al'fa Bank, "Annual Report 1994" and <http://www.alfa.ru> 1997; Association of Financial-Industrial Groups, "Svedeniia o finansovo-promyshlennykh gruppax, vnesennykh v reestr FPG Rossiiskoi Federatsii," April 1997; *Banki Moskvy* (Moscow: Intelbridge Plus, 1997); European Bank for Reconstruction and Development, Credit Department, "Russian Financial-Industrial Groups," February 1997; Inkombank, "Annual Report 1994" and "Annual Report 1995"; Nikita Kirichenko and Andrei Shmarov, "Vtoraia neftianaia voina," *Ekspert* 2 (May 1997); *Kommersant-Daily*, "Problemy Severno-Zapadnovo parokhodstva," July 30, 1997; Vladimir Kovalevskii, "Gruppa 'Most' stavit na televizionno-izdatel'skii biznes," *Finansovye izvestiia*, January 30, 1997; Craig Mellow, "Russia's Robber Barons," *Fortune*, February 3, 1997; Menatep, "Annual Report 1995" and <http://www.menatepbank.ru> 1997; National News Service, <http://www.nns.ru/business> (1995 and 1996); ONEKSIMbank, "Annual Report 1994"; Robert Orttung, "Chocolate Wars: Moscow Giants Buy Regional Confectionaries," *IEWS Russian Regional Report*, June 5, 1997; Rossiiskii Kredit, "Annual Report 1994" and <http://www.roscredit.msk.su> (1997); and Alessandra Stanley, "A Russian's Sprint from Car Dealer to Tycoon," *New York Times*, June 14, 1997.

tance of accumulating political power in order to wield economic clout had their roots in Soviet times. Russia's transitional conditions exacerbated these tendencies, allowing well-placed individuals to concentrate assets in their own hands in an atmosphere of uncertain property rights, within an underdeveloped legal system, and amidst poor investment conditions. This combination of factors led influential bankers and investment-hungry enterprises to run not to each other, but to the Russian state in order to meet their respective needs. The Yeltsin government then bowed to these desires by agreeing to privatize Russia's leading enterprises through questionable bank-controlled auctions.

As Menatep founder Mikhail Khodorkovskii observed, "In our country, as in Japan, big business can't survive outside the government.... It's much easier for me to give a speech at a factory as a representative of the government."[5] The bank-led FIGs relied on the state to help them acquire and wield control over the most viable Russian enterprises without going broke in the process. The Yeltsin team, indebted to the bankers for political support, desperate for money to keep the government running, and firm in the Western-encouraged belief that trickle-down privatization would forward Russia's market transformation, happily acquiesced in this role. This chapter focuses on the evolution of the bank-led FIGs, examining their bold efforts to further amass political power, their reliance on state favoritism to gain control over leading Russian enterprises, their competition and collusion with each other, and their ineffective, half-hearted attempts to restructure the enterprises they acquired.

To understand the bank-led FIGs, two things must be kept in mind. First, for a variety of reasons related to the intricacies of the Russian legal, tax, and accounting systems (and the desirability of sidestepping them), the precise owner of a bank-affiliated enterprise might or might not be the main bank itself. The primary holding companies (such as Interros) and the leading banks (such as ONEKSIMbank) typically controlled a number of subsidiary companies (such as Interros-Oil). Member companies could technically be owned by the primary holding company, the bank itself, by subsidiary or affiliated companies, or by any combination of these.[6] By September 1998, Moscow banks had amassed 4.4 billion rubles-

5. Interview with Mikhail Khodorkovskii, "Krupnyi biznes ne mozhet sushchestvovat' vne gosudarstva," *Kommersant*, April 16, 1996. Some scholars whose research has concentrated on Southern Europe and Latin America interpret this as an example of corporatist development in Russia. While valuable parallels can indeed be drawn, fundamentally the invocation of corporatism to describe Russia's economic structure seems misleading. In particular, the absence of an effective labor movement in Russia and the intense competition among elite business interests precludes describing Russia as an emerging corporatist state.

6. Therefore, when I refer to a bank "owning" an enterprise, the legal owner may actually be a different part of the bank's empire. For example, if I refer to a company "controlled by

worth of stakes in subsidiaries and affiliated companies, representing 94.5 percent of such investments by Russian banks in total.[7]

Second, the banks' president-founders closely controlled the economic and political activities of these bank-led FIGs. The name "Mikhail Khodorkovskii" is synonymous with "Menatep"; "Vladimir Vinogradov" with "Inkombank"; and so on. Therefore, the bank-led FIGs' successes and failures corresponded directly to the political and business alliances made by the banks' leaders. The bank-led FIGs were managed autocratically from above—in almost all cases, the man at the top made the key decisions. Moreover, in 1996 many of these bankers started leaving their official posts as bank directors in order to head up their holding companies. Khodorkovskii, for example, became director of Rosprom, while Gusinskii became president of Media Most. The leaders of the bank-led FIGs (along with the directors of Gazprom and Lukoil) comprised Russia's so-called financial-industrial "oligarchy," a small group that wielded political power disproportionate to its actual economic importance and public support in Russia.

A Vicious Symbiosis: Bankers in Politics

Without amassing political power, the bank-led FIGs could not have acquired and maintained their industrial empires. The largest banks built on their political origins and their efforts in the 1993 Duma elections to become key political players in Russia. Three factors underpinned this influence: their ownership of media outlets, their continuing financial support for political parties and candidates, and their close ties to the Yeltsin government. The government, in turn, depended on the banks not only for campaign finance but for operating capital at all levels, from local to national organs of power. Bankers used this power to advance their own economic, political, and legal agendas, which were designed to protect and enrich the bank-led FIGs.

Banks and the Media

Bankers had managed to gain control over a surprising number of the most important Russian media outlets by 1995. This gave them the power to mold public opinion—influence which was not lost on any of Russia's politicians. Media Most, the largest such conglomerate, gathered together several media outlets, including a major national television sta-

---

Menatep," the legal owner may be Rosprom (the main holding company), the bank itself, or another subsidiary company.

7. CBR, *Bulletin of Banking Statistics* 2 (1999): 133.

tion (NTV), the publishing house "Sem' Dnei," and the newspaper *Segodnia*. At that time, LogoVAZ controlled both Russia's leading television station ORT (with SBS-Agro) and the now-ironically named newspaper *Nezavisimaia gazeta* (*The Independent*); SBS-Agro supported the financial newspaper *Kommersant-Daily*; ONEKSIMbank acquired major stakes in the popular national newspapers *Izvestiia* and *Komsomolskaia pravda*; and Menatep held a stake in the Independent Media Group, owner of Russia's two major English-language dailies. In fact, by mid-1997 only a few major media outlets, such as RTR TV (state-owned), were not owned at least in part by bank-led FIGs.

Although many newspaper editors, in particular, fought against this trend, the difficulty of raising enough money to finance a major Russian media outlet was so extreme that they rarely won these battles. The most dramatic example of an editor fighting, and losing, such a battle with his paper's owners occurred in 1997 at *Izvestiia*, whose major shareholders were ONEKSIMbank and Lukoil. *Izvestiia* reprinted a story from the French paper *Le Monde* claiming that Prime Minister Viktor Chernomyrdin had amassed a fortune from his dealings with Gazprom. Chernomyrdin had been director of Gazprom before becoming prime minister, and continued to vigorously champion its interests while in office. Lukoil, closely affiliated with both Chernomyrdin and Gazprom, pressured the paper to stop its criticism of the prime minister. *Izvestiia*, rather than capitulating, ran stories denouncing this pressure. Editors of other papers owned by various business interests supported it in this effort. Eventually, though, Lukoil and ONEKSIMbank took control of the paper's board of directors and forced *Izvestiia*'s long-time editor Igor' Golembiovskii to resign. As a parting shot, Golembiovskii ran a story accusing ONEKSIMbank, its partner MFK Bank, and Unikombank of conspiring to defraud the Russian government of over $500 million in two deals approved by MFK's then-president Andrei Vavilov while he had been first deputy finance minister.[8]

Campaign Finance

In the 1993 Duma elections, banks had publicly supported a wide variety of parties. By the December 1995 Duma elections, though, most

8. See *Izvestiia*, "Biznes i pressa," April 17, 1997; David Hoffman, "Editors of Izvestiia Take on Owners," *Washington Post*, April 22, 1997; Gleb P'ianykh, "ONEKSIMbank: Vystuplenie i nakazanie," *Kommersant*, July 15, 1997; and Stephanie Baker-Said, "Vavilov Denies Dubinin Charges," *Moscow Times*, July 16, 1997. Further details of the scandal appear in chapter 7.

large Moscow banks had realized that they could now benefit more by throwing their resources behind Prime Minister Viktor Chernomyrdin's newly created "party of power," Our Home Is Russia. Although Yeltsin himself refused to identify with a political party, Our Home Is Russia received overt backing from the Kremlin. Therefore, banks such as Most Bank and Inkombank chose to support Chernomyrdin's party as well. The prime minister also had significant financial backing from his old friends in the oil and gas industry, particularly Gazprom and Gazprombank.[9] For this reason the party earned the nickname "Our Home—Gazprom," which also rhymes in Russian.

A few other banks continued to support opposing parties. Tokobank channeled financial support to Vladimir Zhirinovskii's misnamed Liberal Democratic Party of Russia. Bank Imperial lined up behind Duma speaker Ivan Rybkin's ill-fated bloc, and bank president Sergei Rodionov appeared on the party list. Even the Beer Lovers' Party, whose slogan was "Beer for Everyone!", had a number of directors of medium-size banks on its party list and was financed by Promradtekhbank and MBTS-Bank. In general, according to ARB spokesman Aleksandr Zagriadskii, "with the help of commercial banks, a group of 10–12 individuals [friendly to the financial sector] made it into Parliament, and we are satisfied with our cooperation."[10] While the Communist Party did well in these elections, earning 22.3 percent of the party-list vote and 34.9 percent of the overall seats, Our Home Is Russia gained parliamentary representation with only 10.1 percent of the party list vote and 12.2 percent of the overall seats. Once again, the stage had been set for a standoff between president and parliament.

For the bankers, though, the June 1996 presidential elections represented the real test of their power. Considering the poor showing of pro-government parties in the December 1995 parliamentary elections and Yeltsin's own single-digit approval ratings at that time, Russian bankers realized that Yeltsin needed a huge boost in order to defeat the Communist candidate, Gennady Zyuganov. According to the bankers themselves, they came to this conclusion while meeting in February 1996 at the World Economic Forum in Davos, where Zyuganov enjoyed some success in persuading Western businesspeople that they could deal with the Commu-

9. In June 1995, Gazprom pulled its accounts out of Bank Imperial and Vneshtorgbank, transferring them to Gazprombank. *Kommersant-Daily* speculated that this was in part to concentrate Gazprom's resources for financing Viktor Chernomyrdin's party. Aleksandr Andrianov, "Gazprombank mozhet stat' mestom sbora 'gazodollarov'," *Kommersant-Daily*, June 27, 1995, 1.

10. Quoted in Alexander Gubsky, "Massaging the System: How Russia's Increasingly Clever Duma Lobbyists Conspire to Get the Legislation They Want," *Russia Review* 3, no. 85 (February 26, 1996): 10.

nists.[11] In March, the bankers encouraged Yeltsin to dump his bumbling electoral campaign committee led by industrialist Oleg Soskovets and presidential security service head Aleksandr Korzhakov, and bring back their ally, Anatolii Chubais, making their financial support contingent on this switch.[12] After Yeltsin did so, Chubais immediately began to recast the election as a black-and-white struggle between old-style Soviet communism and a prosperous, democratic future.

Although Russia's campaign finance laws officially limited each candidate's campaign spending to $3 million, Yeltsin's own team admitted that banks channeled at least $100 million to his presidential campaign, while Russian journalists have estimated the amount to be no less than $500 million. The entire election campaign was fraught with accusations of unlawful spending and influence, which reached a fever pitch when two Yeltsin aides were stopped carrying a box with over $500,000 in cash from the Russian "White House." Allegedly, the money had come from the state budget itself, "laundered" through the National Reserve Bank and Gazprom.[13] Recall too that near the end of the campaign Yeltsin liberated a great deal of money from the Central Bank of Russia, forcing it to sell GKOs to raise fast cash in support of the Yeltsin government.

The support of the bankers extended beyond mere money, as they used their media control to attempt to sway voters. The financiers backed an election-season newspaper called "Ne Dai Bog!" (God Forbid!) that spelled out the potential dangers of a Communist victory, and Yeltsin's campaign commercials featured dark images from the past to frighten voters into thinking twice before choosing Zyuganov. While Yeltsin regularly appeared on television and in the press looking chipper and concerned for the welfare of average Russians, Zyuganov received far less (and far more negative) coverage. In fact, an independent study done by the European Institute for the Media found that Yeltsin enjoyed 53 percent of campaign broadcast time in the electronic media during the run-up to the first round of the elections, compared to only 18 percent for Zyuganov. During the two weeks between the first and second rounds of the election, positive references to Yeltsin outweighed negative ones by 247, while poor Zyuganov's references hit negative 240.[14] Bankers were

11. Lee Hockstader and David Hoffman, "Yeltsin Campaign Rose from Tears to Triumph," *Washington Post,* July 6, 1996, A1.

12. Michael McFaul, "Russia's 1996 Presidential Elections," *Post-Soviet Affairs* 12, no. 4 (1996): 318–50.

13. Hockstader and Hoffman, "Yeltsin Campaign Rose from Tears to Triumph," A1; and Leonid Krutakov, "Budget Money Laundering for NDR Claimed," *Moskovskii Komsomolets,* June 3, 1999.

14. Peter Rutland, "Independent Monitoring Group: Election Coverage was Unfair," *OMRI Presidential Election Report* 15 (July 9, 1996).

also instrumental in engineering the second-round alliance between Yeltsin and presidential candidate Aleksandr Lebed, and began heavily supporting Lebed in the media.[15]

In short, without the support of Russian financial interests, it would have been extremely difficult for Yeltsin to have won the presidential election. Yet the Appeal of the Thirteen that Russian bankers and businessmen had published on April 26 revealed their true feelings about the virtues of democracy. As the appeal attested, if democratic processes had threatened their financial empires, the bankers would have gladly run roughshod over them.[16]

The Revolving Door

Finally, leading bankers moved freely from their corner offices to the corridors of power and vice-versa. Over time, this interpenetration of business and government solidified the bankers' political influence from the inside out. A few examples will suffice. Viktor Khlystun, who was the minister of agriculture from 1991 to fall 1994, was reappointed to that same post by Yeltsin in May 1996. In the interim, Khlystun served as the first vice-president of Agroprombank.[17] Sergei Rodionov, the head of Bank Imperial, used to be the deputy director of the CBR. Until February 1995, former Politburo member and head of the USSR Council of Ministers Nikolai Ryzhkov headed Tver'universalbank's board of directors.[18] Avtobank chair Natal'ia Raevskaia previously worked in the Ministry of Finance.[19] CBR director Sergei Dubinin had served as acting finance minister and the first vice-president of Bank Imperial before his appointment. CBR director Gerashchenko became the chair of the International Moscow Bank after his resignation in 1994.[20] Leonard Vid, former executive director of Our Home Is Russia, and a few years earlier the deputy director of Gosplan, became head of Al'fa Bank's board of directors in early 1996.[21] After his firing in early 1997, first deputy finance minister Andrei Vavilov became president of the ONEKSIMbank-controlled MFK Bank. In February 1997, CBR deputy director Rinat Setdikov resigned

15. Peter Rutland, "Money, Guns, and Votes: The Currency of Power in Russia," *OMRI Analytical Briefs*, June 21, 1996.

16. "Get Out of the Impasse!" *Kommersant-Daily*, April 27, 1996. See chapter 1 for details.

17. Penny Morvant and Laura Belin, "Agriculture Minister Reappointed," *OMRI Daily Digest*, May 15, 1996.

18. "Ryzhkov nachal predvybornuiu kampaniiu?" *Izvestiia*, April 7, 1995, 1.

19. Viktoria Lebedeva, "Evropeiskii bank stanet aktsionerom Avtobanka," *Kommersant-Daily*, October 30, 1996.

20. Viktor Gerashchenko, "Antireiting," *Kommersant-Daily*, September 4, 1996.

21. Marina Tal'skaia, "Byvshie rukovoditeli Gosplana teper' v tsene," *Finansovye izvestiia*, February 20, 1996, 3.

and went to work for SBS-Agro. Yeltsin's former press secretary Viacheslav Kostikov became deputy director of Media Most in July 1997. Al'fa Bank's president Petr Aven was Russia's minister of foreign economic relations until 1992.

In the reverse direction, and most controversially, in August 1996 Yeltsin named ONEKSIMbank president Vladimir Potanin to the post of first deputy prime minister in charge of economic affairs, and a few months later named LogoVAZ director Boris Berezovskii to Russia's Security Council.[22] Both Russians and Westerners recognized these appointments as direct payback for the bankers' active support of Yeltsin's presidential campaign. Potanin lost his post in the February 1997 government reshuffle and immediately returned to head ONEKSIMbank, while Yeltsin fired Berezovskii in November 1997 at the initiative of First Deputy Prime Ministers Chubais and Nemtsov. Berezovskii, it seemed, had been accused of mixing business and politics.[23] This conflict of interest did not prevent Yeltsin from rehiring Berezovskii as executive secretary of the Commonwealth of Independent States (CIS) in April 1998, a post he held until March 1999.

The Loans-for-Shares Scandal

Bankers showed little restraint in using their political power to press the state for further privileges. They remained eager to lobby for and accept state investment support, and some bankers (especially Mikhail Khodorkovskii) complained that the state did too little to encourage long-term investment by banks.[24] Bankers particularly took advantage of their political influence by acquiring enterprises cheaply in the "loans-for-shares" program, which gave the most privileged of the emerging bank-led FIGs control over key Russian export and raw materials enterprises.

As we have seen, during the first years of the transition, Russia's big, politically connected banks had little reason to invest heavily in industry and were not important players in the initial privatization process. Bank-led FIGs first began to emerge quite tentatively in 1993 and 1994. In the

---

22. For analyses of the significance behind Potanin's appointment, see Stepen Kisilev, "Gosudarstvo—ta zhe firma, tol'ko ochen' bol'shaia," *Izvestiia*, August 16, 1996; and *Kommersant-Daily*, "Iz interviu Vladimira Potanina," August 16, 1996.

23. Christian Lowe, "Kremlin Dumps Billionaire Berezovsky," *Moscow Times*, November 6, 1997.

24. This claim seems especially disingenuous on Khodorkovskii's part, as his Yukos oil received over 1.4 trillion rubles in subsidies from the state in 1996, trailing only Gazprom and AvtoVAZ as a recipient of state largesse. Michael McFaul, "Russia's 'Weak' and 'Privatized' State as an Impediment to Democratic Consolidation" (ms, July 1997).

early stages, the banks focused on acquiring enterprises in consumer goods, construction, textiles, chemicals, and other kinds of light industries in which they could gather significant packets of shares. Inkombank, for example, invested in confectioneries and timber, while Al'fa Bank became involved in construction, Rossiiskii Kredit in metals, and Menatep in food processing and textiles. The banks formed holding companies for their acquisitions during this period as well (although Interros had preceded ONEKSIMbank). During this process, the banks found that their evolving groups served many useful purposes, including providing a bank with guaranteed enterprise customers, tax havens, less uncertainty in lending, and enterprise revenue with which to carry out short-term financial dealings.

Then, as inflation subsided and their sources of easy money dried up, the big banks looked toward investing in the largest export-oriented Russian industries (particularly oil and metals). Yet they faced major obstacles—most companies remained poor credit risks, with opaque books, Soviet-era managers, and little desire or ability to repay loans. As Sergei Osiniagov, chairman of the board of MFK Bank, observed, "MFK undertakes strategic investment. But there are very few like us. Not least because in order to do something with an enterprise you need to buy it outright, and not just some packet of its shares."[25] The banks, therefore, tried—and to a great extent succeeded—in gaining actual control over many companies. By using their political connections, several favored banks took this process to a new level by acquiring some of the biggest state-owned enterprises in the 1995 loans-for-shares auctions.

These auctions represented the most famous—or, more properly, infamous—privatization episodes in Russia. In March 1995, a consortium of banks led by ONEKSIMbank developed a scheme to lend the Russian government 9 trillion rubles (about $2 billion) in exchange for getting management control over the state's shares of several large companies for five years and (possibly) gaining eventual ownership.[26] The Yeltsin government, eager to acquire financial resources through the cash privatization process, expressed interest in the plan. Although the consortium itself fell apart, this concept evolved into the loans-for-shares auctions. After a series of exploratory meetings between bankers and the Yeltsin team, the blow dealt to the bankers in the August 1995 interbank credit crisis and the Yeltsin government's need for banker support in the upcoming December 1995 Duma elections sealed the deal. Masterminded by Anatolii Chubais and State Property Committee director Alfred Kokh, twelve

---

25. Aleksandr Polianskii, interview with MFK Bank Chairman of the Board Sergei Osiniagov, *Delovye liudi* 74, February 1997.

26. "JP Morgansky?" *The Economist*, April 15, 1995.

loans-for-shares auctions took place in November and December 1995. The Duma opposed such auctions from the beginning but proved powerless to stop them, as Yeltsin authorized them by decree. These loans-for-shares auctions allowed several banks to acquire significant stakes in key Russian export companies for rock-bottom prices.[27]

The main beneficiaries of the auctions were ONEKSIMbank, which acquired packets of shares in Sidanko oil, Noril'sk Nickel, and Novolipetsk Metallurgical Combine; Menatep, which won control of 45 percent of the shares of Yukos oil, another 33 percent of Yukos in a simultaneous investment tender, and 24 percent of Murmansk Shipping; and LogoVAZ, which gained influence over 51 percent of Sibneft' oil by proxy (with the participation of SBS). After the auctions, ONEKSIMbank, Menatep, and LogoVAZ markedly increased their influence in these companies through additional share purchases by their subsidiaries, holding companies, or affiliates.

The loans-for-shares auctions themselves were riddled with allegations of fraud, as the Yeltsin government allowed favored banks both to organize and to bid in the share auctions. Not surprisingly, the bank organizing an auction usually managed to win it. In particular, the auctions favored ONEKSIMbank, MFK, Menatep, and SBS over Inkombank, Al'fa Bank, and Rossiiskii Kredit. In the most contentious case, ONEKSIMbank won control over Noril'sk Nickel after the disqualification of Rossiiskii Kredit's higher bid. Similarly, Menatep won control over Yukos after the disqualification of a joint competitive bid from Inkombank, Al'fa Bank, and Rossiiskii Kredit. Moreover, during these auctions the State Property Committee permitted ONEKSIMbank and MFK to guarantee each other's "competing" bids and to guarantee loans that totaled over 20 percent their combined capital.[28] The loans-for-shares auctions catalyzed the bank-led FIGs' leap from important players in the Russian economy to dominant financial-industrial conglomerates, while at the same time discrediting the privatization process in the eyes of the Russian public. In reaction, the Duma repeatedly called for investigations into the legality of the auctions. For example, a June 1997 resolution stated that "Privatiza-

---

27. There has been a wealth of information published on the initial loans-for-shares deals. For contemporary accounts, see Alessandra Stanley, "Russian Banking Scandal Poses Threat to Future of Privatization," *New York Times*, January 28, 1996; "Financial-Industrial Groups," *Russian Economic Trends* 5, no. 3 (1996): 118–24; and Peter Lee, "Piling High to Meet the Quota," *Euromoney*, February 1996. For lengthier accounts, see Janine Wedel, *Collision and Collusion: The Strange Case of Western Aid to Eastern Europe, 1989–1998* (New York: St. Martin's Press, 1998); and Rose Brady, *Kapitalizm: Russia's Struggle to Free Its Economy* (New Haven: Yale University Press, 1999).

28. Anton Prishvin, "Lucrative Deals Split the Banking Community," *Business in Russia* 63 (January–February 1996): 38–41.

Table 6.2. Selected loans-for-shares auctions in 1995

Date	Company	Minimum bid	Bidders	Winning bid
11/17/95	Noril'sk Nickel	$170 million (38% stake)	1. ONEKSIMbank[a] (MFK guarantor) 2. MFK (ONEKSIMbank guarantor) 3. OOO Reola (ONEKSIMbank guarantor) Disqualified: TOO Kont (Rossiiskii Kredit guarantor)	$170.1 million, ONEKSIMbank
11/17/95	Northwest Shipping	$6 million (25.5% stake)	1. MFK (ONEKSIMbank guarantor) 2. ONEKSIMbank (MFK guarantor) 3. Karat (MFK guarantor)	$6.05 million, MFK
12/7/95	Sidanko oil	$125 million (51% stake)	1. MFK (ONEKSIMbank[a] guarantor) 2. RTD (ONEKSIMbank guarantor) Disqualified: Al'fa, Inkombank, Rossiiskii Kredit	$130 million, MFK
12/7/95	Novolipetsk Metallurgical Combine	$30 million (15% stake)	1. MFK (ONEKSIMbank guarantor) 2. Mashservis (MFK guarantor)	$31 million, MFK (ONEKSIMbank)
12/8/95	Yukos oil	$150 million (45% stake)	1. Reagent (Menatep,[a] Tokobank, and Stolichnii Bank guarantors) 2. ZAO Laguna (Menatep, Tokobank, and Stolichnii Bank guarantors) Disqualified: Konsortium-2 (Inkombank, Rossiiskii Kredit, and Alfa Bank guarantors)	$159 million, ZAO Laguna (Laguna wins tender for 33% of Yukos for $150.1 million on same day)
12/28/95	Sibneft' oil	$100 million (51% stake)	1. Tonus (Menatep and Stolichnii Bank guarantors) 2. Oil Financial Company (Menatep, Stolichnii Bank guarantors; associated with Berezovskii and Sibneft') Disqualified: Inkombank; Withdrawn: Sameko	$100.1 million, Oil Financial Company
12/28/95	Nafta-Moskva	$20 million (15% stake)	1. Nafta (ONEKSIMbank[a] guarantor) 2. Nafta-Fin (ONEKSIMbank guarantor)	$20.01 million, Nafta

Sources: Organization for Economic Cooperation and Development, *OECD Economic Surveys: Russian Federation 1997* (Paris: OECD, 1997); and Anton Prishvin, "Lucrative Deals Split the Banking Community," *Business in Russia* 63 (January–February 1996): 38–41.

[a] Auctioneer

tion was carried out with disregard of Russia's cultural characteristics and the principles of social justice." The resolution passed 288–6, with one abstention.[29] Under heavy political pressure from the Duma, on July 25, 1997, Yeltsin signed a law banning future loans-for-shares schemes.[30]

Importantly, the bank-led FIGs not only restricted their domestic competition in these and later auctions, they took various measures to restrict the influence of foreigners as well. This allowed the FIGs to narrow the number of competing bids, ensured that they could acquire property at fire-sale prices, and made it easier to attempt to arrange the outcomes of auctions beforehand. At the same time, it deprived the Russian government of desperately needed revenue that it might have gained through open, competitive bidding and foreign participation. This protectionist pressure kept foreign companies completely out of the 1995 loans-for-shares auctions. In fact, the government earned only $779 million from all twelve loans-for-shares auctions, merely 7 percent more than the total of the minimum starting bids.[31] Later, in 1997, Al'fa Group won a contested tender for 40 percent of Tiumen' oil in a process that once again barred foreigners.[32] Here the bank-led FIGs found unaccustomed moral support from the Communists and nationalists in the Duma, because for them the only thing worse than selling strategic enterprises to the bankers might be selling them to foreigners. For example, a Duma resolution of February 21, 1997, named over 100 strategic industries that should have no or limited foreign stockholders. These included energy, telecommunications, precious metals, television and radio, shipping and aviation, and financial services, precisely those industries in which the bank-led FIGs already had extensive interests.

Bank-led FIGs were not innately hostile to foreign investment in Russian companies or banks. For these FIGs, the desire to exclude foreigners was a temporary phase that allowed the bankers time to establish their bases without the threat of competition from outsiders. The Russian bankers preferred foreigners to take minority rather than majority stakes in the most promising Russian enterprises and to grant loans to enterprises (Russian banks often served as middlemen in such operations), but also saw foreign companies as potential profit sources. Indeed, the FIGs often expressed interest in selling some of the stakes they had acquired to foreign companies (at a significant profit, of course). For example, in 1997 ONEKSIMbank-affiliated Interros sold a 10-percent stake in

29. Christian Lowe, "Deputies Attack Yeltsin, Sell-Offs," *Moscow Times*, June 6, 1997.
30. *RFE / RL Newsline*, "Yeltsin Signs Privatization Law," July 28, 1997.
31. Prishvin, "Lucrative Deals," 38.
32. Maksim Puchkov, "Al'fa-Grupp gotovitsia k novym priobreteniiam," *Kommersant-Daily*, July 25, 1997.

Sidanko oil to British Petroleum for $500 million, a fraction of the price Interros had originally paid. Bank-led FIGs also appreciated Russia's desperate economic straits and the concomitant requirement for foreign funds to help restructure. As the head of equity sales at Al'fa Kapital noted in response to the 1997 Duma resolution, "I don't think people will take it seriously. It is obvious Russia needs foreign funds in these capital-intensive sectors."[33] However, the FIGs did remain wary of subsidiaries of foreign banks opening in Russia, and continued to lobby against greater inclusiveness. Moreover, in 1995 they found an ally in new CBR director Sergei Dubinin.[34] Dubinin, previously a commercial banker himself, reversed Gerashchenko's longstanding CBR policy of supporting foreign banks in Russia and actively began lobbying the government to maintain restrictions on foreigners.

In the transitional period of mid-1997, these escalating tensions between the need for foreign capital and the desire to control foreign competition manifested themselves most notably in the initial terms for the sale of 49 percent of Sviaz'invest, Russia's leading telecommunications company. Although the Italian telecommunications company STET had won an auction for 25 percent of Sviaz'invest in November 1995, Sviaz'invest went back on the block after the deal rapidly and embarrassingly fell through in the wake of uncertainty over various regulatory and ownership issues. While the first subsequent auction in 1997 (for 25 percent + 1 share) was open to all bidders, the second (for 24 percent) was slated to be open only to Russian investors—meaning the bank-led FIGs.[35] This represented a clear compromise between the bank-led FIGs, which wanted to make sure that they could acquire a part of the 49 percent of Sviaz'invest that was up for auction, and Yeltsin's team, short on money and tired of dealing with allegations of their unseemly favoritism towards the bankers. In the first auction following the collapse of the STET deal, held in July 1997, Russian bank-led FIGs teamed up with Western partners to bid, resulting in bid prices significantly higher than the minimum (in marked contrast to previous cash privatizations). The winner, with a bid of $1.88 billion (59 percent above the starting price), was the Cypriot consortium Mustcom Ltd. created by ONEKSIMbank, Deutsche Morgan Grenfell, and George Soros' Quantum Fund.[36] The auction proved notable both

33. Reuters, "Duma Urges Ban On Foreign Investment," February 22, 1997.

34. Karl Emerick Hanuska, "Are Foreign Banks a Real Threat to Russia?" *Russia Review* 4, no. 23 (December 1, 1997): 33.

35. "O realizatsii aktsii otkrytogo aktsionernogo obshchestva 'Sviaz'invest'," Regulation of the Government of the Russian Federation #618, May 23, 1997.

36. John Thornhill, "Russia: Telecom Stake Sold for $1.88 Billion," *Financial Times*, July 26, 1997; Ivan Cheberko and Aleksei Ionov, "Soros okazalsia partnerom Potanina," *Kommersant-Daily*, July 29, 1997.

because it was open to foreigners and because of the vicious public responses it provoked from the losers. The second auction, planned for late 1998, was cancelled because of the financial crisis.[37]

Competition and Collusion

The bank-led FIGs systematically built their empires by using their political power to gain special privileges from the state. But they also colluded and competed with each other in pursuit of political and economic gain. Their cooperation during the presidential elections, the consortium that proposed the loans-for-shares auctions, and their successful efforts to deny confirmation to former acting CBR director Tat'iana Paramonova are just a few examples of such political collusion. They had no qualms about attempting to corner markets, either. Examples included Al'fa Bank's cement interests, Inkombank and confectioneries, Most Bank and media, and Menatep in food processing and fertilizers. Indeed, Menatep's acquisition of vast holdings in food processing led to Russia's first, though unsuccessful, attempt at a hostile takeover when the company tried to purchase a controlling share in the mammoth Red October chocolate factory in June 1995.[38]

Yet their alliances with each other remained opportunistic and unstable. Boris Berezovskii and Vladimir Gusinskii were bitter rivals until they joined forces to promote Yeltsin in 1996. As we have seen, ONEKSIMbank and Menatep managed to engineer victories in the loans-for-shares auctions by dismissing competing bids from Inkombank, Al'fa Bank, and Rossiiskii Kredit on technicalities. The losing banks responded by publishing a declaration in late November 1995 denouncing the loans-for-shares auctions and accusing Menatep of using the Ministry of Finance's own money (held by Menatep, its authorized bank) to back up its bids.[39] Other bank-led FIGs complained about the terms of the tender for Tiumen' oil, which favored Al'fa Group because the government required the winner to purchase $40 million in oil refining equipment that a sub-

37. By June 1998 it had become clear that domestic banks did not have the means to purchase this second stake in Sviaz'invest (changed to 25 percent minus two shares, and initially valued at the ruble equivalent of $1.035 billion). At that point, the State Property Ministry recommended that Yeltsin rescind his decree prohibiting foreign participation. The point, however, became moot after the August 1998 financial crisis. See Katy Daigle, "Ministry Wants Foreign Bidders for Svyaz," *Moscow Times,* June 17, 1998; Katy Daigle, "No Svyazinvest Sale," *Moscow Times,* October 14, 1998; and Igor Semenenko, "Svyazinvest Plans to Boost Its Value," *Moscow Times,* November 25, 1999.

38. Julie Tolkacheva, "First Hostile Takeover Bid Targets Red October," *Moscow Times,* July 12, 1995.

39. Joel Hellman, "Russia Adjusts to Stability," *Transition,* May 17, 1996, 6–10.

sidiary of Al'fa Group happened to own.[40] In January 1998, Berezovskii and Khodorkovskii announced an impending merger between Sibneft' and Yukos, with the new conglomerate to be named Yuksi. Although then-Prime Minister Chernomyrdin personally gave his blessing to the merger by speaking at the signing ceremony (which, not coincidentally, Smolenskii of SBS-Agro and Gusinskii of Most also attended), the merger fell apart a few months later after continuous squabbling between the two financiers.

Bankers competed over other areas as well, including authorized bank status, large customers, and acquisitions of less successful yet desirable banks. Bank-led FIGs regularly used the courts to undercut each other, bringing lawsuit after lawsuit to prevent one another from gaining control over various enterprises. Therefore, although this small group of bank-led FIGs managed to concentrate much political and economic power into its own hands, rivalry within this financial-industrial fraternity was often intense.

Furthermore, the bank-led FIGs began to face increasing competition from wealthy, politically connected financial-industrial conglomerates formed by Lukoil, Gazprom, and the city of Moscow. These groups combined strong banking, industrial, and service enterprises, and subordinated the banks involved to the founding organizations. The conglomerates acted in ways quite similar to the bank-led FIGs, bankrolling political parties, investing in the media, lobbying, and acquiring companies, but they limited their interests by sector (for Lukoil and Gazprom) or by region (for Moscow).

Lukoil, run by director Vagit Alekperov, was the most successful oil company to emerge from the breakup of the Soviet oil producing and refining industry. Its major shareholders included the Russian state and the Bank of New York. It created its own powerful pocket banks, won an ongoing struggle with Gazprom for preponderant control over Bank Imperial, and expanded its reach to include, among other interests, an important stake in the newspaper *Izvestiia*.

Gazprom, still majority state-owned yet run quite independently by its president, Rem Viakhirev, wielded even greater power in Russia. Gazprom controlled all gas production, distribution, and export operations in Russia, and was the largest and wealthiest enterprise in the country. Former prime minister Viktor Chernomyrdin had previously served as Gazprom's director and protected its interests in Moscow. By 1998, Gazprom held a substantial interest in at least eight banks, the most important being Gazprombank, National Reserve Bank, Bank Imperial,

40. "Alfa Group Wins 40% of Tyumen," *Moscow Times,* July 19, 1997.

Promstroibank, and Neftekhimbank. Gazprom purchased 12.5 percent of Neftekhimbank, a previously autonomous ministry bank, in December 1997.[41] It bought into the suffering Promstroibank Russia at about the same time, further expanding its financial reach. Gazprom made substantial investments in media outlets as well, and controlled *Rabochaia tribuna*, *Vek*, Open Radio, and over 100 regional papers.[42]

Gazprom's influence, though, can best be appreciated by the meteoric rise of National Reserve Bank.[43] Oleg Boiko of Natsional'nyi Kredit Bank originally bought National Reserve Bank (then called Cairos Bank) in 1994 and resold it to a group financed by Gazprom and led by Aleksandr Lebedev in 1995.[44] The bank then emerged from complete obscurity to take a leading position in the Russian banking community after it came under Gazprom's influence. Most notably, in late 1996 National Reserve Bank president Lebedev proposed creating a high-powered banking consortium to finance Russian industry. This consortium, centered around gas and oil-affiliated banks, would invest in selected projects by providing bank and government resources at the rate of one budget ruble to two bank rubles. Although the effort eventually failed, it was supported by Chernomyrdin and clearly had been aimed at challenging ONEKSIMbank's political and economic power. Simultaneously, National Reserve Bank led a consortium with Gazprombank and Imperial that bought an 8.5 percent stake in Unified Energy Systems, Russia's national electric-grid operator, from the government at auction in December 1996.[45] Gazprom's group had thrown down the gauntlet to ONEKSIMbank and the other bank-led FIGs, challenging their supremacy as Russia's most powerful industrialists.

Finally, Moscow mayor Yurii Luzhkov used the vast resources of the city to form his own group, identified with the holding company "Sistema." Directed by Luzhkov's close associate Vladimir Yevtushenko, Sistema united over 100 companies, including several banks, electronics firms, media outlets, the Intourist group, and the Manezh shopping complex. As Yevtushenko told *Euromoney* magazine, "Our goal is to enter the list of the world's top 500 companies."[46] The most important affiliated banks

41. *Thompson Bankwatch*, "Thompson Bankwatch Assigns Debt Ratings to Neftechimbank," (http://www.bankwatch.com).

42. RFE/RL, "Russian Media Empires V," (http://www.rferl.org).

43. See Gleb Baranov and Mikhail Loginov, "Armii postroilis'," *Kommersant-Daily*, December 27, 1996; and Yaroslav Skvortsov, "NRB gotovit nalet na gossobstvennost'," *Kommersant*, February 7, 1997.

44. Igor Semenenko, "Fraud Alleged in 1994 Sale of NRB," *Moscow Times*, February 10, 2000.

45. Interfax, "Russian Banks Buy Unified Energy System Shares," *Russia Today*, January 20, 1997.

46. Ronan Lyons, "The Waltz of the Living Dead," *Euromoney*, September 1999.

were the Bank of Moscow, Guta Bank, and the Moscow Bank for Reconstruction and Development. In particular, the Bank of Moscow, Moscow's municipal bank, threatened the bank-led FIGs.[47] Almost all of the leading bank-led FIGs (most notably Most Bank) served as authorized agents of the city of Moscow, so when Luzhkov created the Bank of Moscow in March 1995, they stood to lose access to Moscow's extensive budget funds. In any event, by late 1997 Luzhkov had only transferred 30–40 percent of the city's resources to the bank. In doing so, the mayor demonstrated his political acumen. On the one hand, he had created a bank he completely controlled, which by virtue of the transfer of budget funds immediately became one of the strongest banks in the country. On the other, he not only retained Moscow's extensive system of authorized banks, he expanded it. This ensured that the largest Moscow banks would continue to support Luzhkov, and would vie with each other and with the Bank of Moscow to maintain his favor and funds. Thus, at least in Moscow, Luzhkov managed to tip the balance of power away from the bank-led FIGs.

In late 1996 and early 1997, the competition among the leading bank-led FIGs grew stronger, as the changing dynamics of the second round of loans-for-shares auctions demonstrated. According to the terms of the 1995 loans-for-shares auctions, the government had the option of reclaiming the shares by paying off the loans within a certain period of time. When the cash-strapped government had to decide whether or not to do so, it declined. The 1995 agreement then required the bank-led FIGs to "sell" the shares for the government via a tender, which would complete the privatization process. The government would receive 70 percent of the profits, and the banks 30 percent. In all four instances, the bank-led FIGs sold the shares back to themselves for minuscule "profits" in auctions that they also organized. These incestuous transactions released the bank-led FIGs from their obligations to the state and left them free to sell these companies later and keep the real profits for themselves if they so chose. Conducting such closed auctions necessitated some collusion among the bank-led FIGs, because it required that no other group be willing or able to submit a competitive bid.

The first two such auctions went smoothly for the FIGs. In December 1996, Menatep's subsidiary Laguna "sold" its stake in Yukos to Monblan, another Menatep shell corporation, for only $100,000 over the starting price. ONEKSIMbank's partner MFK, the legal owner of the Sidanko

47. On the Bank of Moscow, see Aleksandr Polyansky, "Bank of Moscow a Boon for the Budget," *Business in Russia* 81 (September 1997); Elena Makovskaia, "Domashnii bank Moskvy," *Ekspert* 34 (September 8, 1997): 24–27; and Andrei Mochanov, "The Mayor's Favorite Banks," *Business in Russia* 82 (October–November 1997): 42–43.

stock, actually sold its share in Sidanko to Interros-Oil in January 1997 for *less* than the value of the original loan.[48] However, in May 1997 ONEK-SIMbank decided to shake up the privatization game and seriously compete in the auction for the LogoVAZ-controlled 51 percent stake in Sibneft' by submitting a bid through the company KM-Invest. Although the Berezovskii-affiliated Financial Oil Company (with the cooperation of its ally, SBS-Agro) managed to win the stake by having ONEKSIMbank's bid disallowed on a technicality at the last moment, a new precedent had been set.[49] This unsuccessful attempt to participate in the Sibneft' auction and ONEKSIMbank's victory in the Sviaz'invest auction occurred shortly before the required auction for the shares of Noril'sk Nickel that ONEK-SIMbank held. Despite calls by Prime Minister Chernomyrdin to halt the sale and complaints by other groups that conditions for the auction were unfair, ONEKSIMbank-affiliated Svift won the auction.[50]

The most serious sign of the growing tension among the bank-led FIGs came immediately after ONEKSIMbank's consortium won the Sviaz'invest auction in July 1997, when Potanin claimed that he had rejected an attempt by Boris Berezovskii and Vladimir Gusinskii to fix the outcome of the auction beforehand (Chubais and Gusinskii later confirmed that such a meeting had occurred).[51] Immediately following the auction, ORT, NTV, *Segodnia,* and *Nezavisimaia gazeta* all viciously denounced the sale, accusing Potanin of having untoward links with Nemtsov and State Property Committee director Kokh (who resigned soon after the auction), arguing that ONEKSIMbank's group only bought the shares as a speculative venture, and in general complaining that "The Money Stank," as a headline in *Segodnia* read.[52] Gusinskii also threatened to sue Potanin for slander.[53] With money tight, the government no longer pandering to their every wish, and no threatening presidential election to unite them in common cause, the leaders of the bank-led FIGs turned on each other. In response to this unprecedented public falling-out, Yeltsin hypocritically blamed Kokh for showing preference to certain banks and declared that "This is no way to do things. . . . Any banks, not only the

48. "Financial-Industrial Groups," *Russian Economic Trends* 1 (1997): 149–53.

49. Yaroslav Skvortsov, "Degustatsiia Sibneft': Porazhenie obiazyvaet," *Kommersant-Daily,* May 20, 1997.

50. Sergei Kniazev, "V konkurse po 'Noril'skomu nikeliu' ne moglo byt' proigravshikh," *Kommersant-Daily,* August 9, 1997; Mariia Rozhkova and Leonid Skabichevskii, "ONEKSIM prokhodit kak khoziain," *Kommersant-Daily,* August 6, 1997.

51. Andrei Bagrov, "Vladel'tsy ORT i NTV proigrali pervyi boi," *Kommersant-Daily,* July 30, 1997.

52. Alastair MacDonald, "TV Lashes Out at Russian Privatization Bid Winner," Reuters, July 26, 1997, and "Mud Flies in Growing Russian Privatization Fight," Reuters, July 28, 1997; and Marina Shakina, "Scandal with the Sale of Svyazinvest," *RIA Novosti,* July 31, 1997.

53. RFE / RL Newsline, "Gusinskii to Sue Potanin," July 31, 1997.

largest ones, must be allowed to take part in auctions."[54] Of course, the damage had already been done.

Enterprise Restructuring

While the bank-led FIGs had clearly acquired their empires through dubious means, Western and Russian observers alike thought that they might turn over a new leaf and use their resources to restructure these large Russian enterprises. The theoretical logic behind trickle-down institutional design underpinned this belief, as it held that private ownership of any sort would naturally prove superior to state ownership. In 1996–97, with macroeconomic indicators relatively stable while production levels continued to fall, bank-led FIGs did take a few small steps toward attempting to restructure the enterprises under their control. At Noril'sk, ONEKSIMbank used its political clout to get Prime Minister Chernomyrdin to fire director Anatolii Filatov in April 1996. In May, the bank also removed Filatov from his position as chief executive and replaced him with ONEKSIMbank board member Aleksandr Khloponin. ONEKSIMbank began, with the help of the central government, to shed some of Noril'sk's social expenses and to relocate workers and pensioners.[55] At Yukos, in April 1996 Menatep's Rosprom began instituting a restructuring plan that involved cutting the workforce and improving the refinery network.[56] Then, in February 1997, Rosprom and Yukos agreed to divide management functions at the oil company. Rosprom took over general management and finance, leaving Yukos to concentrate its activities on oil production and refining. As part of the deal, Rosprom director Mikhail Khodorkovskii became chair of Yukos's board of directors.[57] ONEKSIMbank began directing a similar reorganization and share consolidation at Sidanko oil in 1997 aimed at streamlining operations and raising profits.[58]

54. Interfax, "Yeltsin Calls to End Preferential Treatment of Leading Banks," August 15, 1997. For Kokh's own analysis of the process, see Alfred Kokh, *The Selling of the Soviet Empire* (Sure Seller, Inc., 1998). Kokh produced this slim volume after it became widely known that a company associated with ONEKSIMbank had paid him $100,000 as an "advance" on the book before the Sviaz'invest auction.

55. Mark Bradford, "Novolipetsk Metal: Lines Being Drawn," *Skate Press Corporate Action Watch*, March 20, 1997 (http://www.skate.ru/watch); and Carol Williams, "Prisoners of Legacy of Repression," *Los Angeles Times*, July 20, 1997.

56. Paul Hofheinz, "The Big Fig," *Russia Review*, April 22, 1996.

57. *Kommersant-Daily*, "Reforma upravleniia v YuKOSe i Rosprome," February 26, 1997; and Sergei Svistunov, "'Menatep' i 'Rosprom' pristupaiut k upravleniiu kompaniei 'YuKOS'," *Kommersant-Daily*, February 20, 1997.

58. Mark Bradford, "Novolipetsk Metal: Lines Being Drawn," *Skate Press Corporate Action Watch*, March 20, 1997; and Aleksei Sukhodoev, "Naznachen prezident neftianoi kompanii SIDANKO," *Kommersant-Daily*, April 11, 1997.

However, most "restructuring" merely involved shaking up management rather than investing in capital improvements.[59] From 1995 through 1997, long-term credit represented a paltry 1.3 percent of total commercial credit to non-financial structures. Not only did this measure remain stagnant during three years of relative macroeconomic stability, but the banks involved in bank-led FIGs invested no more in industry than did other banks.[60] As Menatep's own vice-president Aleksei Golubovich stated in June 1996, "I believe that there are two sources of capital for industry—the state and foreign investors, and none other."[61]

Moreover, many of the enterprises acquired in the loans-for-shares auctions began performing worse than they had before. For example, after ONEKSIMbank took over, Noril'sk Nickel's profits actually fell, calling into question the effectiveness of the measures the bank had taken. For the first half of 1998, it reported losses of $257 million.[62] Other enterprises held by the bank-led FIGs experienced similar problems: ONEKSIMbank's Northwest Shipping owed $22 million to the Leningrad oblast' budget, Inkombank's SAMEKO lost $28 million in 1996, and Noiabr'skneftegaz (part of Sibneft') was $340 million in debt, to note but a few examples.[63] Cash privatization, in short, had changed little but the faces at the top.

Why did the bank-led FIGs fail to meaningfully invest in and restructure the enterprises they had acquired? To the extent that they attempted to improve these companies at all, they faced four main roadblocks: (1) the enormity of the task; (2) their lack of experience; (3) recalcitrant enterprise managers and regional politicians; and (4) a shortage of cash.[64] Noril'sk Nickel, for example, controlled approximately 35 percent of the world's nickel reserves, with a potential market value of $6 billion, but it

59. Aleksandr Tutushkin, "Bankiri priobshchilis' k neftianym problemam," *Kommersant-Daily*, April 23, 1996.

60. Pekka Sutela, "The Role of Banks in Financing Russian Economic Growth," *Post-Soviet Geography and Economics* 39, no. 2 (February 1998): 96–124; and Organization for Economic Cooperation and Development, *OECD Economic Surveys: Russian Federation, 1997* (Paris: OECD, 1997).

61. Quoted in Andrei Shmarov, "Min menatep," *Ekspert* 24 (June 24, 1996): 22–28.

62. Sarah Mae Brown, "Noril'sk endures a tough prosperity," *Russia Review* 5, no. 19 (November 1998): 18.

63. *Kommersant-Daily*, "Problemy Severo-Zapadnovo parokhodstva", July 30, 1997; Vladimir Ul'ianov, "Pokupka 'SAMEKO' vyshla Inkombanku bokom," *Delovoi Mir*, February 21–24, 1997; Rustem Yakhin, "Sibneft: Gazprom Connection a Lifeline," *Skate Press Corporate Action Watch*, July 17, 1997.

64. For an interesting overview of the difficulty of addressing such issues, see the interview with Interros president Yevgenii Yakovlev in Marina Shpagina, "Banki ne mogut upravliat' proizvodstvom," *Ekspert*, May 1997. In general, he states, "Reforming Russian enterprises is terribly difficult, thankless work."

was a badly run, top-heavy company with indebtedness of over \$1.2 billion to federal and local governments.[65] Moreover, in company towns like Noril'sk, the major enterprise traditionally employed all of the town's residents (either directly or indirectly) and paid to maintain the social service network. Cutting costs meant moving newly unemployed workers to other cities, reducing or eliminating company subsidies for housing and local service enterprises, and so on.[66] In company towns, simply firing workers meant that the enterprise would just end up supporting them financially in some other way.

Nor did bankers have any clear idea of how to restructure these companies. The banks had grown quickly, feeding on financial speculation, and often had a hard time managing their own internal affairs, much less those of large industrial enterprises. Although a common conception in Russia pinned the problems of many companies solely on backwards, Soviet-era management (as Yeltsin's 1997 desire to send thousands of young Russian managers to study in the West attested), simply replacing such a manager with a banker did not go very far towards solving the deeper structural problems of Russian enterprises. Moreover, as discussed earlier, the tendency of the directors of the bank-led FIGs to make all major decisions (and many of the minor ones as well) slowed down the restructuring process.

The bankers, to their unending frustration, also ran into numerous roadblocks when attempting to make changes at "their" enterprises. Enterprises, especially the bigger ones, often resented the upstart, outside shareholders or, alternately, saw them as potential cash cows because of their legendary wealth. The bankers' problems mirrored the problems that all outside shareholders faced in asserting ownership and control rights over Russian enterprises. For example, Noril'sk Nickel managers took ONEKSIMbank to court, challenging the legality of the loans-for-shares auction and the bank's attempts to change the composition of Noril'sk's board. After ONEKSIMbank gained control over Noril'sk, workers went on strike several times, with employees demanding back wages and expressing "no confidence" in the new management.[67] ONEKSIMbank also had trouble with the Novolipetsk Metallurgical Combine: the bank was forced to sue the plant's managers (successfully) in a Lipetsk court after the enterprise refused to give ONEKSIMbank and other key outside

65. Craig Mellow and Simon Baker, "North of the Border," *Russia Review*, March 11, 1996; Ekaterina Botvinova, "Noril'sk Nickel: Problems and Prospects," *Skate Press Corporate Action Watch*, June 19, 1997.

66. Reuters, "Noril'sk Nickel to Let Thousands Go," April 18, 1997.

67. Natalia Gurushina, "Conflict within Noril'sk Nickel," *OMRI Daily Digest*, February 4, 1997; and Aleksandra Semenova, "Sudy prepodnesli investoram nepriiatnyi siurpriz," *Kommersant*, April 9, 1996.

shareholders seats on the company's board.[68] Lebedinsk Ore Processing in Belgorod did everything they could to block Rossiiskii Kredit's takeover: "Company directors diluted the bank's stake from 23 percent to less than 6 percent, manipulated proceedings to deny the bank a seat on the board, and hustled one of the visitors off the stage when he tried to speak."[69] In another case, the administration of Kursk oblast' tried to take the Mikhailovsk mining company away from Rossiiskii Kredit, accusing it of not fulfilling its obligation to invest in the company. Rossiiskii Kredit claimed in turn that the company had wasted $20.5 million that the bank had already invested in it, and that the only mistake the bank made was waiting too long to involve itself in the company's management affairs. The two sides finally made a deal in April 1997, with the oblast' administration agreeing that it would no longer attempt to take over the enterprise and the bank agreeing to work with the administration to develop a joint plan to overcome the enterprise's problems.[70] Banks also had trouble managing even the smaller enterprises that they acquired, although these problems were usually not as severe.[71]

Last, and most importantly, the bank-led FIGs faced a shortage of capital. They simply did not have enough money to both purchase and restructure a great number of Russian enterprises. As of January 1997, the Russian commercial banking system held only $62.5 billion in total assets, about eighty times less than United States commercial banks then had.[72] The bank-led FIGs were so concerned with putting their limited resources toward acquiring new companies that little remained with which to improve the affairs of the enterprises that they already owned. Given the gap between the resources necessary for restructuring and the resources available to the banks, the inescapable conclusion is that the banks did not intend to conduct extensive investment and restructuring in these enter-

68. Mark Bradford, "Novolipetsk Metal: Lines Being Drawn," *Skate Press Corporate Action Watch*, March 20, 1997; and John Thornhill, "Russia: Telecom Stake Sold for $1.88 Billion," *Financial Times*, July 26, 1997.

69. Natalia Mileusnic, "Shareholders Evolve as 'Proactive' Class," *Moscow Times*, April 25, 1996. For further information on the Lebedinsk tale, see Blasi, Kroumova, and Kruse, *Kremlin Capitalism*.

70. Kirill Vishnepol'skii and Dmitri Khakhalev, "Aleksandru Rutskomu ne liub Rossiiskii Kredit," *Kommersant-Daily*, February 18, 1997; and Kirill Vishnepol'skii, "Aleksandru Rutskomu liub Rossiiskii Kredit," *Kommersant-Daily*, April 24, 1997.

71. For example, see the comments of Inkombank president Vladimir Vinogradov on restructuring SAMEKO and Magnitka in Vladislav Dorofeev, interview with Vladimir Vinogradov, "Nikto ne znaet, s kem my rabotaem," *Kommersant*, March 11, 1997.

72. This figure represents the total consolidated balance sheet of the Russian commercial banking system, excluding the assets of Sberbank, Vneshtorgbank, and Vneshekonombank (Central Bank of Russia, *Biulleten' Bankovskoi Statistiki* 45 [1997]); and Federal Reserve Bank Statistical Release H.8, "Assets and Liabilities of Commercial Banks in the United States," April 18, 1997.

prises, at least in the short term. In fact, the bank-led FIGs probably had more interest in acquiring the accounts and resources of these enterprises, profiting from their day-to-day operations, and gaining the political clout that went along with ownership of Russia's flagship companies. In addition, they potentially stood to profit a great deal from reselling these cheaply won enterprises in the future. This "capital gap" explains why the bankers scrambled to gain control over enterprises at extremely low prices, using political leverage and fixed auctions. Fortunately for the bankers, the Yeltsin government proved to be a willing partner in this process.

The Ties That Bind

In the heady economic environment of 1997, the bank-led FIGs appeared to have the potential to establish themselves as permanent, powerful players in the Russian economy. Russia's GDP had finally begun to grow again, the ruble corridor held firm, and stock and GKO sales boomed, bathing the bank-led FIGs in an optimistic light. In the best-case scenario, the bank-led FIGs would have come to fill a similar economic niche in Russia that bank-centered *keiretsu* like Mitsubishi or Sumitomo did in Japan, but without the ability of the *keiretsu* to restrict foreign access to their markets. Germany's system of universal banks, where enterprises typically receive long-term financing from a single bank while the bank takes an active role in developing the enterprise's business strategy (particularly if the enterprise appears to be ailing), represented another attractive developmental pathway. Russians often pointed out that many robust economies had developed successfully in conditions of highly concentrated financial power and close ties between financial-industrial alliances and the state.

However, Russia's bank-led FIGs could not aspire to such a rosy (and prosperous) future. Public distrust, a lack of structural economic reform, political instability, imprudent investment policies, shortsighted protectionism, greed, corruption, legal insufficiencies, and financial inadequacies, among other factors, stood in the way of bank-led FIGs becoming powerful, lasting, positive forces for Russian economic recovery. Indeed, in taking on such extensive acquisitions in large, troubled companies, the bank-led FIGs knowingly bit off more than they could chew. Superficial comparisons with Japanese *keiretsu* or South Korean *chaebol* neglected major institutional differences between Russian FIGs and these conglomerates. While the highly integrated Asian groups actively participated in state-led industrial development and the banks involved invested heavily in their affiliated enterprises, Russian bank-led FIGs invested little, never achieved effective control over many of their "partner" enterprises, did not establish extensive cross-holdings among their various components, and received no investment direction from the weakened state. In fact, the bank-led FIGs were regularly accused of asset-stripping and short-term exploitation of their acquisitions.

No less important, the widespread belief that the bank-led FIGs profited from a criminalized privatization process and the obvious interpenetration of the bankers and the government threatened Russia's economic and political future. As political scientist Michael McFaul has observed, this explains the divergence between the "apparent achievements" of the democratic process in Russia at this time (successive and reasonably fair presidential and parliamentary elections whose results were peacefully accepted by all parties) and the "real perceptions" of most Russians, who felt that they did not live in a particularly democratic country.[73] The economically vulnerable yet politically powerful bank-led FIGs could not turn to serious, long-term, and competitive investment and restructuring in Russia because they relied on the state for financial sustenance. The state, for its part, could not fulfill its task of providing the fair, democratic institutional framework for economic interaction that Russia required while it remained under the influence of bank-led financial-industrial groups. Unfortunately, neither the banks nor the state could pry apart the parasitic bonds that joined them, dragging both to financial perdition in the financial crisis of 1998.

73. Michael McFaul, "Russia's 'Weak' and 'Privatized' State as an Impediment to Democratic Consolidation" (ms, July 1997).

CHAPTER SEVEN

The Crash of 1998

These are very, very unusual times. One can't look in the book and find a solution to these problems.

—**Bruce Bean, president of the American Chamber of Commerce in Moscow, 1998**

What a difference a year makes! In 1997, banks such as Menatep, Inkombank, ONEKSIMbank, and Tokobank occupied the financial pinnacle of Russia. ONEKSIMbank arranged to build a lavish new $400 million headquarters in downtown Moscow, Menatep appeared poised to gain further control over leading Russian oil companies, while both Tokobank and Inkombank boasted the European Bank for Reconstruction and Development as a shareholder.[1] All four appeared prominently on any top-20 list of Russian banks. But by mid-1999, all four banks had lost their licenses. Inkombank had so many angry depositors that it reserved a Moscow sports stadium for a public meeting. The EBRD posted a loss of over $100 billion in 1998, primarily due to Russian banking investments gone bad.[2] Menatep, the former Komsomol darling, became an empty husk dogged by mass layoffs and tales of cover-ups. When a truck carrying documents from Menatep's Novgorod branch office fell into the Dubna river in May 1999, few believed it to be accidental.[3]

1. See Boris Aliabyev, "Uneximbank [ONEKSIMbank] Plans $400Mln Headquarters," *Moscow Times*, November 25, 1997.
2. Matt Bivens, "EBRD to Post $100M Loss," *Moscow Times*, January 21, 1999.
3. Gleb P'ianykh, "Kreditnye dogovora MENATEPa pokoiatsia na dne Dubny," *Kommersant*, May 29, 1999.

What had happened to the high-flying Russian banking system? Despite claims to the contrary, the crash itself was not "accidental" either.[4] Like Icarus, Russian bankers flew towards the sun masquerading as birds, yet armed only with homemade wings. When intense heat hit them, their beautiful plumage melted away and the bankers plummeted back to Earth. Although unforeseen circumstances such as the Asian financial crisis and the drop in world oil prices affected the timing of the crash, its true roots lay in the institutional deformities of the Russian financial system.

Western capitalists, governments, and international financial institutions aided and abetted the bankers' folly. In 1997, Western capital flowed into Russia as the government opened the GKO market more fully to foreigners and the country's stock market became the most profitable in the world. Both Russian and Western analysts widely predicted that the stock market would continue its expansion, growing by 40 to 80 percent during 1998.[5] The Russian government issued Eurobonds, and Russian banks attracted foreign loans. The CBR appeared to have stabilized the ruble in its corridor, and felt so confident of its victory that it knocked three zeros off the ruble on January 1, 1998, making the redenominated ruble worth just under six rubles to the dollar. The West hailed Russia's turnaround, believing that the fruits of Western economic advice and the policies of re-ascendant government "reformers" such as Boris Nemtsov and Anatolii Chubais had finally taken hold in Russia.

Yet this apparent triumph belied painful realities in the Russian banking system and in the economy as a whole. Bank profits fell and continued to fall after the presidential election in July 1996, even as the concentration of capital in the top Moscow banks increased. Meanwhile, by late 1997 overdue loans to Russian banks topped 16.6 trillion rubles, while total loan-loss reserves measured only 15 trillion.[6] The government itself fared no better at collecting taxes or paying overdue bills than it had before. Against this backdrop, the noncash economy continued to grow. By May 1998, approximately 50 percent of economic transactions were conducted in barter, and another 25 percent in veksels.[7] The West misinterpreted the active and successful attempts of the government and the banks to attract foreign capital in 1997 as a positive sign of market transformation; of increasing financial integration and maturity. In reality,

4. For example, see Ben Slay, "An Interpretation of the Russian Financial Crisis," *Post-Soviet Geography and Economics* 40, no. 3 (1999): 206–14.

5. Boris Aliabyev, "Analysts Predict Market Boom Ahead," *Moscow Times*, December 10, 1997.

6. "Skvoz' tolshchu l'da," *Ekspert* 11 (March 23, 1998): 20–24.

7. Jacques Sapir, "Russia's Crash of August 1998: Diagnosis and Prescription," *Post-Soviet Affairs* 15, no. 1 (1999): 1–36.

though, both the government and the banks turned toward the West for continued financing because they had exhausted the resources of the rest of the economy and of each other.

This resulted in a dangerous situation for all parties involved, but one that few recognized in time. Problems in industrial restructuring and limitations on direct foreign investment, combined with the artificially high profitability of the GKO and stock markets, meant that the vast majority of foreign money flowing into Russia was short-term, speculative capital. The strategies of Russian bankers rested upon short-term considerations as well: they relied on access to political favors and foreign financial resources instead of on domestic investment. The Russian government came to depend more and more upon the GKO market for financing its day-to-day expenditures. The CBR, influenced by the IMF, by domestic constituencies, by its own investments in GKOs, and by its desire to retain tight monetary control over the country, committed to maintaining the ruble's value whatever the cost. These developments culminated in the crash of August 1998, when the government defaulted on its internal and external debts, the ruble exchange rate corridor collapsed, and the biggest Russian banks came face to face with their unsustainable financial situations. This led to a GDP decline of 4.6 percent in 1998, a rapid outflow of capital, and the *de facto* bankruptcy of hundreds of Russian banks. The chickens had come home to roost.

Prelude to a Crisis

Although Russia's banks and the Yeltsin government briefly basked in the rosy afterglow of the July 1996 presidential elections, the tension between them began to increase rapidly by the end of the year, and accelerated through 1997. This occurred for two reasons. First, the Yeltsin government was no longer as desperate for the political and financial support of the bankers. With no elections imminent, the monetary and media power of the bank-led FIGs carried less immediate weight. Moreover, the government's financial requirements began to outstrip the banks' ability to provide them. The bank-led FIGs had tied up much of their limited capital in enterprise purchases, and could not afford to buy the ever-increasing number of treasury bills emitted by the cash-starved state. Second, a series of financial scandals, political fallout from the loans-for-shares auctions, banker infighting, and perceived challenges to Yeltsin's authority made continuing, overt favoritism towards the bankers politically problematic. These two factors encouraged the government to pull away slightly from the banks and begin to embrace foreign capital in 1997.

As a signal to the West that the Russian government was serious about continued financial responsibility (read creditworthiness), in March

1997 Yeltsin rehired Anatolii Chubais as first deputy prime minister in charge of the economy. Boris Nemtsov, the high-profile governor of Nizhnii Novgorod oblast', soon joined the government as a first deputy prime minister as well. Yeltsin sent these signals because by 1997 the Russian government had big bills to pay, and soon. Most notably, it needed to pay wage arrears—50 percent of state employees were not paid their full salaries for the third quarter of 1997. Prime Minister Chernomyrdin publicly promised to catch up on these payments by January 1, 1998. In addition, the government needed to cover state enterprise arrears and agricultural procurement, among other pressing issues. Meanwhile, Russia's deficit continued to expand as the executive battled the Duma over the 1998 state budget, while efforts to improve tax collection were ineffective. Tax collection reached only 52 percent of budgeted levels, and tax arrears soared to $13 billion. Therefore, the government's reliance on the "non-inflationary" GKO market (and on the parallel six-month OFZ—Obligatsii federal'nogo zaima—bond market) grew by leaps and bounds, outstripping domestic commercial bankers' capacities. As the EBRD notes, "by October 1996, the sale of GKOs and OFZs had exceeded the total stock of the ruble deposits in the banking system."[8]

The government turned to Sberbank and to foreigners to make up the difference. Sberbank, prompted by the CBR (its major shareholder), made by far the most purchases on the GKO market. In fact, it regularly invested well over 80 percent of its total household deposits in government securities through 1997 and 1998. During the quarter beginning July 1, 1997, Sberbank had 97.3 trillion rubles invested in government securities and only 104.4 trillion rubles in household deposits.[9] By January 1, 1998, Sberbank's holdings represented 62.6 percent of all investments in government securities. Instead of taking in household deposits and redistributing them to the economy as investment through loans, Sberbank massively—and dangerously—subsidized the government directly. State-owned Sberbank's Soviet-era dominance of the household savings market, persisting in the post-Soviet era, proved to be an all too-tempting source of easy money.

At least Sberbank managers had an excuse for their excessive level of government security purchases—the state made them do it. Foreign investors, alas, allowed greed to overcome good sense when Russia sought to draw them into the expanding GKO pyramid. The treasury bill market remained all but closed to foreigners as yields skyrocketed before the

8. European Bank for Reconstruction and Development, *Transition Report 1998* (London: EBRD, 1998): 13.
9. CBR, "Annual Report, 1997," 165.

1996 presidential election. About 20 domestic banks dominated the auctions, reaping windfall profits from their activities. However, in August 1996 the government began to allow foreigners to participate directly in the auctions. Once they opened a so-called "S" account with an authorized Russian bank, foreigners could buy, sell, and expatriate their earnings at will. At first the government capped the yields that foreigners could receive (preserving the privilege of high yields for domestic banks), but as the government needed more and more money, foreign investors met with a more and more level playing field. By July 1997, foreign purchasers controlled about 22 percent of the GKO market, and this rose to 33 percent by the end of 1997.[10] This expanded participation initially had the desired effect; not only was the government bringing in more money, but it was doing so more cheaply. Although yields had hit 170 percent before the July 1996 elections, by mid-1997 yields had fallen to 20 percent in nominal terms and 7–9 percent in real terms.[11] As a result, the Yeltsin government no longer felt quite as financially reliant on Russia's top banks.

At the same time, the scandals that rocked the Russian financial system in late 1996 and 1997 made a mutual cooling-off period politically attractive. As we have seen, the second round of loans-for-shares auctions, the immediate post-election decision to bring Potanin and Berezovskii into the government, the public rancor over the Sviaz'invest auction, and the perceived political influence of the bankers led to a backlash among the public and in the Duma. Chubais himself came under fire again for his role in cash privatization in November 1997, especially when it was alleged that he and four other officials had received a $450,000 "advance" on an unwritten book from the *Segodnia* publishing house (controlled by ONEKSIMbank) not long before the Sviaz'invest auction.[12]

In combination with these ongoing debacles, three other events heightened the sense of political tension in the financial system. First, in November 1996, after Boris Berezovskii was appointed to the Security Council, *Izvestiia* reported that he had applied for and obtained Israeli citizenship. Although Berezovskii initially refused to confirm the story, eventually he admitted that he did hold an Israeli passport.[13] On one level, this revelation raised important questions about why a member of Russia's Security Council had formal ties to a foreign government. But on another, more sinister level, it encouraged an ugly strain of anti-Semitism that has

10. *Russian Capital Markets Watch,* July 31, 1997; and EBRD, *Transition Report 1998*, 13.
11. Andrei Illarionov, "The Roots of the Economic Crisis," *Journal of Democracy* 10, no. 2 (April 1999): 68–82.
12. Daniel Williams, "Parliament Seeks Probe of Chubais' Book Deal," *Washington Post*, November 14, 1997, A29.
13. "Berezovsky Admits Israeli Citizenship," *Moscow Times*, November 14, 1996.

historically plagued Russia. This anti-Semitism was directed not only at Berezovskii, but more broadly at the "Jewish bankers" that some ethnic Russians perceived to be ruining the country at their expense.[14]

Second, in spring 1997 the United States Agency for International Development (USAID) began investigating an allegation that its grantee, the Harvard Institute for International Development (HIID), had been misusing funds intended to help develop an independent securities market in Russia.[15] Specifically, they accused the two project heads, Jonathan Hay and Andrei Shleifer, of using their positions for personal gain. The scandal escalated on May 19 when Anatolii Chubais (who had previously worked closely with HIID) wrote a letter to USAID asking that they terminate HIID's aid contract, stating that "because of changing conditions, continuation of these agreements is not consistent with Russian interests."[16] USAID subsequently pulled HIID's grant, and Hay was fired. This took place in the context of an ongoing battle between the CBR and the Federal Securities Commission for control over Russia's securities market. The HIID team had helped develop and champion the securities commission, whose mission was to create a U.S.-style securities market in Russia under its control. The Central Bank of Russia preferred a bank-led, German-style system under its own control. HIID's fall, as Russian observers clearly recognized, represented a defeat for the Federal Securities Commission. While the HIID team had certainly been acting in an inappropriate manner, the timing of the revelations had far more to do with internal Russian politics than a sudden realization of HIID's wrongdoing. The immediate effect, however, was to create the impression that the Russian "oligarchy" had gained control over the securities markets and that Western advisors, the Russian government, and financial interests had been mutually involved in a corrupt scam to put money into their own pockets and defraud the Russian people.

Adding insult to injury, another banking scandal broke in July 1997 at about the same time as the contentious Sviaz'invest auction. CBR head Sergei Dubinin publicly accused Unikombank and former First Deputy Finance Minister Andrei Vavilov of mishandling $237 million in government money that had been funneled through the bank to pay MAPO to

14. Many of the top Russian bankers had Jewish backgrounds. Most prominently, Vladimir Gusinskii of Most headed the Russian Jewish Congress and contributed heavily to building a synagogue at the Victory Park complex on Poklonnaia Gora in Moscow (to complement the Russian Orthodox church and the mosque already in place). Others included Mikhail Fridman of Al'fa Bank, Vitalii Malkin of Rossiiskii Kredit, and Aleksandr Smolenskii of SBS-Agro.

15. For details on the scandal, see Janine Wedel, *Collision and Collusion: The Strange Case of Western Aid to Eastern Europe* (New York: St. Martin's Press, 1998).

16. Cited in Mark Whitehouse, "What Went Wrong?" *Moscow Times,* June 3, 1997.

produce MiG fighter planes for India.[17] Moreover, Dubinin also accused Unikombank itself of "disappearing" another $275 million in back wages for state employees in Moscow oblast'. Both Vavilov and Unikombank had interesting histories. Vavilov had served in the Finance Ministry from 1992 through early 1997, when he was fired and joined MFK bank. During his tenure at the Finance Ministry, Vavilov made key decisions about choosing federally authorized banks, earning him good friends and bitter enemies in the banking community. Unikombank itself had teetered on the edge of bankruptcy in early 1996, and was put under temporary CBR administration until the Moscow oblast' government and its affiliated banks "rescued" Unikombank. Unikombank then became the *de facto* municipal bank of the oblast' government and, like most banks with a powerful government patron, immediately returned to solvency. Not only did this public scandal contribute to the general feeling that "banker" meant "thief," but it increased pressure on the government to do away with the endlessly problematic system of authorized banks.

Indeed, it appeared that in their public rapaciousness the bankers had killed (or at least severely wounded) the goose that laid the golden egg. No longer reliant on the bankers for electoral support, burned by accusations of collusion, and by this point needing far more money than even Russia's wealthy bankers could supply, the Yeltsin government began to withdraw some of its most overt favoritism from the Moscow banks. Most importantly, the controversial practice of authorized banks came under increasing scrutiny. By mid-1997, the IMF and influential officials such as Viktor Chernomyrdin, Boris Nemtsov, and Sergei Dubinin all publicly advocated abolishing authorized banks at the federal level. Earlier in January, Vladimir Potanin (in his capacity as first deputy prime minister) had tried to stave off this mounting political pressure on the biggest authorized banks by shaving down the list. Potanin, who then chaired the Commission on Financial, Credit, and Monetary Policy, slashed the number of fully authorized banks from 85 to 16 (the group of "universal agents"), while the total number of federally authorized banks fell to 54. Although some of Russia's biggest banks (including Promstroibank and Moscow Industrial Bank) did not make the top list, all eight of the banks at the center of bank-led FIGs (ONEKSIMbank and MFK, Inkombank, Rossiiskii Kredit, SBS-Agro, Menatep, Most, and Al'fa) retained their fully authorized status. Potanin lost his job in February 1997, though, and Nemtsov came to power fully intending to do away with authorized banks at the federal level (announcing, for example, that the Customs Service accounts would be taken away from ONEKSIMbank). Therefore, while au-

17. Valeria Korchagina, "2 Arrested in MiG Payments Scandal," *Moscow Times*, September 12, 1997.

thorized banks still processed almost 90 percent of government resources in mid-1997, the banks could not be certain that their political connections would guarantee them the same level of free state resource flows in the future.[18]

As a result, most of the largest banks survived in this period of political turmoil by buying government securities, playing the stock market, accumulating loans from Western banks, and drawing up "dollar-forward" contracts with Western GKO investors (in effect covering the foreigners' currency risk by locking in a ruble-dollar exchange rate three to six months in advance). Such a combination of speculative activities temporarily kept them solvent and helped them maintain the lifestyles to which they had become accustomed. This became even more important for the bank-led FIGs, which needed money not only to manage their huge new acquisitions, but to participate in the anticipated privatization auctions in late 1997 and 1998 for the remaining stakes in the state-owned oil companies and Sviaz'invest. From 1995 to 1997, the percentage of securities in Russian banks' asset structures rose from 5.7 percent to 18 percent.[19] In short, the largest banks became even more dependent on politically contingent, speculative means of making money.

Despite falling yields, the government securities markets remained an important funding source for Russia's banks. Through 1996 and 1997, Russian commercial banks held 20–25 percent of all domestic government debt, and in late 1997 government securities (GKOs and OFZs combined) yielded 41.2 percent of the total income for the top 100 banks.[20] With the exception of Most Bank and Al'fa Bank, all of the banks at the center of bank-led FIGs held massive stocks of state securities, and several banks had over 30 percent of their assets in such securities (see Table 7.1). By September 1998, Russian banks held 1.61 trillion rubles of government securities, of which Moscow banks held 95.9 percent.[21]

Similarly, the Russian banks' search for short-term, high-yield investments helped to fuel the stock market boom that began in late 1995. In particular, when GKO yields began to sink, Russian banks needed another avenue to sustain their hunger for fast cash. Although in 1994 banks held less than 2 percent of the shares of privatized enterprises, by mid-1997 Russian banks accounted for up to half of the trading volume

18. Denis Cherkassov and Yaroslav Skvortsov, "Upolnomochennye banki—ukazy na vyzhivanie," *Kommersant*, April 29, 1997.

19. Organization for Economic Cooperation and Development, *OECD Economic Surveys: Russian Federation, 1997* (Paris: OECD, 1997).

20. Pekka Sutela, "The Role of Banks in Financing Russian Economic Growth," *Post-Soviet Geography and Economics* 39, no. 2 (February 1998): 114.

21. CBR, *Bulletin of Banking Statistics* 2 (1999): 133.

Table 7.1. Banks with the largest holdings of government securities, July 1997

Bank	Government securities (million dollars)	Percent of assets in government securities[a]
Sberbank	$16819.2	57.80
Bank of Moscow	589.0	45.16
Avtobank	560.9	35.01
Vneshtorgbank	512.1	13.12
Inkombank	463.6	13.53
Mosbiznesbank	432.8	26.63
Rossiiskii Kredit Bank	270.3	15.42
National Reserve Bank	269.8	13.43
ONEKSIMbank	228.6	6.36
Mezhprombank	185.5	12.33
Mezhkombank	181.6	45.57
International Moscow Bank	148.6	11.43
Promstroibank St. Petersburg	147.8	20.04
Bank Menatep	147.0	7.73
Copf	122.7	34.09
Promstroibank Rossii	121.5	11.67
Bashkreditbank	112.2	25.65
Sovfintrade	104.4	30.06
Toribank	90.1	14.76
Unibest	86.1	39.33

Source: Russia Review, 1997
[a]Assets according to CBR methodology

on the Russian stock exchange.[22] Foreign investors rapidly joined in as well, attracted by the cachet of Russia's "emerging market" and looking to profit from the huge leaps in stock valuations. The stock market rose 146 percent in 1996 and another 184 percent in the first eight months of 1997.[23] It peaked in October 1997, when the Russian stock market became the most profitable one in the world. By late 1998, Russian banks held 8.77 billion rubles worth of stock investments, with Moscow banks accounting for 84.5 percent of the total.[24]

Moreover, throughout 1997 the biggest Moscow banks attracted funds by accumulating extensive liabilities in hard currency. They did this by raising money in Western markets directly (for example, issuing dollar-

22. Timothy Frye, "Governing the Russian Equities Market," *Post-Soviet Affairs* 13, no. 4 (October–December 1997): 366–95.

23. EBRD, *Transition Report 1998*, 12.

24. CBR, *Bulletin of Banking Statistics* 2 (1999): 133.

Table 7.2. Russian bank debts to foreign creditors (Top ten, in million dollars, as of July 1998)

Bank	Debt
SBS-Agro	1,196
Inkombank	820
Rossiiskii Kredit	648.1
ONEKSIMbank	557.9
Gazprombank	549.9
Vneshtorgbank	474.1
Menatep	419.1
Imperial	388.9
Sberbank	355.9
National Reserve	276.7

Source: Kommersant Daily, 1998

denominated American Depository Receipts—or ADRs), by taking out loans from foreign banks, and by issuing dollar-forward contracts. Menatep, Inkombank, and Vozrozhdenie all offered ADRs to Western investors in 1997. Far more took out hard-currency loans from Western banks. Russian banks had accumulated $32.4 billion in foreign-currency liabilities (about one-third of official bank assets) by the end of 1997.[25] By 1998, debts to foreign banks represented over 20 percent of the liabilities of half of Russia's 20 largest banks (see Table 7.2). SBS-Agro took on the most foreign loans, with over $1 billion in debt representing 28 percent of its liabilities. Rossiiskii Kredit followed close behind with loans accounting for 26 percent of its liabilities, while Inkombank, ONEKSIMbank, Menatep, and Most Bank all had foreign loans measuring between 12 percent and 17 percent of liabilities. Much of this hard currency, of course, went straight into the GKO and stock markets.

Why was the West so willing to loan to and invest money in these young, overextended, nontransparent Russian banks? Partly because greed got the best of them, and partly because the big Russian banks had accumulated a veneer of international respectability. In May 1996, the CBR started a system called OPERU-2, which designated certain banks as "vital" to the stability of the Russian banking system. These banks traded a higher level of oversight for privileged status with the CBR and the implication that they would be specially protected in times of trouble. While fourteen of the most prominent banks made the early list, by 1998 the

25. Illarionov, "The Roots of the Economic Crisis."

CBR covered all major federally authorized banks and those licensed to provide foreign investment accounts for treasury bills and government bonds. The OPERU-2 designation reassured potential creditors not only that these were the leading banks in the system, but that they enjoyed the confidence of the Russian government.

The EBRD, World Bank, international auditing firms, and international rating firms contributed to this perception. First, the EBRD bought equity stakes in banks like Tokobank, Inkombank, and Avtobank. Since the EBRD had access to detailed information about the conditions and practices of these banks, purchasing a stake appeared to be an official stamp of approval. Second, the EBRD and World Bank accredited 41 banks to the Financial Institutions Development Project (FIDP). The FIDP, a noteworthy attempt to bring world-class credibility and standards to the Russian banking system, intended to "twin" selected Russian banks with foreign banks in order to foster the professional development of the Russian banks. Despite the earlier success of a similar twinning program in Poland, though, the FIDP in Russia proved an utter failure because of the fundamentally different political and institutional environments in the two countries. Nevertheless, the international financial community interpreted the anointing of a bank at the beginning of the FIDP project to be a sign that things would turn out all right in the end. Finally, prominent Western firms began to audit the biggest Russian banks (albeit typically to Russian accounting standards), and as a result the banks earned Western debt ratings. For example, in March 1998 Thompson Bankwatch rated 15 Russian banks a healthy "B+" for long-term senior debt (including the soon-to-collapse Imperial and Tokobank), and gave 26 banks ratings for short-term ruble debt.[26] Therefore, the Western financial community not only admired the Russian bankers' Potemkin village, but helped them to construct it.

Just as importantly, as foreign investors entered the GKO market, they made deals with Russian banks to shield their currency risk. In these dollar-forward contracts, the banks guaranteed to pay off maturing ruble-denominated GKOs in dollars at a previously fixed exchange rate, usually between 6.5 and 7 rubles to the dollar. In theory, the CBR had placed limits on the amount of such contracts a bank could make, but in practice the banks routinely flouted these regulations. More than 20 banks, including all of the largest banks at the head of FIGs except Al'fa Bank, held a total of about $40 billion of dollar-forward contracts. Inkombank extended itself the furthest by far, holding almost 140 billion rubles worth of forward contracts by August 1998. ONEKSIMbank held 35 billion, SBS-Agro 28.6 billion, Menatep 19.4 billion, and Rossiiskii Kredit 18 billion.

26. "Tiazhelye den'gi," *Ekspert* 11 (March 23, 1998): 42–54.

Some questions exist about how exactly to describe the value of each bank's post-crisis debt in dollar terms, but analysts at the Troika Dialog investment fund measured it at $1.88 billion for Inkombank and $1.44 billion for ONEKSIMbank.[27]

The banks did sell ruble-forward contracts to attempt to cover this risk, but of course they sold them to each other, creating an untenably intertwined chain. In effect, the banks bet big on ruble stability. If the ruble stayed within its corridor they would have made handsome trading profits, but if it slipped, they would be financially exposed. Therefore, the seeming prosperity of the banks came to rest on fragile foundations—the stability of GKOs, the stock market, and the ruble—in a country with a substantially de-monetized economy and a nearly bankrupt government.

The Crisis Unfolds

The Asian currency crisis and the drop in world oil prices served as the catalysts that brought down Russia's financial house of cards. The rolling Asian crisis began in Thailand in July 1997, but did not hit Russia until October 28 of that year, when alarmed foreign investors began pulling out of the Russian stock market, causing it to drop over 20 percent in one day. Then in November, when foreign investors got their first opportunity to cash in government securities since the Asian crisis began, about $5 billion fled the GKO market.[28] The flood continued into the new year, as, according to Chubais, $2 billion of Southeast Asian money left Russia between January and March 1998.[29] The *Moscow Times* stock index, which had reached a high of 379.3 in September 1997, would fall all the way to 28.7 by September 1998.[30] At the same time, international prices for oil and metals continued to plummet, reaching a 10–year low in the case of oil. World oil prices fell from $135 per metric ton in October 1997 to $67 per metric ton in October 1998.[31] In 1997, in dollar terms oil represented 46 percent of Russia's exports, and metals represented 17 percent.[32] The export price for Russian crude oil in the first half of 1998 fell by 31 percent compared with the first half of 1997, and total export earnings fell by $2.2 billion in comparison to the previous year.[33] For the Rus-

---

27. Margaret Coker, "Help from Afar," *Russia Review* 5, no. 19 (November 1998): 30–31.

28. Dmitry Zaks, "Russia's Biggest Stories of 1997," *Moscow Times*, December 30, 1997.

29. Anatolii Chubais, "Democracy Is Never for Free," statement submitted to the U.S. House Committee on Banking and Financial Services, "Hearing on International Economic Turmoil," September 15, 1998.

30. Slay, "An Interpretation of the Russian Financial Crisis."

31. "The Oil Lobby," *Business in Russia* 100 (April–May 1999): 35–36.

32. Sapir, "Russia's Crash of August 1998."

33. Illarionov, "The Roots of the Economic Crisis."

sian government, the flight from treasury bills threatened its solvency and raised the yields it had to offer, while the fall in commodities prices cut into its already meager tax revenue from exporters. For the largest Russian banks, especially the bank-led FIGs, the situation had become even more dire. While foreign flight did cause GKO yields to rise, the fall in the stock market hurt those who had invested heavily. Moreover, the bank-led FIGs, many of whom now controlled large oil and metals enterprises, faced an immediate loss of revenue from these companies. The decision to postpone the scheduled November 1997 privatization auctions for 34 percent of the Eastern oil company and 50 percent of the Tiumen' oil company spoke to this lack of liquidity.

This combination of stresses naturally put significant pressure on the ruble, and almost led to a devaluation crisis in early 1998. To stave off collapse, the CBR defended the ruble by selling dollars and raising interest rates from 21 percent to 42 percent over a three-month period. Although at this point whispers about the inevitability of devaluation began to be heard, the CBR steadfastly held firm in its intention to maintain the ruble corridor regardless of the cost to itself (in running down its foreign exchange reserves) or to domestic banks (in raising interest rates). Dubinin's CBR, with the hearty encouragement of the IMF, certainly believed in the abstract need to defend the currency from speculative attacks. In addition, though, the CBR's own financial interest in the GKO market through its connection to Sberbank and banks like FIMACO gave it a private incentive to go all-out in protecting the ruble. Unfortunately, rather than prudently building up its reserves as foreign money flowed into Russia in 1996–97, the Central Bank had spent and invested it.[34] It could defend the ruble once on its own, but not twice. By July 1, 1998, it had reserves of only about $15 billion (with $4.5 billion of that in illiquid gold), down from $23 billion in October 1997.[35] With reserves down and GKO revenues falling, the government started borrowing money wildly on the international market. From January through July 1998 alone, Russia's overall foreign debt increased by $18.5 billion.[36] During this period the government attracted $10.5 billion in new foreign loans alone, up 40 percent from the $7.6 billion it had borrowed in 1997.[37]

34. Ibid.

35. Anders Åslund, "Russia's Financial Crisis: Causes and Possible Remedies," *Post-Soviet Geography and Economics* 39, no. 6 (1999): 309–28. If we look at net international reserves (NIR), the situation was even more dire for the CBR. On January 1, 1998 it held only $4.2 billion in NIR, while by March the level had fallen to $0.5 billion See Michael Bernstam and Alvin Rabushka, *Fixing Russia's Banks: A Proposal for Growth* (Stanford, Calif.: Hoover Institution Press, 1998), 101.

36. Illarionov, "The Roots of the Economic Crisis."

37. CBR, "Annual Report, 1998," 33.

On March 23, 1998, Boris Yeltsin added fuel to the fire by dismissing his long-time prime minister, Viktor Chernomyrdin. While Yeltsin once again claimed that he did so in order to bring new blood and new ideas into the government, Boris Berezovskii's increasingly public backing of Chernomyrdin as a future presidential candidate seemed the more likely reason. After Yeltsin's reelection in 1996 his health had continued to deteriorate. The Russian public barely saw their president in late 1996 and 1997 as he underwent a multiple-bypass operation, suffered from pneumonia, and seemed to spend far more time "recovering" at his Barvikha estate than working in the Kremlin. With Yeltsin's ill-health contributing to the air of instability, other politicians constantly jockeyed for influence. No sooner had Russia's Central Electoral Commission set July 9, 2000, as the date for the next presidential election than the unofficial campaign began. In Davos in February 1998, Berezovskii revealed that Russia's leading financiers were already trying to decide which candidates to back in the next parliamentary and presidential elections. As he told ITAR-Tass, "Big business cannot permit the situation that occurred last time when we woke up actually five months before the elections having missed parliamentary elections. We are earnestly discussing what is going to happen during the parliamentary and presidential elections. Capital cannot shirk its responsibility."[38] Such statements appeared especially portentous given the forum, since it was at a meeting in Davos in February 1996 that the infamous "Group of Seven" bankers decided to join forces to support the troubled Yeltsin presidential campaign. As Berezovskii wishfully proclaimed in Davos, the presidential elections "will not be—and cannot be—democratic." This not only revealed Berezovskii's continuing contempt for democracy, but led the ailing Yeltsin to perceive this maneuvering as a threat to his power.

After he fired Chernomyrdin, the president nominated a little-known young banker from Nizhnii Novgorod, Sergei Kirienko, to be prime minister. Although touted as an uncorrupted market reformer, Kirienko had made his way up the post-Soviet ladder of success in the same manner as other top bankers and politicians.[39] Kirienko had founded Garantiia Bank using resources from the oblast' pension fund while his close friend from Komsomol days, Boris Nemtsov, served as governor of the oblast'. Nemtsov appointed Kirienko to run the Norsi oil company in November 1996, and in 1997 brought Kirienko to Moscow where he became deputy and then head of the Fuel and Energy Ministry before his appointment as prime minister.

38. Interfax, "Entrepreneur: Zyuganov, Lebed, Luzhkov Don't Suit Presidential Role," February 3, 1998.
39. Dimtry Zaks, "Kirienko Unallied, Unsullied," *Moscow Times*, March 28, 1998.

The Duma was immediately up in arms over this latest government shake-up. It reluctantly approved Kirienko only on its third and final vote on April 24, under threat of disbandment if it had refused. This high-level political uncertainty brought on by the bankers, Yeltsin, and the Duma further frightened already wary foreign investors.

By May 1998, the situation had become critical. The CBR put Tokobank under temporary administration, as it encountered major liquidity problems and had lost access to the interbank credit market in early 1998. On May 18, the stock market went down another 10 percent, and the CBR raised interest rates to 50 percent the next day to send a signal that it would continue to defend the ruble. Finally, the official failure of the Rosneft' auction on May 26 signaled the bankruptcy of the government's cash privatization strategy and fully revealed the poverty of the bank-led FIGs. The Russian government had planned to raise money by selling Rosneft', the last major state-owned oil company, in a fair auction in 1998 that was to be open to foreigners. Russian bankers, as well as Gazprom and Lukoil, had long salivated over Rosneft'. Rosneft' was involved in high-profile oil development projects such as Timan-Pechora, Sakhalin 1 and 2, and the Caspian Pipeline Consortium, and held good proven reserves (fourth among Russian oil majors). Throughout late 1997 and early 1998, the bankers and the two energy companies attempted to line up foreign partners for bidding and to hoard resources for the purchase. After lobbying in vain to limit foreign participation in the auction, Berezovskii tasked Salomon Brothers with finding foreign partners to join in the bidding process with him. Berezovskii both wanted and needed to control Rosneft' in order to shore up the ailing Sibneft', and often expressed his intention to win this auction. ONEKSIMbank planned to participate as well, and its sale of 10 percent of Sidanko to British Petroleum was widely perceived as a fundraising effort to allow ONEKSIMbank to make a competitive bid. Lukoil and Gazprom also joined together to form a formidable bidding consortium. Yet despite all of this sound and fury, by May no group was able to submit a bid above the fair minimum asking price. Cash privatization had failed the government and the bankers. On May 27, the stock market fell again by 10.5 percent, and the CBR raised interest rates to an astronomical 150 percent. Berezovskii, through his newspaper *Nezavisimaia gazeta*, began publicly advocating ruble devaluation.

Only massive injections of foreign capital would now postpone a crisis. On June 4, Russia issued a $1.25 billion Eurobond, and the Central Bank of Russia tried to create artificial confidence in the financial system by lowering interest rates to 60 percent. On June 18, Russia issued another $2.5 billion Eurobond. Chubais, now named Russia's international "loan liaison officer," persuaded the IMF to release a $670 million loan tranche on June 25 that had been suspended because of Russia's failure to collect taxes. Despite these efforts, though, the stock market continued to fall and the government's GKO offerings were undersubscribed. By July 8, the stock market had dropped 78 percent from its peak in October 1997.[40] The CBR raised interest rates again, this time to 80 percent. The end of the ruble corridor was near. As Russian economist Andrei Illarionov observes, "the government program actually being implemented in the summer of 1998 (not the one that was written, discussed, and officially approved), had been designed to save from bankruptcy not the Russian state, but Russia's largest banks."[41] In its last gift to Russia's bankers, in July the IMF sent a $4.8 billion stabilization loan directly to the Central Bank. The CBR, almost out of its own reserves, immediately sold these dollars as Russian banks and enterprises used the capital influx to desperately convert their ruble holdings. Sberbank, not coincidentally, was one of the biggest ruble sellers. Stocks continued to slide, and GKO yields rose to over 100 percent on August 11. On August 13, George Soros publicly advocated ruble devaluation. Dollar shortages appeared throughout Russia.

The now inevitable collapse of the Russian GKO market and the ruble corridor laid bare the glaring structural weaknesses of the country's financial system. On August 17, the government defaulted on GKOs worth 281 billion rubles ($60 billion at the time), and gave up defending the value of the ruble. Before August 17, the exchange rate had held steady at approximately 6 rubles to the dollar; it dropped by over half in two weeks, hit 20.99 at the end of 1998, and by April 1999 had reached almost 25 to the dollar.[42] The crash paralyzed the payments system, tax transfers, the short-term credit market, and currency exchange points as most major Moscow banks immediately became technically bankrupt. Not only did they represent a significant portion of the GKO market, but the crack in the ruble corridor meant that their dollar-denominated debt and dollar-forward contracts became far too expensive to service.[43]

Therefore, in a concession to the worst-off of the still-influential banks, the government also declared a 90–day moratorium on all payments of Russian bank debts to foreign banks. Russia's 30 largest banks had debts to foreign banks totaling $3.4 billion that would mature during the 90–day period.[44] On August 26, the Central Bank of Russia halted ruble-

40. Åslund, "Russia's Financial Crisis."

41. Illarionov, "The Roots of the Economic Crisis."

42. The dollar passed the 25-ruble barrier only in early September 1999, because the CBR committed to keeping the ruble's value under 25 to the dollar until the end of the summer. The end of summer arrived, and the ruble promptly fell. Igor Semeneko, "Ruble Slumps as Central Bank Stops Support," *Moscow Times*, September 2, 1999.

43. Michael Hiltzik, "Virtual banking," *Russia Review* 5, no. 19 (November 1998): 24–25.

44. Interfax, "Russia's 30 Largest Banks' Debt Totals $3.4 Billion," August 26, 1998.

dollar trading entirely, and formally abandoned the ruble corridor the following week. In rapid succession, it revoked Imperial Bank's license and put SBS-Agro and Inkombank under temporary CBR administration. During the last half of 1998, the assets of the Russian banking system (measured by generous Russian accounting standards) fell from $88.7 billion to $34.2 billion, and its capital, excluding Sberbank, fell by five times.[45] According to the CBR, the assets of the largest 29 Russian banks decreased by 19.3 percent and the capital by 57.3 percent in real terms between August and December 1998, and these banks suffered almost 40 percent of the total losses of the Russian banking system.[46] As Natal'ia Raevskaia, director of Avtobank, observed, "Banks now have no source of resources: foreign banks will not give money, their own resources have been drawn down, and the population has been frightened and has returned to putting money in their socks."[47]

Who was to blame for this massive banking collapse? Was it a freak result of the simultaneous drop in oil prices and the Asian financial crisis? Was it the international financial markets, which at the first sign of trouble pulled money out of Russia as quickly as it had earlier swept in? Was it the CBR, which had maintained an overvalued ruble for months? Was it the Yeltsin government, politically unstable and ever-more dependent on foreign capital? Or was it the Russian banks, which madly sold rubles for dollars in the final weeks leading to the crisis, even as they knew this individually rational response would bring collective disaster?

Indeed, all of these factors contributed to the crash of 1998. But the ultimate cause lay in the evolving relationship between the Russian state and the banking system. As institutional legacies interacted explosively with a series of trickle-down policy choices from 1987 on, the wealthy, politically influential banks became ever-more divorced from the productive economy and dependent on the state. Ironically, it was only when the state began to pull its overt support away from the banks after the presidential election that the cracks in this system began to show. The Yeltsin team and the Moscow bankers had built the Ponzi scheme together, with Western investors adding fuel to the fire. In August 1998, it appeared that both might perish in the flames.

After the Fall

The crash of 1998 sent the Yeltsin government into a tailspin. On August 23, Yeltsin, using his tried and tired strategy, fired Prime Minister

45. Alla Barteneva, "Poteriannye milliardy," *Ekspert* 13 (April 5, 1999): 15–20.
46. CBR, "Annual Report, 1998," 90.
47. Quoted in Elena Makovskaia, "Bez paniki," *Ekspert* 44 (November 23, 1998): 38–39.

Kirienko and his entire government. A few days later, he fired Anatolii Chubais from his position as chief debt negotiator, and then orchestrated Sergei Dubinin's resignation from the CBR. While Yeltsin initially hoped to reappoint Viktor Chernomyrdin as prime minister (reportedly under Berezovskii's influence), the Duma would not oblige, and Yeltsin was forced to nominate the formidable Yevgenii Primakov in his place.

The choice of Primakov, a former head of the Russian Foreign Intelligence Service and an important political player in Soviet times, frightened the West but placated the Duma. The Duma confirmed Primakov as prime minister on September 12. Interestingly, it approved the new Central Bank director on the same day—none other than former Gosbank and CBR head Viktor Gerashchenko.[48] The state had come back into the hands of old standbys.

The Moscow bankers reacted to the crisis as one might expect, based on their past behavior: they turned to the state for help, stiffed their clients, and reorganized their holdings so as to minimize their debts. The state immediately responded to the bankers' pleas for help. In an article entitled "Parasites Look to Primakov for Fresh Feed," Moscow-based political analyst Yulia Latynina argued that "Over the last few weeks, the Russian executive branch has consistently followed a course that could be defined as 'Save the lice instead of the sheep'."[49] Right before the crisis, the CBR had given large loans to several banks (most notably SBS-Agro) in an attempt to prop them up. It also allowed banks in five regions (including Moscow) to draw down their Central Bank reserves in order to pay off their debts. The CBR then swapped the frozen GKO holdings of these banks for Lombard credits that it deposited in their reserve accounts and carried out "mutual debt cancellations" among banks through their CBR correspondent accounts. The swaps cost at least 4.2 billion rubles ($265 million) in September and another 10.6 billion ($668 million) in October, and the ultimate amount (including the debt cancellations and the massive swaps of Sberbank-held GKOs) was certainly much higher.[50] The CBR also repeatedly made substantial long-term loans to a small group of favored banks after the crisis. Four of these banks—SBS-Agro, Promstroibank, Vozhrozhdenie, and Avtobank—pledged 75 percent plus one of their shares to the CBR as collateral for these loans.[51] By November, the

48. Natal'ia Kulakova and Elena Kiseleva, "Finansovyi perevorot," *Kommersant-Daily*, September 12, 1998.

49. Yulia Latynina, "Parasites Look to Primakov for Fresh Feed," *Moscow Times*, September 15, 1998.

50. Some estimate the total amount of the swaps at over 65 billion rubles in Lombard credits. See John van Schaik, "The Newly-Wed and the Nearly Dead," *Euromoney*, June 1999.

51. Ibid.

CBR's total post-crisis loans to the banking system had topped 55 billion rubles ($3.5 billion).[52]

The government also supported the bankers by helping them to minimize and delay payment of their foreign hard-currency debts. The 90–day debt moratorium represented the main plank in this strategy, but it was not the only trick up their sleeve. On September 15 and October 15, large sums of these banks' dollar-forward contracts came due. Mysteriously, right before each of these dates, the ruble's value rose. On September 9 the ruble sat at 20.83 to the dollar, yet had reached 7.96 to the dollar by September 15. One hour after the contracts came due, the ruble fell by 30 percent to 12.5. This happened again in October. Foreign contract holders cried foul, but received no satisfaction. It did not matter at the moment anyway, though, since most of the banks had no intention of paying off the contracts on the due dates.

For the ever-innovative enterprises and bankers, the crash also created a new trading market in the debt of distressed banks (especially SBS-Agro, Inkombank, and Menatep). For example, a financial intermediary (often affiliated with the suffering bank itself) might arrange a debt swap for a fee. If a bank owed an enterprise $100,000 and the enterprise did not think it would be able to recover the money, it might sell this credit for $50,000 to an enterprise that owed the bank money. The indebted enterprise could then use the credit to retire $100,000 worth of debt with the bank at half price.[53] Another trading twist involved the banks' own veksels. For example, Mosenergo owed Inkombank $160 million, so at the start of the crisis Mosenergo bought Inkombank veksels at a fraction of their value (about $50 million) and used the veksels to retire its debt to the bank.[54]

With few exceptions, the banks did not use these windfalls and delays to settle debts with their depositors and creditors. Several banks defaulted on foreign debt payments, while Lehman Brothers arranged to freeze the accounts of Inkombank and ONEKSIMbank in Britain in attempt to retrieve $113 million it claimed to be owed from forward contracts. The banks' Russian depositors fared little better. The commercial banks held an estimated $1.5 billion in household deposits, with SBS-Agro having 5 million depositors and Inkombank 500,000. Individual depositors suddenly found it extremely difficult to recover their money, as the banks of-

52. "Special Report: Resolving the Banking Crisis," *Russian Economic Trends*, November 1998.

53. Margaret Coker, "Debt Trading's Debut," *Russia Review* 5, no. 19 (November 1998): 52–53.

54. Vladimir Inozemtsev, public seminar, Harvard University, November 11, 1998.

fered a series of unattractive account conversion deals. On September 2, the CBR "encouraged" the six banks holding 70 percent of commercial banks' retail deposits (SBS-Agro, Menatep, Inkombank, Most Bank, Mosbiznesbank, and Promstroibank) to transfer their retail deposits to Sberbank.[55] It later added Rossiiskii Kredit to the list. In this deal, depositors could either transfer their accounts to Sberbank at a significant loss, or keep "restructured" accounts in their original banks (typically offering no access to the funds for at least a year at interest rates far below the likely rate of inflation). In the end, 7.1 billion rubles of household deposits (12 percent of total household deposits in the commercial banking system) were transferred to Sberbank.[56]

To depositors who remembered the 1991 currency swap, the 1992 inflation, the 1993 currency exchange, and the 1995 banking crisis, this was familiar ground. They were up in arms, protesting at bank headquarters, bringing lawsuits against the banks, and even robbing the banks to recover "their" money. These complaints met sympathetic ears, especially in the regions. In Tula, for example, a judge froze 30 percent of SBS-Agro's incoming funds in response to complaints from local depositors.[57] Only about 20 percent of individuals had any bank savings at all by early 1998, and this latest collapse ensured that the number would diminish even further. Ruble household deposits in commercial banks diminished by 16 billion (47.6 percent) in the last half of 1998, while household deposits in foreign exchange decreased even more dramatically, by $2.3 billion (58 percent).[58]

The August 1998 financial crisis had two major effects on the structure of the Russian banking system. First, it dealt a devastating blow to the banks at the center of bank-led FIGs. All tolled, from July 1998 to December 1998 the list of top 50 banks by assets changed by one-third.[59] As a result, the financiers at the head of these groups shuffled assets away from their crippled banks and reoriented their economic activities towards their industrial holdings.

The bankers first tried to save their empires through restructuring. Immediately after the crash, bankers announced three major mergers. National Reserve Bank, Inkombank, Avtobank, Mezhkombank, and Al'fa Bank declared their plans to merge; ONEKSIMbank, MFK, Menatep, and Most Bank agreed to form a new entity called "Rosbank"; and Mosbiznes-

55. Karl Emerick Hanuska, "Banking on What?" *Russia Review* 5, no. 17 (September 25, 1998): 24–25.
56. CBR, "Annual Report, 1998," 88.
57. "SBS-Agro Funds Frozen," *Russia Review* 5, no. 19 (November 1998): 12.
58. CBR, "Annual Report, 1998," 88.
59. Ibid., 91.

bank and Bank of Moscow arranged to merge. Only the latter merger, however, actually took place. As the bankers realized the extent of each others' debts, the biggest merger plans fell through.

Since mergers did not represent a satisfactory solution to their problems, the bankers began to restructure their own individual operations to minimize their liabilities. The bankers thus preserved as much of their resources as possible while leaving their depositors and creditors holding the bag. ONEKSIMbank, for example, moved many of its assets into BaltONEKSIMbank and the newly created Rosbank, which ONEKSIM-bank assumed control over after the failed merger. Rosbank came up with $500 million as charter capital, and soon opened a branch in Noril'sk and took over Noril'sk Nickel's accounts. SBS-Agro bank changed its name to Soiuzbank, and then opened another institution called First Mutual Credit Society (where it sent its best clients). Menatep shifted its operations to Menatep St. Petersburg, allowing the main Moscow entity to go under. Rossiiskii Kredit created its own new "bridge bank" called Impeks-bank. Moreover, the bankers could move assets to the bank-led FIGs' holding companies, such as Interros, SBS-Agro Holding, and Rosprom. These legally separate holding companies and affiliated enterprises persisted while the banks were cut loose. The original banks might disappear, but the financial conglomerates would remain.

The Central Bank of Russia did little to stand in the way of this subterfuge. In October 1998, Gerashchenko devised a plan to revive the banking system that divided banks into four groups: 1) healthy banks, which would be left alone; 2) regional banks with branch networks, whose losses would be written off in exchange for giving an equity stake to the state; 3) core banks (the most important banks for the system), which would be dealt with on a case-by-case basis; and 4) insolvent lesser banks, which would be liquidated.[60] In November, the CBR and the Yeltsin government created the Agency for the Reconstruction of Credit Organizations (ARKO) to handle bank restructuring.[61] Despite the appearance of action, however, ARKO had insufficient power to deal with the massive banking crisis. The state budgeted only 10 billion rubles for ARKO's work, and six months later had still not transferred even this small amount to its account. ARKO actually existed without a director until March 1999, when the CBR's Aleksandr Turbanov (the former Inkom-

60. Gary Peach, "The Big Bank Bailout," *Russia Review* 5, no. 19 (November 1998): 32–33.

61. Anton Starozhilov, "Glavnyi konstruktor," *Ekspert* 13 (April 5, 1999): 22–26; Viktor Gerashchenko, "Kak provodit' restrukturizatsiiu bankov," *Kommersant*, May 20, 1999; and "Osnovnye polozheniia programmy i printsipy deiatel'nosti ARKO," *Den'gi i kredit* 3 (1999): 11–16.

bank vice-president and Duma member) was named as its head. The Central Bank and ARKO quickly got into disputes over which banks to rescue, and neither stood in the way of the post-crisis redistribution of funds.

Of all the financial-industrial groups, Al'fa and LogoVAZ emerged from the crisis in the best positions. Al'fa had prudently avoided amassing large holdings of GKOs and dollar-forward contracts, while LogoVAZ did not have significant banking interests to weigh it down. Therefore, although both were hurt by the crisis, they eventually managed to maintain and even strengthen their economic positions.[62] Al'fa bank actually expanded its branch network throughout 1999, doubling its branches to 44 at a time when the vast majority of other banks were consolidating their networks.[63] Al'fa Group increased its stake in Tiumen' oil and fought a bitter battle with BP-Amoco over stakes in two major Sidanko subsidiaries that Al'fa won in two questionable bankruptcy auctions in October and November 1999.[64] For his part, in August 1999 Berezovskii announced that he had obtained control over the respected Kommersant publishing house, buying 85 percent of the shares from an obscure company called American Capital that had acquired the shares in July 1999.[65] More dramatically, in February 2000 Berezovskii and his Sibneft' associate Roman Abramovich arranged for affiliated companies to acquire controlling stakes in three aluminum enterprises that accounted for two-thirds of total Russian production.[66]

The halcyon days of the bank-led FIGs, though, had passed. Not only did they lose a great deal of money during the crash, but as a group their grasp on Russia's leading enterprises slipped and their political power waned. Inkombank had its license revoked, and Vladimir Vinogradov resigned as its president. Rossiiskii Kredit lost control over Krasnoiarsk Aluminum and sold its shares of Lebedinsk Ore Processing. Most Bank, although it had not been burdened with participation in cash privatization and ownership of underperforming Russian enterprises, still experienced

62. Berezovskii, for example, saw his business ventures come under heavy fire from the Russian prosecutor's office and lost his government position as Russia's representative to the CIS. As a primary dealer in GKOs, Al'fa lost about $10 million in the crisis, and also experienced a major reduction its capital base. See Ronan Lyons, "The Waltz of the Living Dead," *Euromoney*, September 1999.

63. Andrew McChesney, "Alfa Expands Operations by Ukrainian Bank Buy," *Moscow Times*, February 5, 2000.

64. See Eduard Gismatullin, "BP, TNK End Feud And Split Sidanko," *Moscow Times*, December 23, 1999.

65. Andrei Zolotov, Jr., "Berezovsky: I've Bought Kommersant," *Moscow Times*, August 7, 1999.

66. See Andrew McChesney, "Berezovsky & Co. Buy Up 3 Smelters," *Moscow Times*, February 12, 2000; and East-West Institute, "Russian Aluminum War Reaches Surprising Cease Fire," *Russian Regional Report* 5, no. 13 (April 5, 2000).

financial difficulties and Vladimir Gusinskii increasingly turned his attention towards developing and promoting Media Most. At Noril'sk Nickel, ONEKSIMbank cut staff and production, while Sidanko entered bankruptcy proceedings after Potanin tried and failed to give an unprofitable piece of Sidanko back to the state.[67] Westdeutsche Landesbank and Daiwa Bank gained 30 percent of Yukos shares, which had been the collateral for $236 million in loans to Menatep.[68] Rosprom immediately undertook a series of machinations to retain its control over Yukos, moves which ran roughshod over the external shareholders' rights. At shareholder meetings of Yukos's three subsidiaries in March 1999, plans were approved to allow Yukos to buy oil from them for three years at $1.50 a barrel, about a tenth of the world oil price at the time. Those meetings also approved the issuance of huge quantities of shares to unnamed investors in return for promissory notes issued by other Yukos subsidiaries. Most stunningly, Yukos transferred large stakes in two of its central companies (Yuganskneftegaz and Samaraneftegaz) to several new offshore companies, decimating the value of Yukos itself. The bank-led FIGs had been demoted by the August 1998 crisis (at least for the time being) to just another Russian interest group.

Second, the crash of 1998 brought Russia full circle as the banking system once again came predominantly under state control at both the regional and national levels. In the regions, the crisis provided an opportunity for local governments to increase their influence in the banking sector. Regional banks weathered the crisis better than the Moscow banks. Their bane had become their boon, because regional banks had held only 4.1 percent of all bank investments in government securities, only 16.5 percent of investments in stocks, and only 6.5 percent of bank-owned stakes in subsidiary and affiliated companies.[69] As Moscow-based banks closed their regional affiliates, regional banks stepped in to fill the gap.[70] Unlike the politically powerful Moscow banks, though, most top regional banks were under the influence of regional administrations, a trend which grew markedly stronger after the crash.

Moreover, banks controlled by Gazprom, the Moscow city government, and the CBR dominated the list of Top-20 banks by January 1999 (see

---

67. Maria Tatevosova, "Klinicheskaia smert' SIDANKO," *Ekspert* 8 (March 1, 1999): 26–27.

68. Lyons, "The Waltz of the Living Dead."

69. Calculated from CBR, *Bulletin of Banking Statistics* 2 (1999): 133. Of the non-Moscow regions, St. Petersburg had the most government securities (1.76 billion rubles, or 1.1 percent of the market) and Tatarstan the most stock investments (91 million rubles, or 1 percent of the market).

70. Banks closed 1,695 branches in 1998, almost five times more than in 1997. CBR, "Annual Report, 1998," 93.

Table 7.3. The twenty largest banks (by assets) as of January 1999

Bank	Branches	City	Affiliation (if any)
1. Sberbank Russia	27,799	Moscow	State-owned (CBR)
2. Vneshtorgbank	28	Moscow	State-owned (CBR)
3. Mezhprombank	5	Moscow	
4. Gazprombank	23	Moscow	Gazprom group
5. International Moscow Bank	1	Moscow	
6. Al'fa Bank	22	Moscow	Al'fa group
7. Most Bank	17	Moscow	Most group
8. Vozrozhdenie	60	Moscow	
9. Promstroibank St. Petersburg	43	St. Petersburg	
10. National Reserve Bank	0	Moscow	Gazprom group
11. Promstroibank Rossii	na	Moscow	Gazprom group
12. Bank of Moscow	2	Moscow	Moscow group
13. BNP-Dresdner Bank	1	Moscow	Foreign subsidiary
14. Avtobank	21	Moscow	
15. Guta Bank	2	Moscow	Moscow group
16. Evrofinans	0	Moscow	CBR group
17. Omskpromstroibank	20	Omsk	
18. Moscow Industrial Bank	35	Moscow	
19. Bank Petrovskii	19	St. Petersburg	
20. AK BARS	11	Kazan'	Government of Tatarstan

Source: *Rating* information agency, <http://www.rating.ru>

Table 7.3). Gazprom, which as Russia's leading exporter actually bene-fited from the 1998 devaluation, strengthened its hold over its affiliated banks and saw them shoot up in the ratings as banks with less wealthy patrons dropped out of sight. The Moscow city government's Sistema group assumed direct control over Mosbiznesbank, while Moscow-affiliated Guta Bank absorbed Unikombank.

Finally, not only did the Central Bank of Russia put several banks under its own administration, but Sberbank once again became Russia's near-monopoly savings bank. Sberbank estimated that by April 2000, it controlled 88 percent of the household deposit market again, and it reported a 24–percent rise in profits in 1999.[71] The Russian government took full advantage of the Central Bank's relative wealth by borrowing $4.5 billion from its coffers to help repay the state's mounting foreign debts. Ironically, after ten years of trickle-down liberalization, Russian bankers and the state had become more intertwined than ever.

71. "Sberbank Posts Record Gains," *Moscow Times*, April 5, 2000.

CHAPTER EIGHT

The End of the Beginning

In Russia, only an idiot would make predictions.
—**Yabloko Party leader Grigorii Yavlinskii, 1998**

After the crash of 1998, Russia's banking system deservedly lost the trust of both the international financial community and the Russian people—despite over a decade of economic and political "reform." For the West, the Bank of New York scandal epitomized the nest of financial depravity that post-Soviet Russia had become. In August 1999, U.S. federal officials alleged that certain Russian individuals and companies had used accounts at the Bank of New York to move several billion dollars out of Russia secretly. U.S. authorities ultimately indicted one Bank of New York employee for lying to investigators, while another agreed to plead guilty to money laundering charges.[1] This incident led to U.S. Congressional hearings on Russian money laundering and to finger-pointing at the Clinton administration's Russia policy. Western commentators, once so optimistic about Russia's imminent transition to a free-market democracy, began lamenting that the Western model had proven inappropriate for that infamous enigma of a country and offered answers to the ubiquitous question, "Who Lost Russia?"

Fortunately the U.S. government had not, in fact, misplaced the Russian landmass. But this episode did remind the West that vast sums of

---

1. Lucy Edwards (a senior officer at the bank) and her husband Peter Berlin (director of Benex International, the company that controlled the questionable accounts) both agreed to guilty pleas after lengthy negotiations with federal authorities. Raymond Bonner and Timothy L. O'Brien, "Guilty Pleas Seen in the Laundering of Russian Money," *Moscow Times*, February 15, 2000.

money had vanished from Russia. While much of the cash flowing out of Russia through the Bank of New York and other institutions may well have been exported legally, this scandal illustrated the immense and persistent problem of Russian capital flight. Indeed, after slowing briefly in early 1999, capital flight shot back up to almost $3 billion monthly in the second half of the year.[2] In the face of such damning figures, the West began to ask, "If Russians won't invest in their own country, why should we?" Although it continued to blame the same tired scapegoats for Russia's problems—corrupt and weak-willed officials, the conservative Duma, rent-seeking businesspeople, and stubborn Soviet-era managers—the international financial community no longer trusted in the inevitability of a successful Russian transition.

Similarly, the initial skepticism of most individual Russians towards the Soviet and post-Soviet banking system deepened into a widely shared belief that no bank could be trusted to safeguard one's savings. Given regular commercial bank collapses, the lack of broad deposit insurance protection, Sberbank interest rates that were often negative in real terms, widespread automatic-teller-machine and other financial fraud, and the proliferation of pyramid schemes masquerading as legitimate financial institutions, it was no wonder that people like the elderly pensioner mentioned in the preface preferred to store their cash in rat-infested basements. Putting one's money in a bank did not ensure that it would hold its value, nor even that it would ever be returned. Yet simply avoiding the banking system could not solve the average Russian's savings problems either. Unpredictable inflation and exchange rates, the rise of barter and surrogate currencies, and the monetary reforms of 1991 and 1993 meant that no consistently reliable means of exchange and store of value existed in Russia. U.S. dollars came closest to meeting that standard, and as a result by 1999 Russians held an estimated $40 billion in cash within Russia's borders.[3] Taken together, the high level of capital flight and the minuscule level of individual bank savings demonstrate the terrible cost to Russia of its untrustworthy banking system. Rather than putting their earnings in reliable banks that could redirect the money to productive investment, Russia's citizens and companies typically either sent their earnings abroad or gave the U.S. Treasury an interest-free loan by holding them in cash dollars. Without a viable banking system to mediate exchange, Russia had reached a developmental dead end.

How did this occur? As this book has argued, the problematic emergence, development, and crisis of the Russian financial system resulted from the unhappy convergence of Soviet-era institutional legacies with in-

2. "Flight Takes the Future from Russia," *Moscow Times*, November 24, 1999.
3. James Roberts, "Dollar-Choked Russia," *Moscow Times*, October 8, 1999.

appropriate policy choices. The Soviet and then Russian government's trickle-down policies ensured that any power it once had to direct the development of the financial system gradually slipped out of its hands. By implementing a sequence of liberalizing and decentralizing measures in an inhospitable institutional environment, these would-be reformers asked command-era economic institutions to adapt themselves to the rapidly changing political and economic situation.

Adapt they did, but not as the reformers hoped or expected. Under Gorbachev, the liberalization of the financial system fostered hundreds of tiny, parasitic banks and facilitated *nomenklatura* privatization. In 1990–91, the battle for sovereignty between Gorbachev and Yeltsin led to the commercialization of the spetsbanks, the loosening of banking regulations, and the emergence of a politically autonomous yet technically challenged Central Bank of Russia. Yeltsin's failed attempt at shock therapy in 1992 and the subsequent high inflation and rapid privatization reinforced the growing power of the largest Moscow banks, while impoverishing the majority of Russian industrial and agricultural enterprises. Western advisors exacerbated this process by encouraging rapid liberalization while neglecting the importance of a market-oriented institutional infrastructure. Moreover, the West overlooked the Yeltsin government's abuses of democratic procedure and ongoing favoritism towards the Moscow bankers because of Yeltsin's apparent commitment to the IMF's preferred policy approach of liberalization, privatization, and stabilization.

These bankers had become major political players by the 1993 Duma elections, and used this political power to gain economic favors from the Yeltsin government. When macroeconomic stabilization finally occurred, underlying institutional weaknesses had set the stage for a massive regional banking crisis and the de-monetization of much of the Russian economy. The hundreds of regional banks dependent on inflation-based revenue, centralized credits, and loans to suffering enterprises could not survive in an atmosphere of relatively low inflation and exchange rate stability. Likewise, stabilization combined with institutional legacies such as the *kartoteka* system led perpetually insolvent Russian enterprises to shun banks and resort to barter, veksels, and interenterprise debt as means of exchange. Well-connected Moscow banks, which could tap the treasury bill markets and which held the vast majority of government budget funds, emerged on top and began to use these resources to accumulate enterprise holdings. The loans-for-shares debacle in 1995 completed the creation of politically powerful financial-industrial groups in Russia and the concentration of financial resources in Moscow. The continuing lack of deeper political and economic restructuring, however, meant that both the banks and the state had to rely increasingly on short-term, speculative strategies for their financial survival. In the end, these strategies failed. Giving greater autonomy to Russia's banks had not ensured that they would then undertake market-oriented reforms on their own. Instead, this policy created an irony of autonomy, in which banks exercised their freedom from central control to subvert Russia's long-term political and economic development.

In certain ways, the rise and fall of the banker-oligarchs resembled that of the U.S. Robber Barons to which Russia's bankers so enjoyed being compared. Like the Russian bankers, in the court of public opinion the Robber Barons were victims of their own success. As economist Miguel Simon observes:

> By 1912, 18 financial institutions sat on the boards of 134 corporations with $25.325 billion in combined assets. Of these 18 institutions, five banks held the lion's share: J.P. Morgan and Co., First National Bank, National City Bank, Guaranty Trust Co., and Bankers' Trust sat on the boards of 68 non-financial corporations with $17.273 billion in assets. . . . These banks controlled industrial assets (on behalf of others) representing 56 percent of the country's GNP.[4]

As in Russia, this concentration of power led to a public backlash in the United States. In 1914, for example, Louis Brandeis railed against the bankers' power in *Other People's Money and How the Bankers Use It*. Brandeis argued that such concentration suppressed competition, distorted company development, and harmed minority shareholders.[5] And again, as in Russia, a systemic financial crisis contributed to the bankers' fall from grace. The 1929 stock market crash did in the Robber Barons, as the government no longer remained willing to support finance capital in the United States. The bankers' meteoric rise and fall culminated in the 1933 Glass-Steagall Act, which forced a separation between commercial banking and investment banking activities.

Yet the similarities end there. Unlike the Robber Barons, Russia's bankers did not add value to the companies they acquired. Instead of creating wealth, they merely redistributed it to themselves. Moreover, their ability to do so rested entirely on their cozy relationships with the Yeltsin government and the Western-influenced perception that privatization of any kind would yield meaningful, market-oriented transformations. Russia's banks used the political system to ensure a continued flow of state re-

---

4. Miguel Cantillo Simon, "The Rise and Fall of Bank Control in the United States: 1890–1939," *American Economic Review* 88, no. 5 (December 1998): 1077–93.

5. Louis Brandeis, *Other People's Money and How the Bankers Use It* (New York: Jacket Library, 1914).

sources into their coffers, while the government amassed a massive debt burden, with little economic progress to show for it. This solidified the deep public mistrust of the post-Soviet financial and political systems. As one Moscow real estate broker observed after Rossiiskii Kredit froze over $40,000 in her account, "The moral of my story is that this country is not ready to have a proper middle class. This country is losing its middle class now because we are so frustrated. I am leaving this country."[6] The big Moscow banks, in short, contributed to the gradual evisceration of Russia's fledgling market democracy.

The crash of 1998 marked the end of Russia's first attempt at economic transformation. With the bankers temporarily weakened, it also presented the Yeltsin government with an opportunity to distance itself from the embrace of financial interests and to demonstrate a new commitment to political and economic institution-building, transparency, and the rule of law. Russia and the West, however, had learned few lessons from this debacle. In the economic sphere, much like vampires the "undead" banks and bankers continued to feed on the Russian economy with the complicity of the Russian state. The practice of authorized banks and insider privatization auctions persisted, while the broader battle over property redistribution heated up once again. The government declared SBS-Agro bankrupt, and announced the imminent creation of a new state-owned agricultural bank with an old name, Rossel'khozbank. Meanwhile, the stock market began to boom again, world oil prices rose to the delight of Russian exporters, and the August 1998 devaluation sparked a growth spurt in Russian GDP. The IMF designed a reform program for Russia composed of warmed-over and unfinished recommendations that had previously been offered, while Russia's creditors negotiated over debt restructuring. In February 2000, the Russian government began issuing new GKOs even though it had yet to deal with the problems that caused the old GKO pyramid to collapse.

Politically, Yeltsin continued his capricious and undemocratic ways by firing two successive prime ministers (Yevgeny Primakov and Sergei Stepashin) before settling on the obscure former KGB agent Vladimir Putin in August 1999. Buoyed by popular support for the renewed war in Chechnia, the Kremlin used its influence over the media and state finances to heavily support its new "party of power," Unity, in the high-stakes December 1999 Duma elections. According to the European Institute for the Media, Kremlin-affiliated media outlets conducted an unprecedented smear campaign against Unity's closest rivals—the Fatherland-All Russia block created by Primakov and Moscow mayor Yurii

6. Quoted in Adam Tanner, "Frozen solid," *Russia Review* 5, no. 19 (November 1998): 27–29.

Luzhkov—while presenting Unity leaders and supporters in a consistently positive light.[7] Although the Communist Party actually won a plurality in the party-list voting (with 24.29 percent of the vote), Unity's strong showing of 23.32 percent combined with Fatherland-All Russia's disappointing 13.33 percent contributed to the perception of a massive victory for Prime Minister Putin and Unity.

A few prominent financiers also resumed their political activities with the December 1999 Duma elections. Boris Berezovskii declared himself a Duma candidate in the Northern Caucasus Republic of Karachaevo-Cherkessia, while his associate Roman Abramovich ran in Chukotka. Both won seats. Moreover, Berezovskii-controlled media also supported Unity party candidates, while Al'fa Group increased its influence within the presidential administration and the Duma as well.

Yeltsin's surprise resignation on New Year's Eve, December 31, 1999, completed the victory of the Kremlin team. By granting Putin the status of acting president and accelerating the presidential elections to March 26, 2000, Yeltsin all but ensured the victory of his chosen heir. Backed by major financial and industrial interests, riding on a wave of unstinting media support, and with all of the advantages of the presidency at his command, Putin swept to a first-round victory with 52.64 percent of the vote. He achieved this victory despite his refusal to debate his rivals, campaign openly, or put forth an economic program for the country. After the elections, Al'fa Group director Petr Aven expressed his expectations for the Putin presidency:

> The only way ahead is for fast liberal reforms, building public support for that path but also using totalitarian force to achieve that. Russia has no other choice. . . . I'm a supporter of [former Chilean dictator Augusto] Pinochet, not as a person but as a politician who produced results for his country. . . . You can't always fight criminals by staying within the law. You can't always do it peacefully.[8]

Putin himself appreciated this parallel, saying that he would deal with corrupt elements in the economy in the same way he had dealt with the Chechen rebels. Once again, Russia's leader and his financial backers supported using extreme, undemocratic means to achieve liberal economic ends. Once again, these proclamations appeared to exclude from scrutiny those connected to the Kremlin. The new world turned out to be

7. Gillian McCormack, "State Media Won Elections, but at What Cost?," *Moscow Times*, December 29, 1999.

8. Petr Aven, quoted in Ian Traynor, "Putin Urged to Apply the Pinochet Stick," *Guardian*, March 31, 2000.

much the same as the old—truly depressing, yet maddeningly stable in its own twisted way.

While Grigorii Yavlinskii rightly warns of the dangers of peering into Russia's crystal ball, one prediction seems eminently safe. Continuing the policies of the past will reproduce the same types of perverse institutional outcomes we have witnessed in the 1980s and 1990s. Liberalizing economic policies carried out in politically authoritarian ways did not and can not yield their intended results, because Russian leaders and international financial institutions have misconstrued the fundamental nature of the Russian transformation. Marketization advocates in Russia and the West mistakenly thought that they were fighting the twentieth-century battle of the budget, when they were actually fighting a nineteenth-century battle of state-building. The Russian state that emerged from the Soviet breakup did not have the means to administer itself, and lacked institutionalized control over its territory, its money supply, and its regional and local bureaucracies. It looked, in short, like a textbook "late developer."

Therefore, the Russian state as it developed in the 1990s could not provide a stable, fair institutional framework for the development of a market economy. As Karl Polanyi understood decades ago, the market needs a regulatory underpinning in order to work its magic.[9] Moreover, financial globalization has made the state's role in this endeavor more important, not less, because the state is responsible for building the institutional framework that mediates interactions between the domestic economy and the international one. There is no "market solution" to this problem; enforcing widespread bankruptcy, increasing tax collection, carrying on with privatization, firing state workers, and cutting pensions cannot create this infrastructure. Nor does Putin's nationalistic and authoritarian vision of a "strong state" offer Russia any hope. What Russia needs is a strong state in the Weberian sense—supported by and supportive of the rule of law. What Russia has is a strong-armed state, with an executive that has ruled by decree, reserved for itself the right to punish perceived economic offenders regardless of legal niceties, carried out a war of annihilation against its own citizens in Chechnya, and controlled much of the national media.

Without regulatory underpinnings, economic liberalization fosters an environment characterized by extreme uncertainty and short-term thinking. This economic uncertainty—when combined with the ever-present political uncertainty of rapidly changing governments; the sudden New Year's eve resignation of the increasingly capricious Yeltsin; and an unstable party, electoral, and constitutional order—comprised a recipe for the venality and corruption that overwhelmed Russia's banking system.

9. Karl Polanyi, *The Great Transformation* (Boston: Beacon Press, 1944).

Rather than rule by presidential fiat, in order to achieve lasting stability Russia requires economic and political institutions that transcend individuals. Economically, this means fairly enforcing existing laws concerning transparency and property rights, while confining economic actors to political roles as formal interest groups rather than as informal patrons and clients. This difficult economic institution-building task, in turn, will now only be possible and sustainable in a politically democratic Russia. This means a state that allows parties to contest for power on equal terms, holds its officials accountable for their actions, and builds public support for a representative constitutional framework. Unfortunately, none of this is inevitable—or even likely—given the developmental trajectory on which post-Soviet Russia has embarked.

One of the saddest ironies of the Russian transformation is that the West directed the bulk of its advice and aid in exactly the wrong direction. In particular, the IMF, which might have helped Russia to develop appropriate new market-oriented institutions within a democratic framework, instead exacerbated the problem by encouraging Russia to undertake further accelerated, damaging economic decentralization while subverting democratic norms. The IMF, of course, was founded in order to deal with short-term balance of payment issues in developed market economies, not to create market economies where none existed before. Therefore, it naturally saw Russia as yet another nail to be driven into place with a firm whack of the austerity hammer. Yet after a decade of careful attention from the IMF, the Russian state still found itself incapable of raising money and paying its bills, the CBR still could not control the country's means of exchange, and the commercial banks still could not make profits reliably without exploiting state connections. In fact, the Russian state expected to collect less tax revenue in 1999 than the City of New York.[10] In any case, much of this revenue (upwards of 90 percent) must be used to service Russia's foreign debts—if Russia actually paid them all on time.[11] In sum, IMF aid and advice has led to few improvements in Russia's economic condition while undermining its nascent democratic institutions and burdening it with billions of dollars in debt. In this light, the IMF's recommendation that Russia cut its budget back further and "live within its means" seems ludicrous, as these means are either in barter, in hidden cash, or are fleeing the country at a rapid rate.

We in the West have been slow to grasp Russia's status as a late developer, even in the face of its persistent difficulties, because Western misperceptions about the nature of institutional change allowed observers to

10. Harper's Index, *Harper's*, December 1999.
11. Garfield Reynolds and Matt Bivens, "Following the Same Old Map," *Moscow Times,* July 31, 1999.

discern a rapid developmental trajectory where none, in fact, existed. By assuming that Russia was an institutional *tabula rasa,* and by assuming that trickle-down policies could create only desirable institutional forms, the West assumed it knew what the endpoint of Russia's transformation would look like. As a result, we mistook the familiar and superficial trappings of a Western-style market democracy for the reality. Russia, after all, introduced elections, political parties, an executive and a bicameral legislature, a Supreme Court, and a constitution. It created a stock market, a central bank, and commercial banks; privatized its industries; liberalized its prices; made its currency convertible; joined Western economic organizations; and set state budgets. Although the political and economic institutions failed to function in accustomed ways, many Western observers nevertheless believed that their mere existence meant that Russia was "on the right track." Unfortunately, reform is not a railroad, and the expected light may not appear at the end of the tunnel. Scholars should be humble before the creativity of individuals, the power of institutions, and the infinite ways in which they may be combined. As Hamlet warns Horatio in Act I, Scene V, "there are more things in heaven and earth, than are dreamt of in your philosophy."

Index

235

Central Bank of Russia, 2, 4–5, 64–97
  ARKO and, 221–222
  battle for sovereignty and, 4, 27, 43–54,
    61–63
  commercial banks and, 46–54, 69,
    71–73, 80–81, 101–103, 112–113, 116,
    134–135, 137, 145, 157–158, 164,
    206–207, 210–211, 215, 218–222
  conflict with executive and, 5, 65–66,
    69–71, 85–95, 182
  credit auctions and, 134
  crime and corruption and, 76–77, 83–84
  currency reform of 1993 and, 90–91
  directed credits and, 80–81, 93–94,
    101–104, 140, 147–150
  exchange rate and, 7, 69, 93, 134, 199,
    201, 203, 213, 216–217, 219
  Federal Securities Commission and, 206
  FIMACO and, 64–65, 76–77, 213
  foreign banks and, 120, 189
  foreign loans and, 209–210
  GKOs and, 64, 81, 123–125, 182, 203,
    218
  government borrowing from, 81–82, 86,
    89–90, 224
  independence and, 65–73, 92–97
  inflation and, 88, 96, 134
  institutional legacies and, 66, 74, 77–86
  interest rates and, 6, 48, 72, 80, 93–94,
    100–102, 134, 148, 215–216
  law and, 67–69, 78, 95, 103–104, 153
  monetary policy and, 66, 69, 71, 74,
    80–82, 85–89, 94–96
  parliament and, 70–71
  payments system and, 73, 77–78, 80,
    82–85, 88, 93
  personnel and, 74–75, 77–80, 118,
    183–184
  regional divisions of, 75–76, 102, 147,
    151, 153, 166–167
  reserves of, 7, 76, 213, 216
  ruble zone and, 77–78, 85, 87–92
  Sberbank and, 110, 204, 218, 223–224
  secrecy and, 74–77, 83–84
  technical capability of, 67, 77–85
Central Electoral Commission, 214
Centralized credit. See Credit
Chaebol, 161, 199
Chazprombank, 135
"Chechen Affair," 76–77, 130
Chechnya, 229–231
Cherepkov, Viktor, 155
Chernomyrdin, Viktor, 24, 93, 180–181,
    191–192, 194–195, 204, 207, 214, 218

Chernow, Ron, 14
Chimkent Union Bank, 34
China, 170–171
Chubais, Anatolii, 24, 182, 184–185, 194,
    202, 204–206, 212, 215, 218
Churbanov, Oleg, 165–170
Civic Union, 160
Command economy, 29, 128
Commonwealth of Independent States
    (CIS), 63, 76, 184
Communist Party of Russia, 95, 111,
    117–118, 160, 181–182, 188, 230
Communist Party of the Soviet Union
    (CPSU), 4, 19, 27, 29, 40–41, 59, 62,
    64, 165–166
Congress of People's Deputies, 43, 47
Congress of Russian Communities, 160
Constitution of the Russian Federation, 67,
    92
Cooperative banks, 5, 33–35, 42–43
Cooperative enterprises, 32–33, 35–36, 38,
    42, 82–83
Copf, 209
Council of Ministers (USSR), 27, 32, 34,
    45, 62, 183
Coup attempt, 62, 85
"Crash of 1998," 9, 17, 38, 201–203,
    212–217, 229
  reaction of bankers to, 218–222
Credit
  Central Bank of Russia and, 80–81, 86,
    93–94, 101–104, 134, 140, 147–150
  commercial banks and, 6, 45, 100–106,
    140, 144–145, 147–149, 168–169,
    196, 202
  cooperative banks and, 35
  specialized banks and, 31, 35, 48
Credit Commission, 70, 93–94
Credit Lyonnais, 119–120
Crime and corruption, 17, 36, 73, 76–77,
    83–84, 102–103, 127–134, 148. See also
    Pyramid schemes
Croatia, 19
Currency
  devaluation of 1998, 213, 216–217
  hard currency licenses, 38, 57–58, 141,
    168
  hard currency purchases, 106, 128–129,
    226
  parallel, 87–88, 90
  reforms in FSU, 91
  reform of 1991, 61–62
  reform of 1993, 90–91
  reform of 1998, 202

Monblan, 193
Monetary overhang, 28
Monetary policy, 66, 69–71, 74, 77, 80–82,
    85–89, 93–96, 103
Money laundering, 128–129
Montazhspetsbank, 41
Mosbiznesbank, 50, 58, 109, 135, 209,
    220–221, 224
Moscow, 84, 118–119, 157, 191–193
    city government of, 37–38, 50, 122,
        223–224
    dominance of banks from, 6, 8, 57–58,
        136–140, 142–145, 150–157,
        171–172, 208–209
    municipal bank of, 144, 193
    See also Luzhkov, Yurii; Sistema
Moscow Bank. See Bank of Moscow
Moscow Bank for Reconstruction and De-
    velopment, 193
Moscow Industrial Bank, 109, 207, 224
Moscow Narodny Bank, 28
Mosenergo, 219
Mosstroibank, 42, 58
Most Bank, 37–38, 117–118, 122, 154, 174,
    181, 190, 193, 207–208, 220,
    222–224. See also Gusinskii, Vladimir;
    Media Most; Most Group
Most Group, 174. See also Gusinskii,
    Vladimir; Most Bank; Media Most
Municipal banks, 132, 143–144, 170, 193,
    207
Murmansk, 116
Murmansk Shipping, 186–187
Murrell, Peter, 103, 160
Mustcom, Ltd., 189

Nafta-Moskva, 187
Nalichnye (cash money), 28, 82. See also
    Dual monetary circuit
National Banking Council, 70, 116
National Reserve Bank, 182, 191–192,
    209–210, 220, 224
Natsional'nyi Kredit Bank, 117, 135, 192
"Ne Dai Bog!" 182
Neftekhimbank, 41, 45, 58, 192
Nemtsov, Boris, 163, 184, 194, 202, 204,
    207, 214
New Economic Policy (NEP), 32–33
"New Russians," 133
Nevzlin, Leonid, 173
Nezavisimaia gazeta, 180, 194, 215
Nizhnii Novgorod, 156–157, 162–163, 204,
    214
Noiabr'skneftegaz, 196

Nomenklatura privatization, 36, 40–41, 44,
    58–59, 99, 227
Nomenklatura system, 27, 36
Noril'sk Nickel, 174, 186–187, 194–197,
    221, 223
Norsi oil, 214
Northwest Shipping, 187, 196
Nosko, Anatolii, 124
Nosta-Truby-Gaz, 159, 162
Novgorod, 201
Novolipetsk Metallurgical Combine, 174,
    186–187, 197–198
Novosibirsk, 143–144, 158
NTV, 180, 194
Nuti, Domenico, 95

OFZ, 204
Oil, 151, 155, 174, 179, 186–191, 193–196,
    212–215, 222–223
Oktan, 167
Olbi, 117
Oligarchy, 9, 173, 179, 206, 228
Omskpromstroibank, 224
ONEKSIMbank, 109, 121–122, 151,
    153–155, 174, 176, 178, 180,
    183–190, 192–197, 201, 205, 207,
    209–212, 215, 219–221, 223. See also
    Interros; Potanin, Vladimir
Open Radio, 192
OPERU-2, 210–211
Organized crime. See Crime and corruption
ORT, 180, 194
Osiniagov, Sergei, 185
Our Home Is Russia, 181, 183

Paramonova, Tat'iana, 74–75, 83, 94, 116,
    190
Paris Club, 64, 82
Parliament. See Supreme Soviet (through
    October 1993); Duma (December
    1993 and after)
Party of Russian Unity and Accord, 117–118
Patent Bank, 34
Pavlov, Valentin, 61
Payments system, 73, 77–78, 80, 82–85, 88,
    93, 128, 142, 216
Pereiaslavl' Bank, 143
Perestroika, 29, 33, 37
Perm, 144
Personnel, 31–32, 44–45, 57, 59–61, 74–75,
    77, 105, 118, 131–132, 183–184
Petrovskii Bank, 224
Petrozavodsk, 144
Pigilova, Tamara, 31, 165